Motifs

Motifs

The Transformative Creation of Self

Don J. Feeney, Jr.

Westport, Connecticut
London

#44914371

Library of Congress Cataloging-in-Publication Data

Feeney, Don J., 1948–
    Motifs : the transformative creation of self / Don J. Feeney, Jr.
      p. cm.
    Includes bibliographical references and index.
    ISBN 0–275–96844–8 (alk. paper)
    1. Individuality. 2. Self. 3. Personality. I. Title.
BF697.F44   2001
155.2—dc21   00–064957

British Library Cataloguing in Publication Data is available.

Library of Congress Catalog Card Number: 00–064957
ISBN: 0–275–96844–8

First published in 2001

Praeger Publishers, 88 Post Road West, Westport, CT 06881
An imprint of Greenwood Publishing Group, Inc.
www.praeger.com

Printed in the United States of America

The paper used in this book complies with the
Permanent Paper Standard issued by the National
Information Standards Organization (Z39.48–1984).

10 9 8 7 6 5 4 3 2 1

Dedicated to my daughter Kelly,
who persists and perseveres in enhancing her
unique core motifs' formativeness
through moment to moment improvisational solutions.

Contents

Acknowledgments

Inspiration for exploring and expounding on profound core qualities inherent in human beings evolve from larger ecological paradigms of existence and the nature of living formativeness. Drawing from the roots of such domains as physics, biology, psychosocial dimensions, evolution, genetics and spirituality; consistent themes of emerging formativeness persevere in their presence. I am grateful to my many professors and colleagues over my years of training and experience who have offered such a mosaic range of learning. I am deeply moved by the continual evolution of unique formativeness in my enriching family relationships and especially in the artistic and healing improvisations of my daughter Kelly. I am very thankful for her contributions in the final chapter on spirituality and her perspectives from a Reiki healer's point of view. I am extremely thankful for the sustaining literary assistance of my editor, Nita Romer, who believed in the undertaking of this project and to the production staff of my publisher who have worked so affectively and efficiently to move this project towards completion. Finally, I want to express my sincere gratitude to Susan Dziedzic for her tenacity, persistence and "above and beyond the call of duty" attitude in always being there throughout the countless hours of arduous manuscript revisions and its final production.

Introduction

Imagine the motion of a spinning gyroscope. After winding string around the center rod and pulling, the inner spinning wheel keeps it upright. Whether it is held in the palm of the hand or on the tip of a pencil, it sustains its position and orientation for the length of time the spin lasts. Human beings also may have their own unique spin and gyroscopic movement that keeps them on some life course, resilient against outside influences. This unique inner gyroscopic movement having its own unique signature is what I have termed the sensory motif.

Artists have motifs in the way they move their paintbrush or sculpt a statue. It is the unique artistic movement and design that allows us to distinguish a Picasso from a Michelangelo. Each has his own motif. Motifs are not static. They evolve and shift, as exemplified by evolving states of Picasso's or Chagall's work.

Each individual human being is actually a marvelously unique, artistic motif with his or her own movement, way of being, and unique signature of self. It is that inner movement or motif that gives such gyroscopic stability and structural design in anchoring an individual on his or her life course. The inner movement of such a gyroscopic motif is actually a signature and formulation (having some uniquely personal pattern and/or design that manifests itself as a highly individualized shape and form) of each human being's core self. Such a signature of self is illustrated in unique character themes and patterned behaviors persistent throughout the self's developmental states. Persistence of an organizing motif (the self's signature) emerges throughout the development of an individual's life character.

This book presents a novel perspective related to the inherent presence of a third force (motif) operating within each individual. Exactly how such a third force (the motif) operates within each individual, providing a superstructure or epigenetic dimension to both genetics and environment, is explored. Such a metastructure or framework incorporates genetic coding and environmental influences as participants in the motif's higher ordering of creativity and transformative change.

Motif involves epigenesis, which is the organism (or whole) being greater than the sum of its component genetic and environmental parts. This work demonstrates that the inherent organizing properties of motifs propel their unique, complex holism at multiple levels of the organism. The motif's complex wholeness at each level is the guiding epigenetic dynamic influencing the genetic and environmental synergy of interaction. Such motif complexities can be developed from unique themas of the organism at multiple levels and their interconnections into a coherent web-like archetexture.

The manuscript will explore how motifs are manifest throughout the multiple levels of higher, hierarchical organization in the human being. Such levels range from the most microscopic DNA molecule to the macroscopic cosmos and spiritual levels of worship and meditation.

Motif is the essence of the self's uniqueness articulating in unfolding artistic-like formative flow patterns the idiosyncratic design of the individual's archetexture. Such formative patterns of motifs are operative at multiple levels of human functioning ranging from the DNA molecule to the cellular metabolism to the choreographed functioning of the heart and its connection to the brain as well as the central nervous system and many of the electromagnetic fields that operate from that region. Motifs are also manifest through many of the psychosocial functions of human beings as in the ways memories are stored, motivation is elicited, decisions are made, and emotions and social interactions are engaged in. Like sections of an orchestra meshing and flowing together, motifs operate throughout the human system in harmonic and highly choreographed timings of precise flow and unfolding patterns.

The uniqueness unfolds with an intelligence guided by the design structure of motif. At the cutting edge point of being oneself is the essence of the uncategorizable uniqueness of each self in its own becoming.

The motif is archetextural, not archetypal, in that motifs are not a matter of fitting the self into a type or category, but rather each individual is a unique "type" of being — one of a kind. Motif is the essence of individuality. It is the archetextural design structure that is the subtle substructure of overt behaviors, patterns, feelings and expressions. Yet, it is a complex array of interacting life forces that flow and interlace with one another moving in an orchestrated and uniquely timed series of occurrences. Such a complex of interaction gives rise to unique features of emergent self contrasted with the innumerable possible patterns providing the ground of its expression.

The book reviews in depth the construct of what motifs are and how they operate throughout the self-organization of spirit/mind/body structure and function. The chapters further explore, from the perspective of motif, the nature-nurture continuum of determinants in the self's growth and development.

Motif is neither a concrete blueprint nor an aloof abstraction. Motif is the orchestrated resonance of formative flowing design structures culminating in a unique archetexture of unfolding unification. Motif is unique, unfolding integration as seemingly isolated parts develop inherent relationships of rhythm, harmony and design structure. There is some proportional connection based on some whole or partially shared attribute or set of attributes. The metaphor of the university is appropriate at this point. Is there a building on some campus that says "university"? Is it the administration building or athletic field? Is the university simply a collection of buildings and books? How does one distinguish an Ivy League university from a "Big Ten" university? Indeed the characteristic attributes of the distinguishing features relating or uniting (or universalizing) all the constituent parts becomes the resonance or relatedness of that particular university. Note that the logo of the university somehow captures the unique design or trademark signature that distinguishes it from another. Note also that such a trademark is manifest at all levels of the university organization. It can range from the massive university seal arching over the entrance to the campus to the tiniest symbol on a number two lead pencil sold at the bookstore. In similar fashion, the motif is infused throughout the archetextural skeletal design of structure of the individual organism from the subcellular level up to the highest level of mental organization.

The evolution of the individual's motif enhances his or her unique identity. Such evolution necessitates nurturing and resonating (aligning with) one's own organizing motif in the transformative creation of self. The evolution and growth of the individual's motif throughout life is inherently a unique work of artistry. Each life is a precious work of art with its own characteristic motif. When there is alignment of behavior, attitude, biology and psychosocial functioning in ways that nurture and harmonize with core motifs, creative self-transformations evolve. Implications of alignment, how this may or may not occur, and the immutable presence of autonomous design structures essential to the motif's dynamics are all discussed in later chapters. The final chapter on soul and spirituality depicts how motifs, imbued throughout multilevels of self, illustrate the all-pervasive presence of the soul's spirit.

This study is designed to present a multitude of facets related to motif focusing on such aspects as healing, body shape, temperament, brilliance, purpose and family as they each reflect on one another. With the discovery of a genetic basis as a major influence on patient character traits, any exploration of human behavior needs to review the interaction effects of temperament and environment in light of the individual as self-formative and self-regulating. The manuscript explores how the etiology of human behavior involves the perspective of an internal archetexture pressing for its own manifestation as a third force in the individual's identity and behavior manifestations.

An additional focus of this book deals with such issues as treatment related to individuals who appear to have characteristics that are immutable. For example, alcoholism, once labeled a disease, allows the recovering person to accept his or her liabilities and inherent needs to respect how to behave in ways that control for a permanent condition such as this. In a similar fashion, once one accepts one's inherent core condition not as a disease but as an inherent unfolding of a unique set of core archetextures, one begins to no longer resist who one is. The person can work with these unique identities in ways that allow healthy utilization and validation of self. Individuals can rally to the cause of their own unique constellation as a manifestation of their archetextural uniqueness.

Unfortunately, many individuals are labeled as disordered and impaired when in reality they fail to grasp in the early stages of development the core organizing forms of inherent self motif. Individuals with unique temperaments and dispositions, or a motif of their own, are sometimes labeled as having a disease to work around, as if the larger social structure does not grasp what the unique core designs of that individual truly are.

This work will further examine the use of motif as a major contribution to dealing with a variety of genetically predisposed temperaments, character traits and behavioral manifestations. Further, the motif will be related to research findings on twins. Illustrations will demonstrate the high degree of synchronicity present in identical twins as exhibited in mental, emotional and psychosocial behavioral expressions having their origins in the construction of an archetextural motif. The very articulation of identical structures within twins is a manifestation of the motif's precision and work. By the same token, it will also be illustrated that the slight differences noticed in the idiosyncratic physical, mental and behavioral manifestations of twins indicate the presence of the motif's uniqueness with its subtle differences in each individual even when they have identical genetic components.

Motif will be related to the individual's pursuit and discovery of a sense of purpose and meaning in his or her own life and in relating to the lives of others. The empowering capacity of motifs and how to bridge gaps of alienation and confusion will be elucidated. Motifs can enhance the intimate value and respect both within the individual and between individuals in their own family context. The entire focus of the book is how motifs assist not only in the guidance, organization and evolution of the individual human being but that the motif, as an expression of the individual evolution of the human being, depends for its own manifestation on the individual person's choice to align oneself with one's own innate core structure and nature.

The extent to which this alignment occurs is the extent to which the motif becomes fully operative and affirmative in that person's life and related functions. Indeed, this may require a sense of faith, even spirituality and commitment to an archetextural formativeness of structure and unique core of self that may not always be clearly visible or concrete. It may be found in flowing experiences of artistic and unique sensory and imaginative constructions that allow these manifestations of underlying substructure to express themselves in unique, creative manifestations. Examples of this type of imaginative and creative structuring will be given in terms of individuals who, for example, are performers, musicians or scientists and how they have common capacities to give. For example, a singer aligns herself with voice pictures of the actual physiological structure of vocalization and how the vocal cords and attenuated anatomical components operate in patterns, which assists her to create beautiful music, harmony and rhythms.

We find that many remarkable discoveries in science and creations in art have involved the invocation of motifs, models, metaphors, patterns and various metastructures as ways of capturing the complexity of some event, performance or experience. Yet far from being purely states of creative imagination, these reflect deeper, core archetextural structures of that formative, individual self who is able to inherently relate to his or her particular field of chosen life work. Motif facilitates an inherent relatedness with others through the use of one's unique, core design structure (as a singer can structure a picture of her vocal cords actually moving and vibrating as she sings, performs and relates under great pressure).

This can also be found in scientists. For example, the double helix in carbon rings was discovered by one scientist's dream of snakes consuming one another's tail ends forming circular design structures. He awoke one night realizing such imagery was symbolic of the shape of the benzene ring which involves a cyclical constellation of molecules. Indeed, this book will seek to elucidate and elaborate on how core structures are operative in many of the creative breakthroughs in individuals' lives as a way of manifesting their own unique structures and how that entrains and interconnects with their careers and endeavors in their behavioral and social environments.

Finally, the concept of motif will be related to what is referred to as "entelechy," which is Greek for realization and bringing to life that which lies within. The motif is the design structure that is the embodiment of the inner guidance that "assists the acorn to become more of what it already is everyday of its existence into an oak tree." Such embodiment is the sacred uniqueness of the soul's motif imbued throughout the multilevel systems of the unfolding human archetexture.

Chapter One

Transforming Motifs

Within each individual are inherent, self-organizing properties which constitute and consist of unique design structures (formative patterns). The composite integration of these design structures is the individual's motif (Feeney, 1996). The motif's inherent properties of self-organization are unique to each individual. It provides a novel perspective of a superstructure or epigenetic dimension incorporating but transcendent to both genetics and environment as a third force for transformation. Such a metastructure and framework articulates unique design structures within each individual orchestrating genetic influences and selective, environmental interactions resonant to the uniqueness of each person. The orchestration of complex growth processes is propelled by unique, inherent properties of the human organism's capacity for design and structure at multiple levels of self-organization. The human brain, for example, self-constructs its own structures accessing neural circuits, wiring and honing them to the task at hand (Eliot, 1999). Such properties involve capacities in the human organism for self-organization capable of generating idiosyncratic (uniquely individualized) design structures known as motifs.

THEMAS AND WEBS

Motif is the archetexture of self. Motif organizes and operates throughout the physical and psychosocial development of the individual. Motif is a constancy of unfolding change states manifesting a family of coherent themas or design structures integrated into a web-like lattice of a complex whole. No one thema encompasses the whole, yet each thema interfaces and interconnects with each other such that, like individual threads of a web, when one is pulled the entire complex may resonate in whole or part of that entity. Themas are multifaceted, occurring throughout multiple levels of the organism. At one point in time, an individual may exhibit one formative thema (flexible, easygoing and casual). At another point, he or she may exhibit other themas (compulsive, rigid attitudes, a demanding formal nature). The degree of how themas overlap forms the interactive complexity of unique, emerging motif within that individual. The differential complexity of how an individual moves begins to emerge.

Notice the rich perspectives and modes of operating for someone who has encountered vast ranges of experience and wisdom over the years. His or her motif emerges much more readily than that of an individual with a limited variety of experiences. Varied experiences in living assist in themas' differentiation and the emerging complexity of motif.

Themas or design structures represent multiple facets of each individual's unique personality, physiology, temperament and psychosocial mode of functioning. Taken as a whole, these themas interact and integrate into a complex whole or web-like structure. Such web-like structures have unique design features characteristically represented and repeated with intersecting variations throughout multiple levels of the human organism. These web-like manifestations form unique motifs and indeed are the expression of the self's idiosyncratic motif. The complexity of human personality consists of motifs and its themas that serve as organizing matrices which are influenced by the development of conceptual constructs of self and reality. These constructs are subjectively formed by the age of five and have been found to remain relatively consistent throughout the individual's life span, imperious to educational experiences though they are modifiable and evolve to maturational levels in the adult years (Restak, 1995). Such constructs as safety, how the world operates, who is trustworthy, ways of controlling oneself, what ideals to aspire to and so on are all created by the self at very early stages of development.

The tendency to develop, construct and integrate one set of beliefs over another certainly is affected by the self's temperament and its interaction with the environment (James & Woodsmall, 1988). Yet, the presence of unique web-like structures of motif serves as a metaorganizing third force guiding the foundation for growth. Infused throughout the temperament of the individual and its self-selecting way of responding to environmental conditions and stimuli are inherent organizing principles operating behind the scenes at meta levels above both temperament and environmental interactions. The temperament of an individual represents predisposing orientations (extraversion, aggressiveness, sociability, tempo, levels of emotional sensitivity, etc.). These can all affect cognitive interpretations of the self's interaction with the world. An individual with an outgoing, bold temperament may meet adversity as a challenge and strive to overcome it. Another individual, passive and sensitive with a tendency to feel things deeply, may struggle with adversity, feeling overwhelmed. Yet, operating behind the scenes for both types of temperament is the characteristic of uniqueness within these temperaments. Each individual has his or her own unique nuance, shade of meaning, variation and tempo for how his or her temperament is constructed and manifest. It is to this unique specificity that one's idiosyncratic design structure or motif operates and is manifest.

It is the unique valence, weight and intensity of how each thema participates that reflects the overall unique organizing principles at work. The degree, intensity and juxtaposition of various themes and how they come together are similar to a recipe for a special dish or meal. Each of the ingredients has its own proportion, timing and patterned combination, yet each meal is uniquely prepared by a master chef (inherent organizing principles of unique self motif) who follows no set recipe. Rather, an intuitive, artistic level sense design of what ingredients, in what proportion, combination and sequence would create that unique taste is the formativeness of the recipe. Each time the master chef prepares the exquisitely artful gourmet meal it is never exactly the same. With each new meal preparation, unique similarities emerge as the signature of the master chef but with subtle variations.

The uniqueness of patterning, the unique similarity of recipe in the complex whole design is the guiding motif within the temperament and between its selective, environmental interactions.

FORMATIVENESS IN PERCEPTION AND COGNITION

The motif's themas or design structures are not the self's constructs of reality or the belief system but rather the lattice or web-like skeletal framework upon which such cognitive operations are founded. The motif's themas influence the fundamental formation of the self's beliefs and constructs of reality. Beliefs and constructs of reality result in part from perceptual filters of incoming sensory stimuli and higher cerebral, cortical processing and interpretive analysis. This results in making deletions, distortions and generalizations (James & Woodsmall, 1988) through sensory information processing. Involved is a formative reorganization of information into a meaningful design or motif. Through comparative analysis and cognitizing stimuli (ordering, shaping and organizing data), abstractions are delineated which organize information in relevant or meaningful ways to the individual. Thus, formation of beliefs and constructs of reality involves utilizing a formative way of filtering, organizing and integrating incoming data into a meaningful order. Developmentally, young children follow the Piaget stages of moving from sensory experience to concrete operational ideas and later to abstract formulations. This concrete to abstract development is essentially an organizational development of formativeness, which is exactly the function of motifs.

The unique way a young child deletes, distorts and makes generalizations first involves perceptual filters that skew attention and interest of how incoming sensory data are ordered and grouped. For example, young children will give greater attention and show more positive emotion to symmetrical structures (facial features) than to nonsymmetrical structures (Etcoff, 1999). In addition, novel stimuli of brightness, noise, movement, color and so on are more likely to capture a young child's interest than those lacking such features. How the child pays attention and experiences pleasant or unpleasant emotions to such stimuli contributes to what information is absorbed and how it may be positively or negatively labeled. As each child's brain is unique in subtle ways (Edelman, 1992), what is absorbing and attentive to one child may be boring and uninteresting to another. The way children organize their perceptual filters varies from child to child. Different dimensions of ordering (e.g., color, movement, sound, sequence, the gestalt or whole pattern of how stimuli may be arranged, either in terms of closeness and/or movement, groupings, size, etc.) are all weighted slightly differently for each child.

The perceptual filters themselves are organized by the motif's themas, which therefore determine what is attended to and how the brain receives it. The individual child tends to perceive and conceptualize events in his or her reality according to his or her own motif's design structures. The design structure of the midbrain's amygdala (known to be a center for emotions of fight or flight, arousal and motor activity) affects its threshold level of sensitivity. Studies of four-month-old infants reveal that those who respond to novel stimuli (noise, smell of alcohol, etc.) with high arousal of motor activity and irritability showed low thresholds of stimuli in their amygdalas. The affects of perceiving stimuli with such sensory perceptions and responses later translated into cognitions of danger, fear and withdrawal as exhibited by right frontal lobe activity (dealing with negative emotional material) (Eliot, 1999). The design structure of sensory perceptions and activities translated into higher ordering cognitions. The motif of perception translates into higher organizational levels of thought form cognitions.

The mind/brain system self-designs itself through interactions both between its own neurons and with the external environment. Sensory touch affects and is affected by characteristic design structures in the mind/brain system. While there is adaptation to environmental sensory stimuli, such accommodation is achieved utilizing characteristic motif designs of the assimilating mind/brain system. When confronted with extreme degrees of environmental variations (exaggerations in stimuli that significantly diverge from the preferred mode of perception and conception) the child has difficulty utilizing his or her own rules of perception/cognition. The child's rules of organizing and structuring reality being primitive and underdeveloped, such cases of extreme environmental events (emotional, physical and/or sexual abuse) cause massive environmental discrepancy/conflict to their inherent modes of how to make sense of the world.

Dissonance of stimuli (a child who experiences conflict between his or her preferred design structure for soothing, low noise, soft lighting, and loud, abrasive sounds, etc.) may contribute to negative emotional associations to certain perceptions. Environmental labeling by significant others (parents) can further skew what the child perceives as positive or negative. Parents who exhibit high levels of excitement, novelty, noise and rapid change with their children may skew such experiences in positive or negative ways (laughing loudly or fighting violently), may arouse unique associations and interpretations depending on the child's preferred (motif) way of organizing perceptions, and comparative analysis can create such formative ways of thinking as life is beautiful or life is dangerous.

The essential point is that the motif manifests its influence of structuring and ordering at both the perceptual and conceptual levels. When the young child takes in new experiences in his or her own way (filters data based on thema selectivity), ordering and perceiving them, this serves as information for the child's cerebral cortex to begin its deletion, distortion and generalization process in creating beliefs and constructs of reality. The cognitive process of construction takes its cue from how the data were ordered, filtered and perceived in the first place (was it pleasant and harmonious or painful and clashing with the child's motif of preferred structuring?).

Through analysis and comparison, the executive functions (judgment, decision-making, etc.) of the cerebral cortex analyze and compare what was experienced and how it was perceptually organized. That is, if the perceived experience had important features consistent with the inherent organizing motif of the child, a positive interpretation and construct would emerge. For example, the young child may perceive rapid movement, loud noise, harsh tones and bright images in parents' and/or siblings' behavior and expressions. The child with a motif for slow tempo, easygoing movements and subtle shades of sensory lighting may interpret his or her world as chaotic and painfully discrepant to personal needs. That child may develop beliefs of pessimism and helplessness. Such beliefs are interpretive, guided not simply by genetics or environmental interaction, but epigenetically by an organizing motif of the child's enjoying quiet, inwardly reflective sensations.

When confronted with discrepant and unpleasant perceived stimuli, the motif organizes that event from the slow-paced sensitizing, magnification perspective of inner reflectiveness. The motif inherently organizes and orients the young child to process the lack of resonance with an inner dwelling and reflectiveness, which if not intervened could induce or structure the child to develop depressive schemas. Notice however that the hidden influence of the motif's unique ordering is at work in affecting the probability of structuring which beliefs and constructs are likely to develop in light of the child's contextual experience. Even the context of the experience is actually framed by how the child structures his or her perceiving process of environmental experiences. Images formed from the way perceived filters (organized by motif's themas) skew reality experiences can influence the formation of beliefs and constructs. The organizing effects of motif influence the perceptual process of darkness, silence and ambiguous spaces in a child's bedroom at night lending itself to cognitive distortions (creations). A child whose motif requires more structure, definition and light would have such an experience.

Perceptions of this nature may exaggerate the quality of darkness and magnify shadows into figures which are cognitively structured into the personal meaning of a child whose motif's design requirements have not been met. In this case, the child might project the presence of monsters and gremlins, and perceive that darkness is filled with unknown terrors.

Indeed, even adults prone to depression tend to use emotionally sensory based reasoning. For example, upon awaking on a Monday morning, if one sees that the day is cloudy, one feels tired and disoriented and perceives it to be the beginning of a long, hard workweek. Such perceptions filtered and designed in this fashion induce an ordering of idea formation and symbolization suggesting a most negativistic emphasis. The person may construct the operating belief that he or she should just stay in bed. Notice that the person's motif emphasizes projecting throughout the whole week a sense of darkness and a personal feeling of disorientation (possible dizziness and lack of mental clarity).

If the person's organizing thema is one preferring to see the long-term nature of things, is linear in thinking and seeks color and diversity, his thema requirements of color, diversity and clarity are not met, which affects the construct and belief formation his motif now has formatted and influenced in the form of thema design structures.

Motifs influence through their design themas the rules of how perceptual and cognitive processes are to be framed and guided. Adler (Ansbacher and Ansbacher, 1956) addressed this issue in part referring to the guiding rules of perception he called apperceptions. They are the structural lattice upon which percepts and cognitive thought forms are self-constructed. Motifs function through their structuring process to increase the probability that their unique design formations and ordering filters will be adhered to. Such is the all-pervasive influence of motifs on mental function.

MOTIFS AND ARCHETYPES

The influence of motif is unique for each person. For example, the image formation that emerges from perceptions and cognitions influenced by motif is unique and archetypal for that individual self. Individualized images are the symbolic representations in their structure and design form (long tunnels, lightning speeds, tornadoes) of the unique self's themas and motifs. Such stimuli, for example, taken as a whole might suggest relativity of movement where one could be moving forward in one perspective or the lights and tunnels could be flashing by in another. This figure-ground reversibility can be an organizing motif thema which influences the schematic structuring the individual may utilize in multiple facets of his or her life tasks (assists in peak performance, has motivational experiences, facilitates decision making, shares intimate experiences, has dialogues, etc.).

The self utilizes its unique core organizing design thema in an idiosyncratic manner which becomes a guiding archeidentity (or recipe) universal only to that individual. The motif's archetexture is universal only to that individual self. Motifs have implications at higher mental levels of functioning. For example, motif's such as reversibility may have the further symbolic as well as structural impact of affecting dimensions involving decision making, creativity, problem-solving and the like. An individual with this unique type of motif may be able to perceive two sides of the same argument, shift back and forth in perspective, generate multiple creative perspectives yet experience difficulty in deciding on only one outcome. The individual's motif (the particular way one utilizes reversibility, for example) is identical to no other and therefore goes beyond Carl Jung's (1971) universal archetypes.

The evolutionary nature of motif images (how the motif develops) are idiosyncratic to the individual and are therefore archeidentities to the unique signature of the person involved. Jung referred to universal archetypes from which all individuals draw. Yet, the uniqueness of the individual self is that idiosyncratic integration and formulation of all the individual themas or design structures evolving into the composite unique picture of motif. It is not unlike a Picasso with his myriad, cubist fragments (or themas) juxtaposed and positioning themselves into unique proportion and relationship to one another. This creates the unique priceless work of artistic motif of self.

The concept of archetypal refers to the oldest archetextural design in history, that of the arch. It was used in ancient times to be the most efficient, all pervasive, structurally stable design that could evenly distribute its weight load at ninety-degree angles (right angles). The arch was considered the core stabilizing design element of the individual building structure. The literal and symbolic implications are obvious when we speak of core motifs as the archeidentity of the individual's all-pervasive sense of self in how it structures and carries the life load.

EVOLVING DESIGNS

The present being of each person's self is manifested and stabilized by the design which also guides the becoming part of the self to unfold in precise but uniquely spontaneous ways. The motif designs movements which interact in unique fashion such that they create invariant variations (alternate variations of consistent uniqueness) of a transformative selfhood or being. This is similar to Martin Buber's "I-thou" where every "thou" is destined to become an "it" in an I-it relationship. This is a reified frozen quality of a thing divested of its unique flow and lifegiving process. Every stage of the human existence is therefore destined towards moving from an I-thou to an I-it or what may be termed positive disintegration where the old breaks down in favor of new replacements. The process of being unfolded into that new being of becoming illustrates that change is constant in the motif's regeneration or renewal of selfhood.

The manifestations of self, self-identity and self-concept are supported by the subtle substrates of the motif's archetextural process patterning that infuse these complex interactive flows of life themas in ways that may not always be apparent to the observing eye. Motifs are similar to the interweaving movements of a multisectioned orchestra where the conscious attention may be hearing one set of notes or another yet it takes the entire range of consciousness to appreciate the full orchestrated flow of life movements in ways that create that artistic musical score of unique human selfhood. Motifs many times present the residual effects of the interacting life patterns or movements as the figure emerging from the ground of their interactiveness. Such figure ground emergence is guided by the self-motif's archetextural design inherent in the nature of selfhood. Manifestation of motifs can be seen and experienced when viewed from the ground of that creative system interacting in an open and creative process with itself and with the environment at hand. Many times the symmetry of the motif's patterns may emerge in asymmetrical imbalanced ways, illustrating its growth and evolutionary nature.

Motifs have a heterogeneous nature in that they are not pure but rather involve a vast variance or even deviance in an ever-unfolding, at times imperfect mixture of the human being, the environment and the becoming process. The motif is not rigidly fixed like something set in stone. Rather, it is an evolving, self-creating interactive dynamic that moves in a holistic self-constructing, self-assembling way. Motif grows and refines itself from the interactions of the individual, the environment and the multiple processes in which it occurs. Motif is never a pure form any more than there is an ideal signature to an individual or an ultimate form. Rather, the motif is hinted at, approximated and always in the process of becoming yet another "ideal." The motif presents the ideal only for the moment of expression in that time, in that place, in that context just as a signature of human being reflects mood, state of mind, and the type of environmental influences one is currently experiencing. Such illusory and suggestive manifestations of the facets of motif are indicative of its hidden archetextural infrastructure, which is something that is never complete but always evolving. It is an archetexture of hidden order imbedded in the chaotic life of evolving events of growth, change and evolution. It is nonplatonic but rather what the Greeks term entelechy, where the essence of the acorn is realized in the becoming of the oak tree.

Motif is not part of the self, it is the whole, unique essence of self. Motif is the archetextural infrastructure, unique and evolving through multiple levels: metabolic, sensory, biochemical, psychosocial, and so on. The motif is similar to the holograph in that no matter how many times it is broken down into pieces, each piece reflects the whole. In other words, no matter what one does or experiences, one cannot *not* be oneself.

In decision making, this holographic character serves the whole of motif as an effort towards its evolution. Free will is the exercise of motif to that which it resonates. Such free will may express itself as an urge or compulsion, but actually the result is an intended effort to resonate to that which most self-selects and entrains the individual to the uniqueness within, connecting with the unique set of experiences without. Decision making is not part or ego driven but derived from the whole self. Motif is not a category or category of categories nor is it a matter of characteristic traits or types. It is the integrated residual culmination of multivaried characteristics interacting together in a uniquely designed work of artistry. Yet, it is a work of art that is never finished as it is ever refining and evolving in its innate signature of development and becoming.

In the senior years of a human being's life, this evolutionary process of evolving and articulating artistic formative designs manifests itself in the unique passions, artistry and elaborate endeavors of people who have honed and refined their motif throughout many decades. What were once merely symbolic acts of interests, endeavors, pastimes or avocations are representations of a core self that now take on attributes of integrative qualities of one's own being. They reflect an inner core that has always been there but is only now coming to fruition. Examples of passions discovered in advanced age include fly fishing, artistic painting, mechanical repair and adventures in remote places.

Expansion in articulation of the grace and beauty of one's own unique, passionate endeavors allows one to discover the motif manifesting itself in remarkable clarity and consistency offering peace, joy and harmony in the years to come. As people evolve, they become more specific in articulating and integrating their motif in everyday life in an aligned and attuned fashion. Anything short of the uniqueness of articulate self is simply a fragmentation and/or larger part of what has been previously called temperament or character traits.

The motif manifests the cutting edge, self-organizing uniqueness of self emerging from the field forces of environment and individual. It orchestrates the self-convergence and transformation through a quantum leap from the science of who human beings are to an artistic appreciation of what they have always been.

Motifs offer a healing quality. The more human beings align with motif, the greater behavioral and psychosocial benefits emerge in their environment. This result promotes wholeness, balance and harmony in healing. Alignment with motifs reduces stress and converts pressures and influences into what may be called eustress. It provides an entrainment of the organism where one's inner core design begins to match and mirror the synergistic connection with appropriate people, places, events, opportunities and capacities that enhance the manifestation of motif in everyday life.

Motif is not a core thing or place. It is an evolving archetexture guided by the boundary and outlines of the self/other contrast and articulates comparison and distinction between the two. It is neither subjective nor objective but the unique archetextural field or medium through which the self is an inherent oneness. It is common to think of being in or out of something observing or being observed. Yet motif is neither observed nor observer but could be both. The transformation is the self moving as one. Motif is at the cutting edge of the uncommon boundary of unfolding self-design. As such it is always at one with itself yet capable of almost infinite unique variations.

When an individual's unique motif of design structure is accessed and resonated, deep levels of rapport and relatedness can be established. Interfacing with motifs in communication involves attunement to the complex organizing design structure of how an individual nonverbally communicates. This attunement involves refining attention and focus to just the right balance of sensory design organization capturing the quality artistry and relational attributes of how individuals sensorially articulate and symbolize their movements, tonal sounds, points of emphasis and so on. Far from simply pacing another's rhythm, resonating with motifs involves grasping their unique hieroglyphic structure, symbol and form. This may involve an infinite number of patterned and varied sequences of short, medium or long movements, frequencies, intensities, duration, juxtaposition of phenomes and so on. Such grasping of motifs in communication is nothing short of resonating with the artistry and form of a master (e.g., Picasso, Chagall, etc.). In each individual's case, such resonance manifests artistic mastery of oneself.

DEVELOPMENTAL MOTIFS

Persistence of an organizing motif (the self's signature) emerges developmentally throughout an individual's lifestyle. Pearce (1986) uses Piaget and Inhelder's (1964) work on early childhood development (concrete to abstract formal operations), suggesting emergence of a postbiological ego identity (Erikson, 1950). Pearce states that this identity emerges through development of sensory-motor connections and emotions toward a fluid mental world of creative power and expression. He notes that this organizing identity exists from the beginning of life but in a latent form that awaits, as a growth blueprint, stage-specific attention and development. He stresses the critical importance of models (motifs) essential for development of this identity blueprint or organizing principle.

Pearce suggests that early developmental learning of language actually occurs in the womb, where small micromuscular movements parallel verbal sounds of the mother. Condon and Sander (1974) found through sophisticated analysis of high-speed sound movies of scores of newborn infants that so-called random movements immediately coordinated with speech when speech was used around the infants. Computer studies verified a complete and individualized repertoire for each infant of body movements synchronized with speech (moving a left elbow slightly on hearing a *k* sound as in *cough* or *cat*). Their studies of older children and adults revealed patterns of synchronization to be permanent and universal. They found movements in adulthood had become microkinetic, detectable only by instrumentation but still unique to each person.

These findings are consistent with other studies (Bernard & Sontag, 1947; Brody & Axelrod, 1970; Klaus, 1972). The only exception to this were autistic children, who showed no body-speech patterning. This exception may only mean suppressed performance of synchronicity, not absence. What is essential about these findings is that the newborn has a distinct, unique repertoire of movements (motif) with the synchronicity occurring within twelve minutes after birth. Pearce accepts the compelling logic that twelve minutes is insufficient time for synchronicity to develop. He therefore suggests that the infant structured this patterned response at some level of design while in the womb. He suggests the drive for this patterning be considered innate. That driving intent (or purpose) within needs only content (stimulation) from the outer environment with which to interact and thus take manifest form and shape. Here is a fundamental example of intent or purpose preceding the ability to "do." This and many other types of *in utero* learning are documented by Verny and Kelly (1981). This inherently unique structuring character of self emerges in varying degrees of refinement (interdependent on environment, early childhood experiences, physiological conditions, etc.) (Dabrowski, 1967, 1970). Chomsky (1967) proposed that language was innate, built into the genes.

Briggs (1988) reports research on nuances of feeling-tone "themes" in creative people's lives. Below the level of language and cognitions lie the complex nuances or shades of feelings between love and hate that organize events along these themes. Briggs indicates how metaphorical and imagery language could access organized feeling nuances of lifestyle themes that are oversimplified in thoughts and language. It would seem that there is a nonverbal structure or lattice below the level of language and thought with its own set of organizing principles. Jung (1964) referred to the presence of archetypes operating in the self.

This nonverbal structure could be expressed in sensory motifs. Motif is an evolving formation of design. The sensory quality in motifs (visual, auditory and kinesthetic) serves as a fundamental expression of thematic or symbolic ideas embedded in the motif. The motif's design may first be expressed at the sensory level (a child's attraction to handling and molding clay into bold, colorful shapes and designs). As the motif develops, it can emerge at the emotional level (child's personality begins to become colorful and charismatic, molding and boldly handling life tasks). The motif can then emerge into cognitive and spiritual expressions. These developmental stages parallel the concept of the triune brain (MacLean, 1973), which depicts developed brain structures that are sensory (reptilian), emotional (limbic) and cognitive (new mammalian).

The preceding material implies that individuals are inherently designed with a motif and intent to harmoniously organize their lives to be healthy and whole. Dabrowski (1967, 1970) and Dabrowski and Piechowski (1977a,b) describe personality development as a progression of five ascending levels. They describe dynamic dimensions facilitating this ascendant self-organization as guided by a personality ideal, creating harmonious unity and integration. The inherent guiding unity of this personality ideal is characteristic of innate motifs and their intent toward unifying wholeness. The unique character of sensory motifs represents the personality that is ideal for that individual self.

Sensory motif is an inherent kind of structural schematic that determines the shape or design of what makes each of us unique. It is ever unfolding. The motif seems to operate as a highly individualized field of energy characterized not by a single pattern or even sets of patterns (in terms of personality and/or behavior patterns), but rather generates what is referred to as a family of interacting patterns. Human beings can be quite complex, and no single pattern or sets of patterns adequately describe the uniqueness of self. That is why most individuals resist being categorized. I advocate using the model of a family of interactive patterns as a step to grasp this complexity.

Such a model suggests that human beings operate in inherent patterned ways, modifiable at the behavioral level yet essentially unchangeable at the core level of self. It is rather like the structure of a tree. The core pattern of the trunk is innate, yet the way it grows and branches outward is modifiable. The unique subtleties in inherent patterns of behavior (speaking, walking, working, loving, relating, etc.) in various areas of an individual's life overlap in their similarity yet express their own specific variations. Such a system of interactive patterns is referred to as a family of interactions. Our work behavior patterns affect and interact with our patterns of relating at home. Yet the way we operate at work is not identical but only similar to our behavior patterns at home (we may be high achievers at both home and work, but be more active at work and passive at home). Our early childhood behavior and belief patterns interact with and affect the way we function as adults. Unique ways in which patterns in one area of our life affect those in other areas (thought and behavior patterns of love and intimacy learned in childhood affect and are affected by those adult learning experiences) demonstrate the interactive effects of sensory motifs.

The wholeness of the motifs lies buried in the myriad patterns and events of a person's life. It is not unlike asking how many faces you can see hidden in a pictured collage of objects and figures. Sometimes standing back, releasing old fixations and opening up to creative ways that reformulate how and what a person is perceiving allows these motifs to emerge. That is why perceiving the family of interactive patterns is so essential in grasping how the motif is perceived. This allows the configuration of the motif to be visible.

These configurations are like the ripple effects of dropping a pebble into a pond. As patterns of waves spread out, some hit the shore and bounce back into oncoming patterns of waves. The interaction and interference effects of these colliding waves create shapes and configurations that repeat themselves in similar but different ways. Such similar but different configurations are called a family of interactive patterns. As motifs are not learned but are inherent structures to be developed, these interactive patterns are the distilled, pure manifestations of what is already innately present.

A very simple example of this can be seen in your own signature. Each time you sign your name, there will usually be some kind of small or large variation in the way you signed. However, you can always recognize your signature from anyone else's, as there are characteristics and shapes that emerge from the patterned variations of all of your signatures combined.

The sensory motif manifests itself in such a family of interactive patterns. Motifs imply unique configurations based on movement. We are always in movement whether we remain in one place or are quite active. Without movement, there is no life. However, the type of movement to which I refer is a special one known as flow. Csikszentmihalyi (1990) discusses how flow occurs through focused sensory and mental interaction, creating qualities of various form and design (a tennis player's flowing back-and-forth movement exhibiting form, skill and art). All people may find their self-existence in flow experiences that evoke qualities of form and art where they say they really feel alive and exist as their true selves. The sensory motif's existence in self is essential for each person's unique sense of meaningful existence. It is equivalent to the essence of self.

Motifs most clearly demonstrate their unique configurations and characteristics in these flow states. Interactive motifs usually, but not always, involve exchange in various activities — either alone, as in reading a book, or with someone else, as in playing ping pong or making love. Flow is a process that is conducive to generating a family of interactive patterns. That is why such a process is so intrinsically rewarding and gratifying. As a result, there is a powerful sense of purpose generated in these states.

Resonance between an individual's unique sense of self and the way one's lifestyle is manifested has been measured as meaning in life. Ebersole and Quiring (1991) discuss meaning in life depth (MILD) as a cognitive content process by using a five-point scale to measure depth of meaning. They indicate that the more precisely interactions of self and environment resonate to that person (design qualities or motifs), the greater the sense of meaning. It is postulated that the self has unique form and design qualities that necessitate resonant interactions (art, music, etc.) idiosyncratic to that self's motif. Experience takes on meaning in terms of what one discovers as identifiable external forms that are symmetrical with internal organizing principles. As the individual experiences a matching of external and internal organizing experiences, he or she feels a sense of meaning and purpose in life.

Frankl (1963) has emphasized the importance of discovering meaning and purpose in life in logotherapy. Each person's organizing properties seem to have a unique differential signature (or designation) such that some experiences will resonate more with some individuals than with others. When there is resonance, the individual feels like there is purpose in his or her self-experience. This, therefore, can be referred to as a purposeful self that resonates or relates when symmetry is discovered in experiences that present properties of their organizing principle. This ordering process, although unique to each client, is essential for the joy of flow experiences to occur in such unself-conscious manifestations (Csikszentmihalyi, 1990). At such times, the individual has a sense of joy, absorption or fascination.

Motifs can be expressed in flowing, artistic forms that are sequenced in unique, sensory syntax. The particular shape or configuration of a person's motif will have unique expressions. For example, some people may use such phrases as "see how they feel about ideas" or "get feelings off their chest." They then begin to share them verbally or auditorily. This could be their syntax of experience.

However, motifs are more than how the senses are sequenced. Motifs are an intricate and articulated type of design that partners begin to manifest in their own life characters. Motifs go beyond mere interests and hobbies. They are the structurally unique signatures of self. Motifs are the templates that generate within us an innate sense of order and beauty. They serve as the organizing gyroscopes that order the syntax of experience. They are fluid, not fixated. They involve a subtle, flowing order and creative design. As a result, they create a sense of purpose. This sense of purpose emerges as these flow states are experienced and transformed into their own unique artistry, form and style of expression. Motifs can be seen in people flowing through some interaction. Yet motifs are more than a style of interacting. There is a unique signature and blueprint in their characteristic ways of moving through life.

For example, some people may become very absorbed and intrigued in abstract symbols of ideas. Albert Einstein was one of those. In developing his theory of relativity, he would become absorbed and intrigued in what he called "thought experiments." That is, he would imagine what the effect of time and space would be if he were riding a beam of light to the ends of the universe and back. His motif was one of manipulating abstract symbols in relative frames of reference where time and space are fluid. Such a motif involved contrast and juxtaposition of different levels of abstraction. Notice the interplay of an absolute, universal oneness contrasted against his emphasis on how relative the universe can be. Indeed, he sought oneness throughout his life as evidenced by his search for a unified field theory of universal forces. His penchant for relative frames contrasted beautifully with his search for pure truth and a universal constant ($E=mc^2$). His motif utilized a paradoxical structure as he pursued unification through relativity. It is interesting that his motif of enjoying the relative nature of a holistic universe never got him to dinner on time with his wife. He was late, but then it's all "relative." Einstein enjoyed the motif of juxtaposing parts and wholes in contrasting designs.

Other people may be much more concrete in their manifestation, such as engineers or tool and die makers. Their focus may utilize motifs in a setting involving physical forms and concrete imprinting. The nuances in these motifs may have their focus more in engineering and maneuvering their ways into physical, manifest forms. Musicians enjoy the tactile feel when playing chords, harmonizing in syncopated rhythms, and the varying interchanges of patterns and arrangements. While these structural patterns may be most visible in certain areas such as music, they are found in many fields. These designing features have a kind of architecture (or archetexture of feeling) in that they act as self-organizing templates. They serve to catalyze and guide the formulation and precise articulation of how these unique patterns can be expressed and experienced in the here-and-now situation. Each person has an intrinsic motif or family of interactive sets of qualities. To the degree to which we are congruent and aligned with sensory motif as an organizing principle of self, the more empowered, harmonious and robust will be our relationship with ourselves and with others.

Developmental stages through which motifs self-organize and emerge is not necessarily without hazards and difficulties. There are many cases of deprivation in early childhood or in later years (trauma, oxygen deprivation, marasmus children, etc.). Many hardships certainly can be viewed as impeding developmental interactions for growth and change. Yet as Frankl (1963) demonstrates, in many cases meaning and purpose can manifest under the most adverse conditions. It would appear that because of how traumatic and deprived life conditions can become, it is even more essential to access one's unique motif in life. As both Frankl (1963) and Csikszentmihalyi (1990) imply, it is in times of greatest adversity when individuals may need to be at their very best, and a sense of meaning and purpose evolves through flow experiences as individuals are compelled to engage their sensory motif. It may be an alcoholic hitting bottom, a child abuse victim confronting a perpetrator, or an earthquake victim discovering firmness in his or her own resilience to survive. In all these cases, it is that immutable sensory motif that empowers people to dare to risk and move through their terrors. It is their motif that allows them to enter into a flow experience, discovering meaning and purpose in their adversity.

The organizing, empowering experience of motif allows the fears, terrors and anxieties to peak and then become incorporated into a larger, holistic, self-organizing identity. One's sensory motif is the experience of an immutable, unshakable reality of self at the core level. It therefore empowers and energizes awesome capabilities of belief, positive expectation and creative imagination for problem solving. It gives one a sense of permanence in an otherwise chaotic world of trauma and turmoil. The degree to which the self can access and resonate with its own character or motif through outside interaction (Csikszentmihalyi, 1990) is the degree to which meaning and purpose are fulfilled.

Impairment of developmental growth through trauma can result in dysfunctional, state-dependent learning. The concept of state-dependent learning (Rossi,

1986) indicates that what is learned, remembered and enacted is state-bound. In reaccessing one's psychophysiological state at the time of experience, memories, learnings and behaviors organized in that state emerge. Cheek (1981) found that severe stress leads to altered states, identifiable as a form of spontaneous hypnosis encoding state-bound problems and symptoms. Lienhart (1983) formulated a theory of multiple personality based on state-dependent learning. She indicated paradoxical messages and chaotic confusion of memory sets both in time and context of events. In treating traumatized clients (Erickson & Rossi, 1980; Rossi, 1980), it was found that by circumventing "learned limitations" and accessing response potentials, integration could occur.

This bypassing of interference from state-bound material required a special design in which creative reorganization could occur. Erickson (1980b) used age regression to bypass present, resistant, state-dependent learning. The client's dysfunctional behavior has its own "functional autonomy" when state-bound material persists against the client's will or ego (Rossi, 1986). It is therefore necessary to invoke that special design or motif to provide the integrative function. When Erickson tapped the client's resources, he could well have been using the motif that has a therapeutic "autonomous function" of its own. The motif, being developmental in nature, occurs at preverbal stages, empowering it with cross-context, state-dependent learning. Motifs can provide the common, unifying denominator in reintegrating dysfunctional, state-dependent learning. Smith and Jones (1993) indicate that traumatized clients can reintegrate with experiences that reverse fear of the "new," allow opportunities for personal choice and restore security in the continuing sense of being one's self.

The developmental nature of motifs provides the capacity to reorganize states of chaos and confusion into integrated experiences. Motifs serve to reorganize and reintegrate dissociated, state-dependent experiences. Csikszentmihalyi (1990) refers to higher-ordering effects that emerge with absorption in pleasurable flow experiences (making love, watching a child sleep, sculpting clay, etc.). The flow experience is an inherent feature in each person's unique sensory motif.

The motif is an open system responsive to fluctuations in nuances, sensations and feelings, perceptions, memories and cognitions. It seems to emerge as an interaction between the inherent organizing character of the individual and the environment in which learning occurs.

The therapeutic value of sensory motifs emerges when their unique design is accessed with clients "stuck" or fixated in limiting life conditions. By accessing the coding and organizing features of sensory motifs, thoughts, emotions and behaviors can be liberated and creatively used. Development of these sensory motifs serves to nurture emergence of powerfully embedded life themes critical to the client's sense of meaning and purpose. When the client accesses these motifs, creative, organizing, thematic processes are set in motion (creating music, growing flowers, building houses, coaching teams).

The intricate organizing principles of sensory motifs can be seen when people are doing their life work. Whatever their field of experience (music, art, business, machinery, etc.), their choice expresses their unique internal organizing principles and manifests their movement in a flow state of purpose.

The experience of this organizing movement within the client when accessing such uniquely personal experiences is a feeling of "I cannot *not* do this." When there is a love of repairing old cars or painting sunsets, there is the sense that one could not avoid doing these activities even if one tried. There seems to be a match or congruence between what the person loves to do and an internal organizing structure or principle of self. When this match between activity and internal organizing forms or structure exists, there is a sense of alignment. As the artist paints a version of a sunset, there can be an experience that all is well with the world (Csikszentmihalyi, 1975).

It is this principle of self-organization as manifest in sensory motifs that aligns the client's resources. This is similar to what Pearce (1986) indicated when discussing the need for models to develop identity. It is alignment and resonance within this larger organizing field that facilitates the individual's empowered mental and sensory integration. It is all too easy to focus on a problem area to be resolved and thus miss the inherent organizing motif.

RESILIENT MOTIFS

The interactive effects of motif with the family and social milieu are well researched in studies of resilient children. Resilience is the ability to recover the unique, psychological shape of oneself after having been twisted and bent out of shape due to adversity. Emma Werner (1992) presented research findings in *Overcoming the Odds* regarding a 40-year longitudinal study of 210 resilient children on the Hawaiian island of Kauai. The findings reveal a complex interaction between child and environment. It appears that resilient children utilize both internal and external (extended family and social connections) resources. The internal resources of resilient children involve vitality, a sense of confidence and self-righting qualities (ability to recover psychological balance). As many resilient children had to help out in dysfunctional family situations, they learned not only self-reliance but also self-knowledge of their intrinsic core abilities and talents. Stripped of conventional family resources, they had to develop and hone their own inner, unique core abilities and characteristics to survive (abilities and skills such as creative writing, art, dancing or carpentry). Such a collision with lost resources left only their inherent, core motif standing. Emphasis on their unique talents and abilities generated a sense of vitality and charisma in these self-directing children. As a consequence, these energetic and self-initiating children were perceived by adults as highly attractive and likable. The synergistic effect of these children's adherence to their own unique motif was not only to develop a sense of mastery and competence, but also to make them more attractive to potential mentors.

Being attractive and likable increased the probability that these children would be "adopted" or sponsored by the right type of mentoring adult to help them succeed on their unique life paths. Werner's research confirmed that resilient children were more likely to recruit the appropriately supportive mentor who would empower them into a positive life trajectory. In addition, such a re-cruited mentoring intervention could occur at any stage of the individual's life cycle (the person could be four years old or forty years old, it was never too late for such mentoring).

External factors such as mentors, guides, coaches, teachers, 4-H club lead-ers and so on assisted resilient children in achieving and overcoming obstacles. Resilient children appear to be good at selecting mentors. For example, one re-silient teenager with exceptional interpersonal skills knew how to talk and charm the mother of his girlfriend and was invited to move in with them for pro-tective shelter. It seems that resilient children learn to "make luck happen" as they are good at selecting mentors as a consequence of having to help them-selves.

Resilient children are challenged to rely on intrinsic self-qualities, honing and sharpening their inner talents and uniqueness. This honing and shaping pro-cess etches out the unique design and structure of the resilient child's motif. I'm reminded of how engineers can strengthen and reinforce the resilience of very thin steel plates used for automobile hoods by stamping in unique angles, shapes, and lines to create texture, design and resistance to impact and damage. In much the same fashion, resilience is enhanced by the challenging times of dysfunctional families where children learn to hone and shape through adversity their unique inner designs and motifs. They only need supportive mentoring to bring this to life.

Resilient children have a sense of coherence and trust that they will over-come obstacles. They seem to have a clear, private sense or shape of who they are and attract abundant support for their motifs and unique abilities. While re-silient children are said to be able to "snap back into shape" after adversity, no-tice that this is more than just a metaphorical way of speaking. The shape and form to which they innately adhere is actually the shape and form of motif. One could say that resilient children snap back into motif. They resume their uniquely structured, resilient form and shape which is actually that of their sen-sory motif.

The powerful attractive qualities of someone making the effort to work one's motif recruits the right mentor at the right time. Witness, for example, African American males with specific athletic talents rising out of dysfunctional settings through the recruited support of a coach or "big brother." In this way, a self-righting or gyroscopic balance throughout life is maintained in aligning with their inner core shape or motif which extends, through mentor attraction, into the external environment.

The interactive aspects of resilience (internal resources of vitality and com-petence stemming from a coherent sense of core motif and external resources of recruiting supportive mentors and enhancers) are similar to the motif's family of interactive patterns model. One can see intricate, interactive patterns of motif both within the individual and between the individual and his or her environ-ment. They are mutually reinforcing and reflexive to one another. The more in-ner motifs are developed and relied upon, the more self-righting or balanced the individual is in staying on a positive life course.

There is a honing and refining of inner motifs with interactive support and encouragement from significant others. This interaction assists in shaping and sculpting of the individual's unique design and core motif. The idea of maintaining one's shape and being able to bounce back from adversity suggests that a coherent, core consistency is operating to bring one back into form. That core consistency is the sensory motif operating as an inner and outer gyroscope allowing a resilience and return to unique form.

The interactive, perpetuating nature of motifs is that they attract and generate on-going development, support and enhanced refinement. In this way, motifs can be healing and self-correcting in the face of adversity utilizing resilient qualities.

SELF-ORGANIZING AND DEVELOPMENTAL MOTIFS

Motifs need to be nurtured and developed from early childhood and throughout life by attending to their unique organizing qualities. The developmental nature of motifs is that they have the capacity to organize and guide the evolutionary development of individuals' lives. Motifs provide the capacity to reorganize states of chaos and confusion into more meaningful experiences. Motifs serve to reorganize and reintegrate what are called dissociated, state-dependent experiences. Individuals who have been hurt either physically, sexually or emotionally in childhood have separated or disowned different parts of themselves and repressed certain memories. These disowned parts, wounds and memories are anchored and fixated to state-dependent experiences that, when accessed, arouse the trauma (sexual intimacy can arouse states which embody memories of abuse).

Motifs can help by enabling the person to discover his or her artistic talents, intrinsic interests, and organizing features of his or her own fascinations and joys. Accessing such powerful organizing structures assists the individual in making personal sense and meaning out of life experiences that intellectually are in conflict. Traumatized clients, for example, can begin to work through and reintegrate painful and detached parts of their life experience and repressed feelings by first accessing empowering core motifs. This can access the joy of their own organizing, artistic talents whether they be music, art, poetry or even the artistry of engineering, mathematics and the like. Motifs offer an inherent scheme or structure that organizes their life experience. While life experiences may not logically make sense, motif has its own unique, creative "logic" that is nonlinear (not a simple cause-and-effect model). This inherent, self-organizing signature of the core self serves as a filter through which conflicting and non-sensible personal life events take on a continuity or meaningfulness all their own.

Many personal losses and rejections, when filtered through one's motif, can assist in meaningful reorganization of such events as times in which one had lost touch and adherence to one's own true self. When relationships suffer, it can be indirectly related to becoming rigid and narrow in one's demands, not being true to one's own principles of mutual growth and expansion. Partners discover that many of their intimate relationship problems leading to entrancement are clearly related to being distracted from their own unique motif in life. When congruent to one's motif, partners feel whole and complete, and enjoy personal freedom they are able to share.

Motifs clearly have an internal gyroscopic structure that assists in the organizing and development of our personal growth and development. They are actually the formative nonverbal structures or templates that affect the shape and form of what we believe and how we make sense out of our world. Computers offer an intriguing model for understanding how this template process works. The computer uses a special template design to rearrange and reorganize written material from its original form to a specialized format. The text will not be changed, just the format, guided by the template. Whatever their chosen field of endeavor, individuals, in discovering their own organizing themes, can experience a coming together and healing of traumatic issues.

Many traumatized people struggle with intrusive memories and denial at the same time. That is, self-repeating ideas and images of painful losses and fears of helplessness in personal relationships may seem to involuntarily come into the individual's awareness. There usually is an attempt to deny and suppress such inner mental experiences. Entrancement is usually operating at this point. Motifs assist the individual in coming out of entrancing, recurrent mental experiences. Motifs empower self-organizing management of an individual's inner, mental experience. Motifs allow and create organizing self-experiences of intrinsic wholeness. As a result, they provide a powerful, organizing "motif-ating" model that gives a safe, stable structure for resolving conscious and unconscious traumatic struggles.

Ironically, the therapeutic aspects of trance occur more readily with uniqueness and individuality as absorption seems to be facilitated by novelty. There is a higher ordering of affect or emotion which emerges through absorption into those pleasurable flow experiences. These are unique to each person's motif. While making love, watching a child fall asleep or sculpting clay may vary in priority for each individual, each offers a sense of flow experience that reflects each individual's inherently unique character structure. The motif is an open system responding to changes and fluctuations of feelings, sensations, perceptions, memories, cognitions and external conditions.

Manifestations of motif seem to emerge as an interaction between the inherent organized character of the individual and the environment in which learning occurs. Differentiating unique signature qualities of one's motif from such interactions assists in identification and access. When Madame Marie Curie was pursuing the discovery of a radioactive substance now known as radium, she had to sort through tons of ore and dirt. She sifted, filtered and distilled hundreds of pounds of excess material, resulting in only a thin, pure concentrate of radium. She had interacted with tons of material mixed with hidden traces of radium. Pursuit of one's multifaceted motif involves sifting through a multitude of manifestations in which it is embedded. Pattern manifestations of motifs are all-pervasive in every area of one's lifestyle (work, love, friendship, etc.) and need to be recognized and differentiated as they overlap from one area to another.

Motifs emerge at the overlapping interface of where lifestyle patterns interact. They are like a multifaceted, crystalline structure where multicolored lights can shine through, yet the purity of the crystal structure is preserved.

Therapeutic values of motifs emerge when their unique design is accessed by individuals stuck or fixated in limiting life conditions. By accessing the coding and organizing features of sensory motifs, thoughts, emotions and behaviors can then be reorganized and utilized. Development of sensory motifs serves to nurture emergence of embedded life themes critical to the partner's sense of meaning and purpose. When partners access these motifs, creative, organizing, thematic processes are set in motion. For example, creating music, growing flowers or building skyscrapers can access unique, inherent abilities and talents, helping one get in touch with a core sense of self. In entranced relationships, this very core motif of self is what has been "lost" in the chaotic whirlwind of entrancement's fantasy ideal. While it, of course, is still present, the motif is now hidden and camouflaged by the luster and fusion of entrancement.

Regaining that musical motif within creates a harmony. Such harmony allows a genuineness or resonance with people's ability to be themselves. This in turn allows resonance and harmony in their relationships. Just as there is a psychobiophysical connection to relationships, there also exists this structural hierarchy of motif in each of us. Accessing the sensory motif taps into these organizing structures at the mind-body level. For example, while men generally may have a hard-wired perceptual-biological-physical response to female proportions, it is also clear that each of us individually has our own inner concept and aesthetic of beauty. These idiosyncratic perceptual-biological-physical wired-in responses to beauty are as much inherent as well as learned. The inherent, structural design of what we find individually beautiful is our sensory motif in action.

Accessing sensory motifs of one's talent, art, ability, aesthetic interests and so on opens doorways to unique character-designing empowerments. These unique, organizing structures suggest what we love to do, play or even become. Sensory motifs provide foundations for identity and self. Knowing that you may have an innate, organizing structure of spatial positions with your hands and fingers, for example, can help you pursue relevant activities (piano, typing, writing, etc.). Motifs can suggest broad areas of endeavor from which refined manifestation of these inherent structures and forms can take shape and expression (from brain surgeon to computer technician). The challenge is to discover these inherent motifs and their specific applications and manifestations.

Growing and developing dexterity, for example, can be discovered and manifested in the way a person lives his or her life and relates to others. An individual may develop greater finesse and become adept at "handling" complex relationships. Recovery from entrancing relationships requires access to self-organizing structures already inherent within ourselves. Indeed, it is for want of developing our unique, character-organizing motifs that we can fall prey to hypnotic entrancement. It is at this juncture that the entranced partner's fear of loss of identity is actually a movement toward discovering their core self, their characteristic motif.

However, the unique characteristics of entranced partners' artistic motifs may be allowed expression only through selective hypnotic experiences. These usually take bizarre and, at times, frighteningly twisted manifestations of their genuine form. In their own way, entranced persons manifest their unique motifs in distorted caricatures and cartoonlike versions of their genuine artistry. Their wild roller-coaster ride threatens the loss of their identity as they know it. However, it is this very process which can lead to the discovery of their real self or characteristic motif. Partners orchestrate their relationship like dramas or scenes from a Shakespearean play. Out of their most survival-oriented and need-based functions (control, power, fear, etc.) partners encounter symbols of their own motif imbedded in one another's physical and personality features.

Partners are oblivious to concrete, commonsense and everyday reality. They prefer a private, illusionary, fantasized reality even if it means drawing on the dark, mystical quality of their own inner minds. This kind of fusion of fantasized reality in that hypnotic dreamlike relationship can wreak havoc when seeking to work out relationships with friends, families, children, and special occasions. In the hypnotically induced relationships, these kinds of real-life issues are lost to partners fused in hypnotic mind-sets with a logic and fantasy all their own. Their problem-solving abilities in real-life issues are as impaired as their perception of real life.

Finding one's life work (purpose in life) through utilization of motifs can be healing for entranced relationships. Whatever the field of endeavor, the choice and application express unique, internal, organizing principles. Accessing internal organizing principles assists the healing process in providing a sense of balance and stabilization for partners lost in entrancement. Such aligned congruence between what the person loves to do and the internal, organizing structure or principle of self can provide a healing sense of integration very much needed by entranced partners. The expressive motif of unique style and structure allows partners to reestablish their unique sense of identity.

It is this principle of self-organization as manifested in sensory motifs that aligns individual resources. It is alignment and resonance within this larger organizing field of structure, design and inherent "architecture" that facilitates the client's empowered mental and sensory integration. It is all too easy to focus on client problems to be resolved and thus miss the inherent, organizing motif already operating within.

As mentioned previously, motifs are profoundly manifested, especially in flow experiences which occur through focused, sensory and mental interaction, creating qualities of various form and design. Flow experiences, which activate the unique, transforming design and structure of motif, activate the sense of self. The sensory motif's existence in self is essential for each person's unique sense of meaningful existence. It is equivalent to the essence of self. Engaging in unique flow states assists in the experience of meaning and self-worth.

It is postulated, using the concept of sensory motif, that the self has unique form and design qualities. These require aligned interactions (with the inner and outer world) such as art, poetry, music or machinery that are idiosyncratic to the self's motif. This is not simply a particular state of consciousness or mood, it is an innately designed set of traits and attributes that are formative expressions of the motif of self. Just as Picasso had his own artistic motif, so does each and every one of us. That means that it is important that we find a medium that matches and reflects our unique qualities, talents and artistry. The danger in addictive relationships is that, instead of reflecting our uniqueness, they tend to reflect our hardened, stereotyped image of what we think we should, ought to or must be. Rarely is this what we are.

As a unique expression of motif, the flow state takes on an experience of meaning. Individuals in flow discover identifiable, external forms that are compatible, symmetrical and reflective of the internal, organizing principles of who their self is. When individuals are in sync with each other and have a rapport, they seem to have a sense of mutually shared harmony. They are able to be and move as unique and sensory selves in the way they talk, act and even dance together. Individuals in flow manifest a particularly unique, back-and-forth timing and movement. This movement is the external flow experience of each person's unique, internal sensory motif coming together to create a synergy all its own.

When a person is doing his or her life's "artistic" work, it could be said that he or she feels a sense of meaning and purpose in life. One does not have to be a painter to be an artist. Indeed, a mechanic can be very artistic in his work rebuilding old engines. There is a sense of resonance where meaning and purpose in life emerge. The internal motif is aligned with the external world of manifest interaction. We express our unique, inner motif in whatever medium, field or life profession or endeavor that allows a meaningful, flowing expression of this motif. Even the interests or hobbies we choose — for instance, steelworkers who enjoy hunting, fishing and woodworking — express our inner motifs with hands-on experiences. The more developed each partner's motif is, the greater opportunity couples have to learn to share and integrate their relationship, thus creating flow and synergy.

Realize that each person's organizing properties seem to have a unique, differential signature or designation. That is, some experiences will resonate more with some individuals than with others. This is because certain experiences will more closely reflect the unique, inner motif of the individual who has design features similar to the experience at hand. An example of this is the steelworker who positively responds to hands-on activities such as hunting, but not to activities that involve sitting and listening (such as the opera). When there is resonance, it can be said that each partner feels as if there is purpose in their experience together.

At that point, one can refer to what might be termed a "purposeful self," which resonates and positively responds when symmetry or balance is discovered. Resonance can occur not only between individuals, but also with tasks at work and play. This occurs in experiences that present features similar to qualities and attributes of an individual's inner motif. Individuals feel more comfortable and together when their motifs have similarities that allow for internal, organizing experiences. In other words, some people might enjoy the schematics of an engineer's blueprint because they relate and find a certain symmetry and harmony with their own internal, networking design. Individuals can enjoy and embrace each other's differences because they actually share a similar template or motif which is made more complete when interacting together.

Symmetrical motifs between people interact in flow, creating purpose and organization of an inner experience unique to each. Such symmetry is essential for the joy of flow experience to occur. We become unself-conscious when we immerse ourselves in identifiable healthy, life-enriching ways of expressing our inherent self. Individuals have a need for a creative variety and flow that occur in these experiences. There is a sense of play and sense of purpose. The flow state is essential in accessing these motifs of design and order. Indeed, matching the unique designs of inner motif with the outer flow of movement and energy creates a sense of power and change for abundance in the future.

The birth of a unique motif experience is not without pain or a sense of loss (witness a mother's labor of love during childbirth). The birth of the motif may involve three phases similar to that of an artist's creations. First, there is accumulation of ideas, visions and data to gather information to start and explore the "project" of discovering one's motif. Second, there is saturation where the artist is taken over by the vision and intensifies his or her work, going through determined discoveries. These discoveries are journeys of the artistic work. It allows this entity to build and shape itself within the character of the artist (witness the exploring and accumulation of Mozart's efforts in writing classical music; he became obsessed with its dictation to him at the age of five). Finally, there is explosion or birth, where completion and emergence of the artistic vision and design take on their own reality. This is manifestation of their work in some form (painting, writing, music, an accounting audit, etc.).

As people work through their vision they can emerge as unique "works of art" in their own individual lives. They can emerge and take on their own unique realities. Termination of the entranced relationship can mean the reawakening, birth and manifestation of motif. People can then give birth to that unique, artistic motif of who they are, allowing its design and character to show through the many facets of their lives.

Chapter Two

Motifs and Fundamental Design Structures in a Physical, Biochemical Universe

A human being's identity is articulated through boundaries lying neither within nor without but at the orchestrated, archetextural skyline of the self/environment interface. Human beings live not in the earth nor above but rather on the edge. Though human beings interact with both the earth and the sky, it is the horizon whereupon we live and die.

The interactive nature of the human identity emerges in part from a physical as well as biological/chemical reality. The late, famous astronomer Dr. Carl Sagan once said that human beings are made of the same physical material (atoms and molecules) as are the countless number of stars above. All physical matter (organic and inorganic) is composed of these atoms and molecules. However, investigation into the nature of physical reality and biological life forms continues to uncover new, core foundations of what composes matter and life itself. The findings to be presented indicate that at the core of physical and biological dimensions are fundamental properties of self-organization, resonance and motif-like design structures. These properties are holographic (holistically present) in the human organism at multiple levels of organization and structure. The nature of physics (subatomic particles, atoms and molecules) as well as biochemistry (organic, metabolic functions and biological growth) indicates the presence of formative design structures infused throughout these levels of physical reality.

Motifs, which are inherent, self-organizing properties, provide unique, coherent guiding principles that maintain the integrity of an entity's structure and function. Such self-organizing properties operate at fundamental levels of physics and biology. Atoms, with their subatomic particles (e.g., electrons, protons, neutrinos, quarks, etc.), are basic building blocks of concrete reality (including human beings).

Physicists pursue ever-deeper levels of what composes particles, and when they find smaller particles they seek what's even smaller and more fundamental beneath that level, as in peeling layers of an onion, going deeper and deeper towards some mythical, absolute core. While the outcome to that experience is obvious (arriving teary-eyed at an empty core), physicists (Green, 1999) are now proposing that the fundamental core of physical matter (subatomic particles, etc.) consists not of smaller particles but rather vibrating strings of energy. String theory, as it is called, proposes that subatomic particles such as protons, electrons, neutrinos, and quarks appear to be solid, concrete matter but are actually oscillating strings of energy vibrating at various frequencies while moving at the speed of light. While it is not clear what the origin of the energy is in these vibrating strings, it is important to understand that the form of a vibrational energy string appears solid and particle-like because of repetitive oscillations. This is similar to the rotation of moving fan blades. They are rotating so fast as to create the illusion of something solid when in actuality it is the effect of the movement on the mind's eye. The movement or vibrating frequency of each subatomic particle repetitiously oscillates in its own frequency curve or design structure.

Each particle has its own vibrational frequency determined by the design structure available, which is its motif. The oscillation of the energy string in each particle is affected by the length (10^{-13} cm) and tension (15 million tons). These design specifications correlate to a quantum level structure of discrete (following quantum mechanical theory) energy levels which accounts for observed experimental results (involving particle collision scatter matrices and dual resonance observations) (Green, 1999).

It is also important to note that strings have two types of vibrations: linear and rotational. The combination of these two vibrations can be varied and are further indications of complexity in a self-organizing design structure exerting its own guiding motif.

String theory also accounts for the diverse and numerous discoveries of a wide range of subatomic particles. The energy string in each particle is actually moving at light speed and is therefore massless. However, the discrete quantum level (the set frequency level for that particle design structure) produces energy which can be converted into mass (which is why particles seem to be solid pieces of matter). Intriguingly, reality involves measurable design structures of motifs consisting of massless emptiness appearing solid. What can give reality substance is its motif, not some mythical content within. Motif is the substance of reality.

The higher the frequency, the greater the energy and therefore the larger the mass of the particle. Einstein's equation of $E=MC^2$ relates the conversion of energy and matter. Heavier sized particles known as hadrons (protons combined with neutrons) have greater mass produced by the conversion of their high frequency string vibration energy into mass.

The light string of energy not only vibrates but also rotates at refined, discrete levels of energy frequencies. Energy strings have two types of frequencies: linear and rotational vibrations. Note that the wire strings in a piano have only linear vibrations. These dual vibrational qualities provide for more and more refinement of frequency and harmonizing. As in a piano, the shorter and thinner the wire with consistent tension, the higher the tonal quality and frequency. Two thousand years ago, Pythagoras discovered the diatonic scale by halving the string of a musical instrument, illustrating how scales and harmonies can be produced. While he utilized a mathematical formula, he was actually operating from the inherent design structure of the instrument's archetexture. Mathematical computations and calculations of ratios and proportions are only made capable by the archetextural design that builds in these constructive qualities in the first place.

As a consequence, the formative pattern emerging in the vibrational frequencies of light strings is reflective of architectural design structures. The harmonic organization of the scales of vibrations reflect a structural architecture which as a composite articulates the operation of motifs. Intriguingly, such organizing motifs are found in design structure which operate like steps of a ladder. Each discrete step up increases the quantum energy level of vibration frequency. Between each quantum level are smaller, incremental substeps (or smaller ladders with steps of their own indicative of rotational frequency vibrations). The character and design of the particle determines which step and substep is to be "played," if you will, on the particle's harmonic scale. The design structure specifications (light string length, tension and mass) all determine the frequency pattern and particle characteristics of linear and rotational vibration.

The motif of subatomic particles manifests itself in terms of energy vibrations and physical characteristics. What applies to subatomic particles also applies to larger objects such as people and planets at the macrocosmic level. When these objects move through space and time, their unique design characteristics involving energy string vibrations influence their external as well as internal environments. The macrocosmic level involves massive energy strings called super strings that are thought to influence galaxies. Massive super strings are a complex of strings with an archetexture that folds in on itself. The complex of strings (super strings) has its own web of vibrational frequency connections affecting cosmic gravitational and electromagnetic fields. The web itself articulates its own archetextural motif. As will be later articulated, web-like design structures of motif manifest themselves at multiple levels of physical and biological realities.

Einstein in his general theory of relativity described how moving objects like the sun warp space and time. Space and time would be altered by the presence of accelerated motions of objects, which would curve and reshape the design structure of an object's time and space continuum. He indicated that the sun created a curvature or bend in space time which accounted for the orbit of earth. His theory of relativity indicated that the mass of an object increased with energy and would therefore never surpass the speed of light. Einstein noted that all objects are actually moving at the speed of light though our relative frames of reference prevent this observation. Relativity in frames of reference is a manifestation of an individual's design structure in action.

As people move and journey through life, they create their own unique curvature through the space of their life and those of others around them. Pace and tempo are also altered. The Nobel laureate Stephen Hawking described how the closer people are to large objects (the earth) versus at a distance (airline pilots), the faster their aging process. Intriguingly, the physical universe itself is a continuum of alterations in space time continuums as the very fabric of reality for each individual is unique and idiosyncratic. People are certainly objects in accelerated motion creating their own unique warp in curvature of space and alteration in tempo and pace. The warps and distortions in four-dimensional reality create motifs which in turn manifest continued warps and alterations throughout an individual's space and lifetime movement.

As Einstein described the ability of an object to create its own unique bend and fold in the fabric of the universe, the architecture of such design alterations reflects the unique characteristics inherent in the object itself. The unique, self-organizing qualities inherent in the motif of the object (person) therefore entrains the physical universe of space and time into its own design. In other words, the inherent organizing motif within individuals exerts its influencing forces in external reality of people, places and physical experiences. Such are the self-perpetuating properties of internal motif manifesting itself in the external reality of an individual's lifeline.

The construction of people and planets out of subatomic particles composed of vibrating energy strings culminates in unique formative motifs of energy. If human beings are over 80 percent water, they are 100 percent energy manifest in formative design structures of motif. The implications of these findings are staggering and will be explored later. Rael (1993) indicates that the nature of all existence is vibration. From human breathing, heartbeat and pulsating energies of subatomic particles to the expansion, constriction and reexpansion of the stars and the universe itself, all is vibration. Vibrations can only exist in design structures. Existence is therefore manifest in motif's design properties of formativeness, which set the ground for the particular vibrations to calibrate and manifest themselves in thought and action.

MULTIPLE DIMENSIONS

According to string theory, the universe has numerous dimensions (up to ten) tightly curled into the folded fabric of the universe. Time and space "fold over" upon themselves as a response to the distorting effects of matter and energy which are contingent on inherent design structures of vibrational energy strings. This suggests the presence of multiple design structures operating in the hidden dimensions of the universe.

Energy strings compose particles. Everything in the universe (at the particle level) is made of electrons, up quarks and down quarks. Nothing is smaller, but there are additional qualities, such as neutrino, muon (similar to an electron only 200 times heavier), more quarks — charm, strange bottom and top, a heavier relative of electrons called tau. Each particle has an anti-particle muon neutrino and tau neutrino. Also, there are anti-particles of electrons called positrons (+1 charge), which when contacted will annihilate one another.

Particles can be divided into three categories or families. All have an electron or one of its cousins, two of the quarks and one of the neutrino species. However, each of their masses varies as a multiple of the weight of the proton. After exploring to a billionth of a billionth of a meter, scientists conclude that these particles are the building blocks of the universe. Many questions remain, however, as to the varying sizes and force properties of these particles. String theory proposes to account for the varying properties of these particles through the various capacities of string vibration. This involves grasping the design structures operating at discrete quantum levels of energy which by their very design determine the vibration characteristics of energy strings and thus the nature of the various particles described.

BIOCHEMICAL LIFE FORMS

Biology involves the study and research of life forms and their evolution. The assertion that living entities involve form and formativeness strikes at the core of what motifs are all about. Indeed, without formativeness and self-constructed organization there would be no life. Self-construction or autopoiesis is a major organizing principle involving living systems. Self-construction in the organization of living forms suggests that there is some boundary and/or cell membrane that defines the life form (note the emphasis on form and its relationship to motif). Such a boundary delineates the first step of development of life from nonlife. This enables a critical mass of organic components to assemble and establish an enzyme-driven web of metabolic reactions.

It has been theorized that the first proto-cells of life forms on earth would involve concentrations of inorganic ions, organic chemicals and polymers out of diluted sea water solution. Their motif needed to be asymmetrical to maintain a 65-95 millivolts negative charge relative to the external environment, which is consistent to most life forms. Concentrations of different compounds inside a membrane of lipids could lead to self-constructive properties of being autocatalytic. Peptides illustrate such properties in cells culminating into an autopoietic (self-constructive) metabolic web. The formation of such a web creates a unique motif even at the proto-cell type level of creation. Motifs could well have existed at the abiotic (nonorganic) synthesis level creating early life forms and self-organizing metabolic webs of chemical reactions. It has been presented (Oparin, 1938) that concentrations of organic polymer compounds enable a critical mass of interrelating chemical reactions among compounds to be achieved. Such proto-cells could reproduce without the presence of DNA by simply splitting in half, continuing their metabolic web of reactions in unique, evolving shapes or motifs. Formativeness is essential in the perpetuation of living organisms at the most fundamental levels.

It is important to note that throughout the evolutionary process, formativeness is expressed through a concept called morphogenesis (the development of the organism's form). The concept implies that there are certain chemical and structural constraints on the possible number of configurations available to life forms. For example, single-celled organisms are limited in size because physically the volume increases proportionally to cubing the radius. The surface area will increase by squaring it as related to the cell's volume.

There will be a problem in the cell's function of disposing waste products towards the external environment. The cell's membrane increases at a slower rate than the volume, setting a limit on how large the cell may grow before it is unable to dispose of the waste. This type of relationship is known as allometric. As the size of an animal increases, the skeletal structure will have a slower rate of increase to support the weight.

Such constraints determine the hexagonal shapes of honeycombs and various crystalline structures. Constraining forces in the physical and chemical world provide the most parsimonious explanation of biological forms. Calculations of constraining forces utilizing allometric formulas present how an organism's body parts maintain consistent congruent proportions from one species to another. As a consequence, species appearing to have different forms are structurally related as to their congruency. Intriguingly, motifs are defined as the unique inherent holism of the individual capable of infinite variations of expressive form yet maintaining a structural congruence among its variations. This is similar to an individual's signature being slightly different with each signing yet preserving the unique congruence of the signature.

There is inherent order in structural constraints as further evidenced by a famous mathematical expression known as the Fibonacci ratio. This ratio of 1:1.68 is found throughout nature (pine cones, Shasta daisy flower head) and has been used by plastic surgeons to construct beautiful faces (such proportions are evolutionarily hard-wired in, where human beings have positive response for such symmetry).

Constraints such as these found in nature imply an order and organizing design structures inherent within them. Goodwin (1994) relates such constraints in morphogenesis to the concept of a law of form. He suggests, for example, that all vertebrates share a characteristic tetrapod limb formation.

Physical and chemical constraints are the parameters of a physical and biological universe setting an inherent, epigenetic stage of formativeness (motif) upon which multiple life forms have possibilities for emergence. These constraints (parameters) can be viewed at even the most elemental level.

For example, biological life forms are made of only a limited number of elements (carbon, hydrogen, oxygen, nitrogen, phosphorus, ions of calcium, sulfur, magnesium, sodium, potassium, iron, copper and zinc) arranged in unique combinations. The key to life forms is not so much in how many elements are involved but rather on arranged configurations of those elements or motifs of design structure. Williams and Frausto da Silva (1996) suggests that such elements lead to compounds that are supportive of biological forms. This is a consequence of both conditions of restraint and the inherent parameters of possible life forms implied. In such ways, motifs are inherent ways of organizing and arranging chemical compounds that eventually lead to a vast range of biological forms.

ZYGOTE AND THE LIFE LINE

The female egg fertilized by the male sperm creates the zygote cell and marks the beginning of individual formativeness. With chromosomes from both male and female, the zygote interacts with its environment beginning the rough etching out of formativeness. The zygote duplicates and cells align with respect to one another, migrating to specific regions of the developing embryo. Genes are switched on or off in various cells in intricate sequences. Such patterning and designing is not simply generated by genes but rather by the interactive choreography of protein synthesis, gene sequencing and cell environment. Unfolding dynamics such as these have their own motifs evolving throughout and constitute the choreography itself.

An essential point here is to note that the zygote's developing interaction within the environment is self-organizing and self-constructive (known as autopoeitic). There is no internal or external place, source or temporalness making it grow. It grows itself. It is life seeking after itself, and motif is its unique life formativeness growing itself, unfolding itself. This theme will be refined and further developed at future points throughout the writing.

As the zygote develops some of its migrating cells become more specialized, lose their totipotency (ability to take various forms as in genetic variation and cell differentiation) and mature as a formative part of the embryo's organization. The organization unfolds from an undifferentiated state to a shaping and carving out of rough large areas to be developed and refined. This is precisely how sculptures are created and emerge through interaction with the hands of the artist. At these early stages of development, cell totipotency is at its highest as formativeness is more essential at this time. Motif is etching out rough areas of organization for later refinement.

Areas that are specialized to become the central nervous system manifest unique design structures of motif, as no two individual brains are exactly the same. The brain contains upwards of 100 billion neurons and ten times as many supporting cells (glial) around them. The brain is organized into numerous, functionally specialized areas. The cells of each are designed into a highly organized pattern. The cerebral cortex has a design structure which is highly convoluted, four millimeters in depth. These neurons of the cortex maintain a cake layer design of six levels. The cells are also arranged in columns and an overall grid-like motif.

The neurons themselves come in various shapes and sizes (pyramids, stars, baskets, etc.). There are fibrous elements at the ends of neurons to make connections. Some fibers (dendrites) receive incoming signals. Others (axons) send out nerve impulse messages to other dendrites at adjoining spaces known as synapses. Neurons are capable of making up to 100,000 synaptic connections each.

The embryo must grow the vastly complex structure prior to birth although a great deal of growth still remains. Many glial cells are not in place at birth and have limited synapses. Approximately 30,000 synapses a second are generated per square centimeter of cortex (about 100 trillion or 10^{14}). In addition, before birth, about one million neurons per hour are created during the gestation period.

The result is an enormously complex communication system among neurons. The neural pathways become more differentiated and unique in their configurations. At about the fifteenth day, the embryo develops a hollow ball of cells with a groove along its surface. The forward end enlarges and is used to map out the formative area of what is to be the brain.

Notice that roughing in of large organ systems like the central nervous system involves developing simpler, outlined design structures into complex, differentiated formative refinements. As the groove deepens, it forms walls that rise and close over to each other to form the neural tube destined to become the central canal of the spinal cord. The head end swells marking out three sections which will eventually become the three major divisions of the brain (fore, mid and hind brain). Notice the gradual differentiation of ever increasing complexity in design structure systems. Dynamic growth such as this is the hallmark of unfolding, differentiating motifs in action.

The design structuring continues to ever-refined levels. For example, precursor cells to the neurons separate from the neural tube and migrate to a distant, designated (design-ated) location. Glial cells begin the migratory pattern spinning out long tails upon which neurons will later attach themselves as a guide (Edelman, 1987). Glial cells contain proteins called cell adhesion molecules (CAMs). Neurons utilize these in their movement of following glial cell progression.

To signal the direction of the glial cells requires a target cell already established towards which migration can be directed. Secretion by target cells of signaling (trophic) molecules called nerve growth factor assists migrating glial cells. For example, axons from the refined neurons which form the optic nerve track their way to their first staging post in the brain (lateral geniculate). Migrating cells are kept in step through a molecular gradient and the presence of a chemosensor on the axon surface. This assists the cells in maintaining formation (motif) in their movement.

With their arrival at the lateral geniculate their formation has now been transposed from the retina to the brain, creating the geniculate map. This topographical transformation is characteristic of motifs generating themselves in the developmental process from one body structure to another. In this way, the design structure has been transformed and transforms (resonates) from one part of the embryo to another. The brain holds multiple map patterns and designs for each of its sensory input and motor output systems. The placement of target cells guiding the process formation may well be following its own precursor formative motif in ways that establish a formative foundation or anchor upon which to further differentiate successive formations.

In addition to transforming topographical formations, the central nervous system has both specificity and plasticity built into it. The body will develop a temporary support design structure while in transition growth phases. The embryo is both being (functioning quasi-independently at current level of development) and becoming (needing to mature and refine its growth for full development and survival). The embryo both needs a specific structural design (to maintain neural retinal connections) yet needs to be plastic (while it grows through its transitions to greater maturity and higher level functioning) (Rosen, 1997). Such being and becoming dynamics in an unfolding process are congruent with the dimension of motifs which are inherent design structures both manifest yet ever unfolding and refining towards artistic differentiations.

PRUNING AND CONSTRUCTION OF MOTIFS

Pruning and streamlining are often required to maintain efficiency of function. This involves the shaping of design structures. For example, there is an overproduction of cells and synapses. If the number of neuron axons arriving at target cells exceeds the number of target cells that are there to receive them, and synapses cannot make functional connections with dendrites, they will be pruned away. There is both selection and competition for resources — trophic factor, target cell and synaptic space. This has been called neural Darwinism. Yet long range order, involving migration of cells and growth of axons over long distances, involves the execution of internal programs both of cells and the totality of cells acting in concert.

The presence of excess neurons and synapses provides the necessary conditions of stability to enable the entire ensemble of cells to cooperate collectively. Each depends on the other to create and preserve the dynamic pattern of connections which maps the world onto the sense organs, the sense organs onto the brain and then via the brain and body structure imposes new patterns. Such pruning and patterning is the organism's mode of maintaining design patterns that function at optimum levels of shaping (literally) its own destiny. Being able to construct that unique design ensemble is indicative of finding balance and harmony that resonate with the organism's unique needs.

There is a neural pathway of networks formed by pruning. The resulting patterned neural network is a mosaic complexity of its own motif. Further, since neurons never actually touch but rather come close together at junctures called synapses, a pathway of spaces between the places of where neurons are present is also created. The spatial or synaptic pathways interlaced throughout the neurons (much like pathways constructed by ants underground) form a field or motif of its own unique mosaic as well. The neural network pathways in the brain create unique motifs contrasting with the spatial synaptic connections creating a juxtaposing figure/ground relationship. That is, the neuron's network pathways can be viewed in relief of the "empty" synaptic spatial network pathways as either in the foreground or background.

Such figure/ground reversals create unique motif formations in the brain/mind functioning contributing to each person's individual electroencephalograph characteristic signature. These neural networks form a unique web with their own characteristic motif capable of multiple levels of inter- and intra-neuron communication. Taken as a totality, such web-like motifs manifest unique oscillations with a character structure all their own. When the neural network motif reaches a critical mass of constructing itself to a certain level of complex design, a quantum leap of functioning occurs. The whole now takes on its unique identity greater than the sum of it neuronal parts. More will be addressed on these web-like motifs as they recur through the mind body human design.

Edelman (1987) indicates that the networking of the brain is similar to the interweaving qualities of a jungle. There is a jungle of interlacing neurons crisscrossing in a maze of entanglements. Yet, each brain's neural network has its own unique, holistic set of connections. The shaping and pruning of our brains can be influenced by the use or nonuse of various brain functions in dealing with sensory input and motor output to the environment. As the perceptual filters of the brain determine what comes into conscious and/or unconscious awareness (posterior and anterior brain structures) the pruning process constitutes formative properties of the brain/mind system creating itself. The cyclic quality of perceptual selectivity influencing what enters the brain and the resulting reshaping of neuronal connections as a response further affect the perceptual process. In this manner, the motif of the brain/mind system creates a holistic shaping process such that continued transformative self-operations can occur.

The central nervous system is not the only one in human biology that utilizes formativeness and design structures in its growth. Edelman (1992) utilizes a selection system on immune system functioning. He indicates that the immune system possesses a wide range of various types (shapes, designs, forms) of antibodies already present. When a potential antigen (toxic agent, virus, etc.) threatens the organism, there is a large production of those antibodies whose design structure best fits the invading antigen. Refinement then occurs in the antibody's protein design structure to exactly match the threatening antigen.

Even in the immune system formativeness (antibody form types) exists as well as a process of unique design structuring (refinement of antibody protein structure). There is the roughing of general patterned design type into uniqueness and specificity. There already exist design structures present at the antibody level capable of functioning at highly unique levels as part of a larger process of refining motifs in service of the body.

To understand the presence of motifs throughout the physical, biological and psychospiritual levels of a human being involves grasping core concepts of the organism. Central to these is the concept of autopoiesis which is the ability to self-construct and self-organize. The biology of the human anatomy has this property to self-create continuously over time, generating a lifeline (Rose, 1997) of growth and life processes from the cellular to the major organ systems integrating in dynamic organizations. The human organism has a process unity, not an object unity (Rosen, 1997), as there is constant replacement of old tissues, cells and so on with new regenerating (for example, new stomach lining every sixty days, new skin and bone structure, etc.), yet constant archetextural design structure is maintained and serves as a guiding motif or template to map out the biological domain. It is similar to soldiers on the battlefield — some are lost and replaced by new recruits while the lines of conflict remain the same. Intriguingly, surgeons have found that they can capitalize on these properties of self-construction by using neonatal cells for skin regeneration in patients suffering from skin trauma. The vast complex biological growth process of the human organism illustrates an incredible degree of well-choreographed timing, sequencing and synchronized metabolic processes. As will be presented, such synchronized organization reflects the articulation of an archetextural motif that unfolds in a self-constructive, dynamic process.

DESIGNER CELLS

The entity of the individual cell is a marvel of orchestrated self-organization and intricate harmonizing of metabolic operations. For example, the cell demonstrates themodynamic properties inherent in its functioning. The internal acidity level remains close to the neutrality level with temperature varying only one degree. The stability of the cells' functions and metabolism is maintained homeodynamically. That is, the set points controlling rates of reactions and other functions are not fixed but rather fluctuate within a range of oscillations to accommodate the lifeline of the cell (Rose, 1997). There is a life cycle of cells (except for neurons in the brain) and when they die, they are replaced by new ones. In addition, the proteins, nucleic acids and other molecules are constantly being replaced. Such a state of change and oscillation involves dynamic stability allowing adaptation to change.

Intriguingly, the formative process of the protein and cell design remains relatively intact while this constant state of component part replacement continues to flow. Were it not for formativeness in biochemistry, the cell and its structures would collapse after the first proteins and nucleic acids disintegrated. Indeed, the cell recognizes proteins by their shapes and forms. Hopkins (1913) indicated that stability results from states where there is continuous flux of component parts. The cell conducts countless chemical reactions on a moment-to-moment basis, forming a web of interactive metabolic operations. The complexity of such metabolic webs involves enzymatic chemical reactions participating in numerous pathways simultaneously (Rose, 1997).

The web becomes stronger and more resilient as interconnections increase. The interweaving creates a tapestry (Rose, 1997) not depending on any one thread. The strength of metabolic webs reaches a quantum level of stability with increased complexity. The resilience is not on the individual parts (enzymes, products). It now is established in the integrity of the entire web which has now emerged as a full unique motif of formative complexity. The web is capable of replacing its parts without risk to the integrity of its totality. The web is self-organizing and stable. The web can reorganize itself as a response to injury. The organizational structuring and restructuring requires the resilience of motif as the web prunes and hones its own formative functions.

The oscillations of metabolic cell sequences indicate a rhythm all their own (Hess, 1994). These oscillations have their own formative design in terms of timing and recurrence. In addition, there are calcium ion signals propagated by spiral wave (design forms) impulses serving as intracellular messengers. The unique formativeness of these timing sequences regarding chemical reactions and wave impulses emerges as a flow of energy throughout the cell, involving enormous complexity.

There is inherent order in the biochemical universe. Webs will emerge when appropriate sources of energy, enzymes, membranes and so on are present within a formative boundary (motif). Such order is also within the structure of the cell itself. There are mitochondria, chloroplasts (plants) and complex networks of internal membranes forming beautiful patterns within the cell (Rose, 1997). Each of these component parts is organized into its own structure with selective chemical reactions operating. There is precise communication between these structural components again in an organized, themodynamic manner.

Yet, cell order is not maintained exclusively by self-organizing properties of webs. Semipermeable lipid membranes with proteins utilize structural recognition to regulate the entry of certain metabolites. Changing the microenvironment changes the protein as their chains fold and curve which therefore alters their shape and thus formative function. The totality of the cell exerts constraints on its structural parts resulting in holistic organization. The cell is in motion with a constancy of spinning nuclei, graceful movements of mitochondria and streaming small particles all occurring in a choreographed, organized whole (Rose, 1997).

The property of self-assembly is a central dimension for constructing cells. Rosen (1998) indicates that this is the result of physical constraint forces leading to proteins constructing themselves into least energy configurations. Ribosomes are an example of this self-organizing activity. The cell utilizes microtubules to create a skeletal structure within cells. Self-assembly also occurs with these structures.

These self-organizing features of cells are indicative of inherent design structures identifiable even at the cellular level. Each level of the human organism is self-constructing and uniquely designing. From the subatomic to the organism each level is composed of organizing design structures interweaving into a holistic system. For example, the cell may be viewed as a part of body tissue yet, as has been noted, is an organizing whole at that level complete with its own infrastructure of membranous microtubules, calcium ion wave impulses and complex metabolic webs. Each "part" of the human organism is actually a subset of a hierarchy of organization with a holistic complexity of design structures at each "part/whole" level. The larger whole of the human organism is composed of smaller wholes (design structures).

The organization of the human brain manifests such complexity of organizations within itself. The three major divisions of the brain (forebrain, midbrain and hind brain) consist of subsystems within each level. The forebrain has four lobes, each with its own characteristic in-folding (parietal, frontal, temporal and occipital). The design structures within each of the lobes are unique to each brain with regard to the degree, number and concentration of folding, peaks and valleys of neurons. Each lobe and region has its own characteristic structure and function. The midbrain involves the limbic system composed of substructures (amygdala, hippocampus, thalamus, hypothalamus, etc.). This system involves mood control and bonding issues. The basal ganglia also in the midbrain are large structures affecting anxiety, panic, fear and avoidance. The cingulate is a substructure of the frontal lobe affecting worry, rigidity and fixations of thought and behaviors. The temporal lobes of the forebrain are related to memory, language, comprehension, mood management and learning among other functions (Amen, 1998).

Each of these systems is composed of subsystems intricately interconnected such that what happens in one resonates through the others. The "parts" of the brain are actually organized subsystems within systems functioning within a metaorganization of unique design structures. The brain models whole systems within larger systems called modules (subsystems like the limbic system) which can be refined to even finer scales (Sperry, 1985). The organization of the brain operates holistically involving higher levels of organization for abstract thought.

The brain can be both holistic for comprehensive, executive functions and modular (localized) for specific concrete operations and emotions. The brain can function as a mosaic of unique design structures and holistically as needed by the dictates of the interactions involved. The point here is that the brain functions and is designed with motif-like qualities and attributes.

Thus formativeness and unique, unfolding design structures that are idiosyncratic and evolving are facets of motifs manifest in the brain. The brain has been found to have body mapping (Penfield) on its surface where various body parts have sensory/motor neuronal connections throughout the brain. The representation of this mapping for human beings is called Homunculus Man. It illustrates the graphic image of the areas and concentration of neurons in the brain which, if stimulated, will produce a response in a body part (hand, arm, leg, etc.). Such a depiction is called a Penfield map.

The organization of brain mapping is not a set nor permanent state. Studies of amputees (Ramachandran & Blakeslee, 1998) reveal that neurons in the brain areas corresponding to lost body parts (amputated arm) will reorganize themselves producing new mapping configurations. In some cases, it was found that touching the amputee's face produced phantom limb phenomena of the lost arm. Findings indicate that remapping and reorganization of brain structures occur in both traumatic and nontraumatic interactions of learning and experience.

The brain is both plastic (can reorganize itself) and redundant (has multiple neurons for similar functions). These neurons sprout new fibers into inactive brain areas (arm amputee's unused arm area of brain) such that facial nerves now innervate in areas formerly used by arm neurons.

There is a vast amount of redundancy of connections with most nerves nonfunctioning. Reserve troops of nerves (Rose, 1997) are thus called into action when needed. The architecture of the brain can be reorganized, sometimes rapidly. There is no fixed, one-to-one permanent wiring of nerves to set body parts but rather an evolving, dynamic state of flux and systematic reorganization depending on need and interactional experience (Ramachandran & Blakeslee, 1998). The redundancy and plasticity of the brain suggest an underlying state of nerves capable of dynamic reorganization, unique in architecture and idiosyncratic for each individual. The brain is a prime physiological example of motif in action.

Plasticity allows each person's individual brain to grow, adapt, reorganize and evolve new design structures (Horgan, 1999) through interactions of its present motif and incoming/ongoing stimuli and response. Each person has a singular integration of social identity, values and biochemistry that is a "unique experiment" (Pressman, 1998). Many debates about such areas of the human organism as the frontal cortex concern whether there is a wholeness in function or a subdivided modularity (separate distinct areas where functions are exclusively located). The conclusion of many scientists is that the truth is somewhere between the two perspectives. This part/whole dialectical tension relates precisely to the construct of motif as there is holistic formativeness generating unique, ever-refining design structures with their own differentiations.

The mind-body motif is uniquely organized through an amalgam of overlapping, web-like integration. For example, the heart, mind, body and brain are not exclusively localized. Design structures of each are interspersed throughout the organism, seemingly autonomous yet intricately orchestrated to serve the complex whole. Neuroscience research indicates that the amygdala of the midbrain's limbic system is a center for intense emotions of rage and fear. Other research (Pearsal, 1999) indicates that the human heart has its own neural circuits independent of the brain yet with pathways to the limbic system. Pearsall (1999) describes how each heart has its own unique signature, which we constantly communicate and receive from others. The cardia synchronized energy pattern (CSEP) is a way of detecting various types of energy associated with the electrical activity recorded by an electrocardiograph. Magnetic activity is recorded by the magnetic cardiograph and cardiac sounds are recorded by an electronic stethoscope. In addition, various pressure and temperature changes are recorded by specifically designed, quantifying instruments. The sum of all these measurements constitute the CSEP signature of the synchronized heart.

When there is a focus on the heart, there is connection with the entire body system synchronizing brain, heart and body vibration energies into its own signature motif. The design structures inherent in synchronized heart vibrations reverberate throughout the mind/body system. Notice that vibration design structures at the subatomic string level are holographic at the biological organ level.

There is also research supporting a "second brain" in the lower chest/stomach region of the "gut" area (Gershon, 1998). So what we seem to be faced with is a human organism with an "emotionalized" heart in the brain (amygdala), an independent brain-like neural circuit structure in the heart establishing its own rhythm and a "second" brain in the body soma (or gut).

Therefore, when human beings have a "heart" in their heads, mindfulness in beating hearts and a body with a head up its "gut," is it any wonder that scientists and philosophers have such difficulty pinpointing where the real consciousness of the human being is? The holistic and yet mosaic-like organization of human beings manifests itself in unique, individualistic motifs with magnificent webs of multiple functionality and plasticity of creative adaptation. Throughout it all is the vast complexity of the organism's motif capable of microscopic refinements of differentiation and simultaneous, orchestrated integration.

Chapter Three

Nature, Nurture and Epigenesis: Motifs in and beyond DNA

The emergence of human identity and behavior has been for decades depicted as the product interaction of varying degrees of genetic and environmental contributions. The human being has been depicted as predisposed towards certain irrevocable tendencies by genetic coding and/or influenced and shaped by environmental affirmations and/or negations. Such a dualistic, polarized illustration of the evolution of human beings suggests that the ultimate identity and behavior of each individual are simply products of the interaction of these two dichotomous forces. Such a perspective reflects a form of reductionistic thinking and analysis, missing the whole for the cumulative addition of its parts. The motif of selfhood may well be inherent in the motif of genomes, chromosomes and subcellular environments in which genes operate. To fully explore the nature-nurture issue, a clarity of thinking and linguistic usage is necessary to comprehend such terms as genetic coding, nature, environment and so on.

While such clarity will be forthcoming, it is important to establish from the outset that the totality of the selfhood's evolution ultimately involves the whole being greater than the sum of its parts. The wholeness or totality of nature-nurture dynamics invokes a higher level ordering of dynamic properties regarding genetics, environmental influences and the relationships operating between and among them. The unique synergism emerging from higher ordering of nature-nurture dynamics is idiosyncratic for each organism and manifests its own signature or design structural motif. The unique design motif of this synergy involves a higher ordering principle beyond cause-effect relationships of genes and environmental influences. As motif operates at a level of organizing principle, it is epigenetic to cause-effect relationships.

Definition of terms is essential at this point and involves clarifying what is genetic and what is environmental, and how they operate and dynamically interface at multiple levels.

THE HUMAN GENOME

The genetic code of a human organism consists of the double helix, spiral-shaped macromolecule known as deoxyribonucleic acid or DNA. DNA involves twenty-three pairs of chromosomes with each pair a matched set in the sense that one of each pair contains the genetic information necessary to make the same set of proteins. Yet, such pairs are not identical to each other. That is, the precise code can vary quite a bit between the chromosome pair. These genetic differences are harmonized from the very beginning of the fertilized egg (zygote) as half the chromosomes are from the mother and the other half are from the father.

There is genetic redundancy as each cell contains twice as much information needed to synthesize proteins. Redundancy allows for tremendous flexibility and versatility in the range of protein types and formations possible.

The chromosomes of the spiraling double helix formation are linked together by four component subunits called nucleotide bases which are adenine, guanine, cytosine and thymine. They are joined together like rungs on a spiraling ladder but only in particular configurations or motifs. These bases are grouped as either purines (adenine and guanine) or pyrimidines (thiamine and cytosine). Only specific purines can join fibrous, hydrogen bonding with specific pyrimidines (adenine with thymine and guanine with cytosine) to form the perpendicular, ladder-like linkages between the spiral chains of DNA. Such specificity is a function of a particular formativeness in the bases themselves known as tautomeric which restricts the conditions of hydrogen bonding to specific base pairs. While the specific linkages between bases are strictly defined, there is unlimited freedom in the range of sequence patterns and formative designs in which series of these base linkages can be arranged.

The resultant contrast in both base-pair specificity and unlimited range in base-pair sequencing are two complementary spiraling DNA chains (themselves composed of sugar and phosphate). These chains are not identical but fit each other like a hand fits a glove. Each chain is the opposite, complementary template for the other. The function of two completely different DNA chains joined together requires harmonizing, epigenesis or organizing motifs to orchestrate complementary functioning of the DNA blueprint.

Each chain of the double helix DNA molecule maintains a separate template complementary to the other. During protein synthesis or DNA duplication, the spiral, double-chained DNA molecule unwinds in whole or part depending on its function. A single chain or strand of DNA, uncoupled from the double helix, presents a template upon which complementary, base pairs of a patterned sequence can be reproduced. Yet, this template is not the whole of the DNA message, as the single chain can only provide half (the complementary) of the complex protein code onto the RNA which is itself single stranded. Complete duplication can be done most simply if single chain DNA takes up the formative configuration of a spiraling helix. Therefore, polymerization of monomers (single chain bases grouped into pairs) is possible if the resulting chains form the proposed structural formativeness of the double helix. The configuration of the DNA molecules is constrained by base pair specificity (referred to as steric reactions). Only through the formative configuration or motif of the spiraling, double helix does the complete totality of the DNA blueprint manifest itself. It is this formative motif that is epigenetic to the DNA molecule itself. For example, the spiraling, double helix design of DNA forms a template that when unwound assists in protein synthesis to reconfigure that protein into a multi-tier complex. Protein configuration requires the template to have emerged from the spiral design.

Formativeness is evident not only within the DNA molecule but in each of the twenty-three paired strands of chromosomes human beings possess. Each pair of chromosome has its own unique shape, length, and overall design (Gonick and Wheelis, 1991). As each pair of unique chromosomes is similar, they are called homologous pairs. During cell reproduction, each homologous pair duplicates through unwinding, template completion, and rewinding into the spiral helix.

The two sets of pairs (tetrads) of each of the twenty-three chromosomes line up preparing to separate into the two-cell nuclei forming during cell reproduction. Each set of two pairs in the tetrads follows spindle fibers formed to guide them (like a temporary scaffolding) towards their destination into their respective nucleus in each new cell. Centromeres divide on chromosomes as fibers pull them apart. The spindle of fibers is similar to a grid forming a structural design mapping out the direction of migrating chromosomes. In meiosis (production of sperm and egg cells), the paired chromosomes migrate in an additional direction as new spindle fibers form from another direction. This results in four cells each with half the number of chromosomes but always one from each homologous pair. The unique motif of each chromosome is thus preserved to pass on its formativeness of that particular chromosome.

Chromosomes obey the law of independent assortment. That is, each chromosome has not one but two genes (alleles) for each position and sequence on the chromosome. There are two copies (not necessarily exact) of any given gene lying at the same point on homologous chromosomes. Formativeness operates at the gene level regarding position and design. It also is involved with cell and gamete reproduction as well as uniqueness with chromosome structure and design. Indeed, the motif of formativeness and unique design structure operates at multiple levels of genetic structure.

THE PARADOXICAL GENE

Genes are not like beads on a string with one gene or bead determining a character trait or protein. The notion of a gene as a unitary particle causing a specific trait to emerge creates a paradox. A gene is actually a sequence of structures. Genes are composed of alternating pieces of DNA, rearranged, reformed and designed in unique motifs. The proteins these genes synthesize (or genomes as they are called) take on alternate forms resulting from cellular metabolism far beyond gene synthesis (Rosen, 1997). Chromosomes may function as twisted ribbon-like structures with irregular but precise patterns of bands. The point is that a gene is in reality a sequence of DNA molecules, not a whole unitary one.

The paradox of confusion occurs when the "gene" is taken as a whole class when it is actually a member of a class of sequences of patterned DNA structures known as genome.

The operation of DNA is not simply a matter of a master-slave relationship where one gene determines one specific characteristic in all cases. Genes are not set in fixed positions in the chromosomes but actually are fluid. They can move from position to position. In sexual reproduction, matching sections of each chromosome pair can exchange. McClintock (in Rose, 1970) discovered genes could jump, relocating at different sites on the chromosome map. Genes can split off from one segment of the chromosome, move to another and recombine with other genes in a variety of fluid and sequenced ways. The sequencing of genes can be split, edited and spliced back together in layer after layer of sequencing. It is possible for gene sequence codes to be organized and reorganized in higher archival structures involving secondary, tertiary and quadranary tiers. They are not unlike musical chords: change one note and the "meaning" of the chord is altered.

Nothing is more striking in how subtle changes produce astounding effects as in the fact that 98 percent of humans' and chimpanzees' DNA is almost identical. The small 2 percent difference is the change of "note in the chord" that shifts formativeness from animal to human. The minute genetic differences are alterations in formativeness of motif. It is not the number of genes involved but the alterations in formative design resulting in subtle gene sequence reconfiguration that produce such human attributes as language, planning and morality.

The smallest units of variation in DNA are referred to as single nucleotide polymorphisms (SNPs, called "snips"). These are units of genetic formativeness that can mutate (for better or worse) over a 300- to 800-year period. Many snips are carried over many generations long after their usefulness has expired. As a result, individuals possess numerous tiny "imperfections" or variants of motif design structures, which may or may not always enrich an individual's life. Honing, harmonizing and design structuring is the province of the formative properties of motif. Complexity of balance is necessary in alignment of healthy formative motifs.

There is not a one-to-one articulation of one gene per human characteristic but that there can be numerous gene sequences and multilayer tiering needed to create such personality attributes. These genetic structures are fluid and have ubiquitous capacities for formative shape and design schemes affecting and impelling future growth. The inherent organizing design structure in genetic tiers has its own unique archetexture and intricate order constituting what may be termed a motif. The DNA molecule interacts with the cell and proteins it synthesizes in ways that further develop archetextural motifs by a singling system. Such a system turns various sections of the DNA molecule on or off at various times (sequences and frequencies), choreographing protein production and building.

Proteins themselves form various tier structures, and their building can trigger other sections of genomes on the chromosome to initiate further production of protein for synthesis and growth. Proteins contain several variant derivative forms of their primary structure. These are called isoforms. They are functionally equivalent as far as the organism is concerned. In such cases the function and form are not perfectly equivalent such that the form can vary without the function being remarkably disturbed as long as there is an approximation of that form. The partial overlap of structure and function becomes critical when a subset of that critical structure component does affect those functional aspects. Notice the transformative variations available at the biological level of motif. If that structural change were related to a unique feature of the DNA protein, substitution of one of 146 nucleic acids would result in a change of properties of the molecule (for example, sickle cell anemia).

Some genes are activated or stimulated on different resonances of activation. Also, genes can be environmentally triggered. Altering a particular feature of the unique structure either from the environmental components and/or protein components can create functional changes as a result of structural alterations.

While form and function have an interdependence, the actual hardware of the DNA is comparable to a computer: the hardware needs of the computer are useless without the program just as the program is useless without the computer or the person to run that program. In the individual, there is a personalized program, if you will, of the motif that seems to manufacture its own hardware such that activation of both program and hardware in terms of the mechanical physical structure of the anatomy itself have their own interactive quality which creates the uniqueness of inherence in that interaction.

While much research has been directed towards the actual hardware or structural design of the DNA molecule, it has been hypothesized that another structure above the DNA structure exists in terms of developing the capacity for speech. Such a metastructure is based on the development of a protein substrate which enables the capacity for structural placements of templates related to speech. Linguistic phonemes can be manifest by the development of templates or foundations where these phonemes can be anchored and later tapped as ways of building word phrases and the spoken word. Such studies of infants and fetuses (Pearce, 1986) have found that indeed phonemes and sounds have been choreographed through the neuromuscular movements of infants and fetuses such that they have their own sensory design, template and archetexture — or motif — that provides that secondary structure which allows children to speak their first word sound nine months after they are born.

It is important to remember that the capacity of genes to restructure and redesign themselves in their own architectural way may have a metaarchetexture or blueprint on how the genome is to operate creatively, and that may well be a motif in and of itself. As indicated previously, genes can jump from one location to another and be quite fluid rather than stable. This capacity for relocating themselves in the chromosome is a constant flow-like state of movement as a map, if you will, is constantly restructuring and redesigning itself. Indeed there are spacers on the chromosome known as introns, which are interspersed throughout the chromosome. They are noncoding regions where they have their own arranged sequence which, similar to motifs, has an asymmetrical, unique articulation in their own formative structure. The introns are spacers that can easily affect design patterns. Proteins are not coded by a simple continuous strand of triplets. The interspersal introns create variability in pattern formation. While introns have no coding properties themselves, they do provide interspersed spacing for design pattern formativeness. As such, they could serve more as delineations in the formative design properties of genomes as a motif in and of itself. Creation of a motif on the chromosome parallels motifs in the self-organism.

Different parts of a protein may be coded for by segments of DNA distributed across long regions of the chromosome, which have to be brought together by complex cellular machinery, a process known as splicing. Once splicing is possible, it also becomes possible to arrange splices sequentially in a variety of ways which are not automatically read off from an originating DNA molecule. Many proteins are products of such alternating splicing arrangements. Many more are synthesized on DNA in one form and subsequently processed further in the cell having components added or removed (shaping, designing motifs) as in editing. There are continual editing processes both with the genes and the proteins. Genes can be assembled from alternate pieces of DNA or rearranged so that their codes are read differently. Proteins take on multiple forms (motifs) as a result of cellular processes a long way down from the DNA stage of initiation itself. Genes are in constant dynamic exchange with the cellular environment. A gene is an active participant in the cellular orchestration in the individual's development.

The ordering/reordering and the secondary and tertiary reordering of sequences is similar to the archetextural motif of designing and redesigning structuring processes of an ever evolving fingerprint of motif. The motif is a blueprint of the DNA blueprint, not necessarily embedded in it, but the motif may be infused throughout it. The motif of selfhood may well be inherent in the motif of genomes on the individual chromosomes; as many times genes become fluid, moving or multilocated and seem to have an endless stream of sequencing and resequencing as if there is a higher organizing principle structuring the molecule in and of itself.

It is important to remember that the DNA needs further development, which is required through interaction with the cellular environment. While many proteins of such spliced alternatives and editing are synthesized on the DNA chromosome and processed, which means they are either added to or subtracted from further down the line of processing in the cell, many more are edited and refined. In this way, both genes and proteins are disarticulated in the sense that there is no direct cause and affect (Rose, 1997). Notice the unfolding weaving of the tapestry of a web of metabolic processes that seem to have their own archetexture, not as a cause and effect from the gene to the cell but from the sequence and coding and rearranging of the archetextural patterns of movement and flow between the DNA molecule, the proteins and the cellular environment in and of itself.

The gene is an active participant in cellular metabolic orchestration, not just a primary cause. The varying sequences of DNA, its fluidity, the strands subject to alternative reading frames, splicing and editing all suggest a constant reorganization and restructuring of motif. Many of the gene's expressions are contingent on the cellular regulation at levels far from the genome in the organismic metabolism. Another intriguing feature about genes is that the genotype of a particular characteristic or trait may sometimes be different than the phenotype of what is actually shown in the physical form. The ontogeny of information which is the developmental projectory of the gene characteristics may unfold in nonlinear ways (Rosen, 1997). Indeed, motifs are not linear, set blueprints but rather unfolding design structures of spontaneous manifestations of formativeness and archetexture. The parallels between the ontogeny of developmental projectory and the operation of motifs are remarkable in their similarity and correlation.

Restructuring and developmental qualities in the DNA molecule and cellular level of functioning are quite influential on phenotypic conditioning. Genes are not simply tool-and-die makers stamping out various kinds of imprints. Genes are more like working through lines of education, carrying out drafting and refining messages, creating, carving and etching out throughout interactions with the cell metabolites what proteins will or will not be synthesized. Indeed, many proteins affect the on and off switches of further DNA sequences whether to be continued, to be uncovered or even to be turned off. Many proteins manufactured through DNA ontogeny or life line (Rosen, 1997) throughout the cellular regions are designed to involve transcribing onto messenger RNA. The transcription process involves spliced and edited messages, translating these into proteins which then provides feedback control to the DNA molecule itself which may switch it on or off for further or lesser synthesis of additional proteins. The DNA sequences are significantly influenced through the splicing and editing steps. In many ways, there is an exquisite timing and sublime balance of this interactive process of DNA protein production, splicing, editing, message translation and determining when to turn it on or off. The entire coordination of this operating motif is very much like a choreographed ballet in which the dancer will hit what spotlight at what time, at what rhythm. Such an artistic and intricate motif becomes quite apparent at this level of perspective. Such orchestration at the cellular level culminates in the synthesis of proteins that begins the process of increasing replication and segregation of chromosomes.

Genes are only partial determinants within the genome structure. Many times the DNA molecule needs signals from the cell from which it is embedded to be active in its production and changes. The fluidity of the genome and how and when and to what extent any sequence is expressed or translated into a functional protein depend on the cell in which the DNA is embedded. This is quite a difference from the abstract idea of a gene having a one-to-one cause and effect; a more realistic view of the complex processing mechanism places the DNA sequences into a larger context or operating archetexture for change and development.

Proteins are not nearly the principal products and productions of DNA sequences. They have complex secondary and tertiary structures themselves which depend not just on their amino acid sequence but on their surrounding environment, presence of water, ions and other small molecules, acidity and alcoholic-ity. The condition and involvement of various orders, complexities and balances indicate that, far from a one-to-one correlation, there are an enormous number of field forces and factors operating in what characteristic traits are expressed, modified or deleted from the gene into the cell and beyond. Accuracy of one gene depends on other genes present in the genome of the organism, the cellular environment, the extracellular environment and the environment outside the organism or even the mental configurations of the imaginal qualities of the individuals themselves (Rosen, 1997). There are continual mediational affects on genetics and evolution.

An important concept known as plasticity is part and parcel of the genetic and evolutionary process. Plasticity refers to the ability of an organism to find alternate routes to achieve its goal if one is thwarted and if other options are available. To achieve this, something called functional redundancy occurs in which there are duplications and replications of many different routes for metabolic reactions, changes and routes of communication to occur so that if one is in some way interrupted or impaired, other routes of chemical communication within the cell can take place. In the genetic construction of the organism, such a route involves a multiplicity of avenues, interactions and pathways. Such multiplicity takes on the form of an archetexture or design, which one could again refer to as a motif. As in archetexture, many biologists and evolutionists refer to genetic and cellular activity as a matter of construction (Rose, 1997). This is very similar to the engineers following the blueprint of the architect in doing the construction of their own building.

Dean Hamer (1994), a molecular biologist at the National Cancer Institute, asserts that long-term happiness levels have a major genetic contribution. However, genetics do not determine every detail in an individual's life. Not only is there gene splicing, editing and rearrangements but also biological processes in which both intra- and intercellular as well as environmental influences determine which genes are switched on or off. In addition, the human genome consists of 90 million DNA base pairs distributed over twenty-three chromosomes. Yet, recent research (Rose, 1997) indicates that more than 90 percent of the human genome has no known purpose. It is therefore quite difficult to determine fully how and where genetic and outside environmental influences interact and interface as a dynamic boundary of change.

THE NURTURING ENVIRONMENT

Recent findings (Begley, 1999) indicate that significant lifelong effects on the human organism can occur in utero. The womb environment can affect the fetus's hormone levels, potential for addiction (fetal alcohol syndrome, cocaine addiction, etc.) and long-term health issues (proneness to heart attacks, high cholesterol and cancer). Such effects are possible without any genetic predisposition.

Environment can refer to what is construed as the surrounding milieu or context of the organism. Immediate and extended family, social peer groups, cultural values and beliefs, community, neighborhood and sociopolitical and religious organizations can all be considered parts of a person's environment.

As may be evident with the way genes function, the cellular environment is essential for appropriate genetic operations and cellular growth. The definition of what is inside (gene) and what is outside (cellular cytoplasm) may be a clear boundary. The issue of what constitutes the organism and its environment is not so clear. The organization of the cell requires the orchestrated functioning of the cell's genetic nucleus and its surrounding cytoplasm. The cell is the whole greater than the sum of its essential parts. The formative whole of the unique cellular organization involves a higher level of ordering (wholeness) in terms of hierarchy of complexity.

The same is true with tissues, as they are organized cell assemblies. Organs are even higher ordered complexities of tissues, and organisms involve a still higher ordering as individual human beings. Continuation of this line of thinking involves couple relationships, social groups, communities, nations, cultures, religions and so on. The point is that the particular level of organized complexity one is dealing with will delineate the inside/outside boundary of interaction that actually represents a higher level of complex formativeness or motif.

IDENTICAL TWINS: SMALL DIFFERENCES THAT MAKE A LARGE DIFFERENCE

Genetic expression can be altered and influenced at many levels of the human organism's growth. Contributing influences of genetic and environment are clearly illustrated in studies of identical twins completed at the University of Minnesota (Allen, 1998). Researchers compared and contrasted identical twins (same genetic material) with fraternal twins (different genetic material from two different, simultaneously fertilized eggs). In studying happiness levels, identical twins reported similar happiness levels 44 percent of the time even when raised in separate families. Fraternal twins demonstrated common mood levels 8 percent of the time. Researchers found that the state of an individual's mood depends half on genetics and half on contextual situations.

While 44 percent is high for such findings, what accounts for the other 56 percent variation in unpredictable mood changes? Clearly environmental factors play a significant role in these cases. The studies at the University of Minnesota involved 120 twin pairs plus the popularized Jim twins. In 1979, the Jim twins demonstrated remarkable detailed similarities and were portrayed on the "Johnny Carson Show." These twins, given the same first name, were separated at birth and after being raised in adoptive homes for thirty-nine years came together with unusual commonalties. They were similar in height, weight, color of eyes and health. They had similar types of professions (law enforcement) and hobbies (woodworking), and had the same name for a dog. Each had a former wife with the same name of Linda and both remarried a Betty. Each built a circular wooden bench around a tree in their backyard, painting it white.

While such similarities are striking, they are not uncommon among identical twins. While a strong case may be made for genetics over environment with twin studies, there is another rather fascinating perspective. Identical twins with identical genetic components also illustrate remarkable differences. For example, identical twins Sharon and Sherry have similar talents as singers, yet Sharon has an outgoing, fun-loving personality and Sherry is more moody, sensitive and serious. Sharon exhibited brashness and resilience to high school teasing whereas Sherry would avoid and strive to escape adolescent critiques.

University of Minnesota psychologist Thomas Bouchard (Allen, 1998), who has conducted numerous studies on identical twins, indicates that they are only 50 percent similar. Twins are not exact replicas of one another but more approximating facsimiles. The effects of environmental influences both in the womb and in early family experiences are contributing factors.

However, the remarkable precision of detailed similarities between identical twins as well as their subtle differences points not to an either/or genetics-environment contribution or even just some combination effect. The precision of detailed similarities (similar singing talent or marrying first and second wives with the same names) reflects refined, organizing principles that harmonize multiple variables of genetics and environmental influences. As in the immune system's ability to hone and refine antibodies to corresponding exact duplicate forms and shapes of invading antigens, so complex, organizing principles of motif in formativeness (where detailed refinements are in form or in-formed or designed in-form-ation) can lead to matched psychosocial transactions among twins. The fact that identical twins have a 50 percent variance of differences is expressive of the individual uniqueness even among twins of the same genetic make-up, manifesting similar but refined differences because of their inherent unique organizing motifs. Motifs account for both striking similarities, as one would expect of artistic designs as well as unique variances. Unique variations in refined expression are quite pronounced even among the most identically similar of biochemical makeup in DNA.

The reconciliation of nature/nurture issues requires the inclusion of a higher ordering principle of complexity, the motif, to account for both genetic and environmental contributions. Such inclusion of higher organizing principles goes beyond a mere additive quantification of measuring proportions of genes and environment towards one of the organism self-constructing (Rosen, 1997) itself utilizing the inherent organizing principles of motif and formativeness.

This can be seen in the concept of genetic selectivity. An individual (predisposed to depression, aggression, etc.) encounters his or her own "subjective (perceived) environment" (loneliness and/or hostile authority figures). It can be said that individuals "genetically select" their own environment according to their own biochemical/perceptual filters, increasing their internal sense of self (alienation and negativity). In such cases, the subjective, perceived environment matches a skewed, deficiently developed motif within the individual. Such deficiently developed motifs intensify and proliferate themselves if not interrupted and realigned with their healthy, holistic formativeness. These realignment issues will be explored in a later chapter.

As the motif of the individual grows and develops, there is a personal evolution. The inside (genetics, self-image, developmental stage) interacts in a uniquely selective formative design structuring process with external environmental factors (cell cytoplasm, social expectations, maturation tasks). Yet the environment is not an absolute, objective reality but rather altered by subject selectivity thereby affecting the quality (motif) of interaction. The self assimilates and accommodates in a subjective, perceptual selective process the new tasks and growth challenges at hand. The self grows, matures and expands what it is and what it is not (differentiation). The result is a renewed sense of self with new boundaries of what constitutes inside and outside (environment) the self. As individuals grow from one stage to another (child to adolescent to adult to senior citizen), there are new stages with which to be challenged and interact.

The self's motif selectively delineates how it perceives the environmental challenge or task to be. For example, is high school teasing perceived as a challenge to develop the determination to cope, or is it incorporated as a learned belief that people are dangerous? The accommodating to and assimilation of new learnings, beliefs and emotional changes become incorporated into the individual's sense of self. Such incorporation may not fully align or resonate with an individual's motif. Take an individual, like the twin Sherry, who has a more reserved temperament. When experiencing harassment and teasing, her motif (preferring a lower key energy stimulation and sensitizing threshold levels) perceives incongruity to what it prefers, but the individual may not know herself or what about the environment is so threatening and may generate irrational, negative self-statements in the process.

The self's motif flourishes in a nurturing environment, matching and enhancing its unique attributes of formative variations and development. Edelman and Tononi (2000) present the need for complexity matching between the internal (brain) and external (psychosocial) environments. Unique complexity in the individual is accelerated when selectively matched with similar but more complex, challenging surroundings. Matching (similar patterning of common themas) the individual with highly complex tasks increases his or her unique complex motifs. Without such matching, motifs become fixated, stilted and restricted. If grossly mismatched and overwhelmed by trauma, abuse and/or perpetual misinterpretation, pathological perversions can result. The latter can occur from the self's irrationality (disordered cognition) and/or it can be imposed by the environment. This result is a lack of what is known as "fitness" between the motif of the self and the environmental contexts in which it moves and operates. Consequently, alignment efforts are involved in the homeodynamic process of reestablishing a fit between the self's motif and environmental experience.

Aligning with inherent organizing principles of motif and its influence on selective perception of its own environment is essential to the lifeline (Rose, 1997) of the individual. The concept of fit is involved here between one's core motif formative of self and creating (selectivity) the environment supportive for optimum growth and development. The Chilean biologist Humberto Maturana illustrates that human beings respond and design their actions to unique environments (Efran, Green & Gordon, 1998). The criteria for this fit of self to one's environment utilizes biological structures (motifs) and the context (motif-ied) they experience. He indicates that it is an illusion that we all experience the same world objectively. It is our inborn, subtle design structural differences in biological form that "attunes" each person to his or her unique, individual perceptual channel. Harvard psychologist Jerome Kagan (1994a) in *Galen's Prophecy* echoes similar concepts in that environments have different effects for each child. The focus needs to be on how a unique environment may affect and be affected by that unique child.

Kagan also supports the concept that biological structures of shape and form are highly correlated with temperament in individuals. The president of the American Psychological Association, Dr. Martin Seligman, expressed his position supporting the enormous effects of genetics, the large effects of recent events in one's life and negligible childhood effects. It is important to clarify that as the motif manifests itself through modes and modalities of environmental experiences, the individual sense of self incorporates the modality of the expressed motif in environmental form. Thus, if Albert Einstein were born and raised in China instead of Germany and the United States, he may still have discovered relativity theory but it may have had a more Eastern philosophy of oneness and unity attached to it. The quality goes in before the name goes on an individual, but what you call him or her can shape what's allowed out into the environment. A psychosocial environment that ridicules individual uniqueness impairs the required self-esteem needed to commit to the motif's expression.

Environmental factors (including parents and teachers) needs to learn how to enhance and work with the uniqueness of the individual. Human beings cope with environmental events based on their present biological structure. Maturana is reported as emphasizing how organisms selectively create their worlds based on fitness between their unique biological structures and their environment (Efran, Greene & Gordon, 1998). In this way, refined manifestations of unique motifs are possible. Enhancing the formative motif of the individual's biopsychosocial structure depathologizes character traits that are rejected because they do not fit a rigid norm. One might call this a hostile environment. If the overwhelming nature of the environment is severely deficient in nurturing motifs (providing meaningful, perceptual possibilities of fitness) then the effect of perceptual selectivity will be diminished. In such cases, a meaningful degree of congruence of self/environmental fitness can be threatened. Criminal behaviors and mental health disorders can result.

The criminal/violent adolescent may inherit not a full-blown criminal orientation but rather predispositional features that, if severely mismatched with poor environmental fitness, could create risk factors to antisocial behaviors. Such predispositional factors include fearlessness, aggressiveness, impulsivity, thrill seeking, lack of planning and lower than average verbal skills (Efran, Greene & Gordon, 1998). These factors are part of a larger, expansive motif of the unique adolescent. Their temperaments are oriented towards risk taking and a need for high stimulation. If they do not encounter congruent environment fits that direct such energies into creative matching or resonating self-expressions in a contextualized setting, then acting-out behavior can result.

The persona (mask) of the individual's personality can conceal or skew discovery and perception of inherent talent and formative characteristics of motif. It is important to develop unique perspectives for each individual regardless of one's presenting features to grasp the deeper perspective of underlying and unifying motifs present but masked over.

Genetic and environmental interactions can occur at micro levels of exchange (moment-to-moment experiences shared with self and others) resulting in positive or negative self and other evaluations. Whether in the school yard, office meeting, or family dinner table, each microinteraction augments or diminishes inherent characteristics in ourselves. When such interactions result in formative self-changes misaligned with core motifs, the mask or persona truncates the developing motif into a fixated stagnation. Pathology can be the consequence to motif stagnation.

The psychopath is constitutionally different but is not born bad. There may be a more complex microenvironment necessary. The difficulty of identifying his or her unique needs may impair fitness congruence of self and environment. It is important to remember that each individual perceives his or her environment idiosyncratically. The twins Sharon and Sherry went to the same school, suffering the same teasing, but each had her own unique perception of what it meant and how to cope with the "environment." Even members of the same family perceive that family differently.

The dialectic of nature and nurture influences is frequently focused on a set of character traits and/or environmental conditions. However, two important points need to be made. First, each human being has a developmental history that continues to build and construct itself on a lifeline (Rosen, 1997) that is a progressive accumulation of self/environmental selective exchanges. Second, to fully grasp interaction affects, one must consider not just a set of traits but the whole uniqueness of the individual as to whether congruent fitness has been occurring along that time line and to what qualitative degree.

For example, by the age of five the novelty seeker has probably been reinforced for daredevil behaviors through aggressive confrontations and direct challenges with peers. A lifeline is being established as well as a congruence of fitness between inner motif and microenvironmental interaction. Note however, that it is the whole of the formative motif which is operative in the organizing principles of perceptual selectivity shaping the idiosyncratic nature of the nurturing environment. When this formative process is aborted through abusive and/or severely deficient environmental resources, the availability of choice selection stemming from the motif is limited.

THE O GOD SYNDROME

The nature/nurture issue needs to embrace the perspective that neither genetics nor environment is capable of being a singular cause in an individual's lifeline. Antisocial individuals do not have a single gene for badness or an "evil seed." Such singularity of thought is referred to as the one gene, one dysfunction perspective. It is known as the O God syndrome (Efran, Greene & Gordon, 1998). The same is true of environmental influences. It is neither a single parent nor a single event that is primarily causal in influencing a person's lifeline.

Research into personality development reveals no causal singularity of individuals with a wide range of temperaments. Kagan (in Efran, Greene & Gordon, 1998) found approximately 20 percent of healthy infants with biological structures for being easily aroused by new experiences or when distressed. Many of such highly reactive children can become anxious, cautious and timid with phobias. He also found that 15 percent had the opposite formative constitution of boldness and social resilience. Yet, there was no evidence of any one gene or one environmental event that caused these temperaments in and of themselves.

Research on alcoholism has found similar predispositional features but no single gene as a causal determinant. Twin studies by Goodwin (in Rutzky, 1999), comparing twins separated at birth and raised either by their biological parents or by their nonbiological adoptive parents, found that sons of alcoholics had a four times greater risk of alcoholism. Blum and associates (1990) conducted genetic-marker studies on alcoholics. They found significant correlations between alcoholism and the D2 dopamine receptor gene. Yet, correlations are not causal, suggesting multiple determinants are involved in the expression of addiction disorders. Singular variables such as a genes, life event or nutritional deficiency may be necessary components to cause a certain condition but are not sufficient in themselves to account for its presence.

It is important to remember that a gene is not a single "bead" on a string but a composite sequence of DNA molecules. The motif of the genome's sequence is more the contributing genetic factor than any single gene itself.

ORGANIZING EFFECTS OF MOTIFS

Formative motifs operate as unique organizing principles within each human being. They function at genetic biopsychosocial levels of lifeline development. From the unique organizational structure of each person's DNA to the idiosyncratic perceptual selectivity, formative motifs are effused throughout these levels of organization. They orchestrate the development of the human being in multifaceted dimensions. These include biological structures, idiosyncratic character traits and psychosocial coping and adaptation styles. When genetic stability (minimal mutations) and immediate and extended nurturing environments are available, inherent organizing motifs can selectively draw from and orchestrate nature and nurture resources in uniquely formative capacities. In this manner the unique integrity of the individual self differentiates and diversifies over time. Witness the multidimensional facets of healthy, mature senior citizens, with active and energetic life styles. Motifs are not fixed or set things, structures or designs but rather evolving formative organizations constantly in the process of evolutionary change and development. The lifeline of the individual aligned with its motif is an accumulation of years of development and refinement.

The orchestrated interplay of genetics, biology and psychosocial environments through organizing principles of motif results in multifaceted and refined manifestations of the individual's uniqueness. Refinements in skills, talents and perspectives grasping the nuances and subtleties of life can become more prevalent. The motif is fluid in its formative expression (not unlike the rearrangement of genes shaping and forming on chromosomes). Through motif, orchestrated selectivity of environmental interaction, diversity and multidimensional facets of personal uniqueness are manifest throughout the lifeline.

The motif of the individual's internal or self-structure selects for resonance features of itself in the immediate and/or extended environments. Individuals with a low threshold of tolerance for sensory stimuli will select environments of soothing, low key activity levels. When thrust into high-energy (as compared to their perceptual motif) environments, efforts to modify, cope and reduce potential stressors will occur (such as avoidance). The more the motif differentiates and is nurtured in its unique expressions, the more adaptable it can become to diverse and seemingly incongruent environments.

Self-esteem and positive expectancy (Kirsch, 1999) can have powerful effects on an individual's willingness to trust and align with one's motif. Extreme environmental feedback from family, friends and the socioculture at large can skew and distort individually unique traits through stigma and prejudice. Artistic, intellectually gifted as well as so-called fringe elements (eccentrics) of society can be mislabeled and misunderstood. Building positive expectancy that aligns with idiosyncratic traits inherent within each individual and that will create a rich and meaningful life is essential in development of the lifeline.

FORMATIVE FIELDS: MORPHOGENIC RESONANCE

There is another dimension of influence on the human being that involves a different type of environmental interaction with the individual self. British scientist Rupert Sheldrake (1988) suggests that learned behavior is passed from one generation to the next through what he calls morphogenic energy fields. He describes research studies of various generations of rats who have learned to run complex mazes with increasing speed from one generation to the next. Sheldrake indicates that learning and behavior can influence succeeding generations through formative fields of energy (morphogenic). Such views are not entirely new; Lamarck (1914) proposed that acquired characteristics (learning and behavior) can be propagated from generation to generation. Lamarck was critiqued and discounted at the time. However, Sheldrake has renewed interest through studies that are suggestive of these possibilities. Morphogenic fields shape the forms of the cells, tissues, DNA molecules and so on. The motif of the field is effused throughout these structures as well as the inherited behavior. Each field has its own unique frequency for each individual as self-resonance.

Morphogenic fields involve an accumulation of learning referred to as the hundredth monkey syndrome. Purportedly, monkeys near the coast of Africa learned that washing sweet potatoes in ocean water improved the taste. When at least a hundred monkeys learned this behavior, monkeys all over the world and in future generations of that species increased the frequency of such behavior (Sheldrake, 1988). Whether these formative energy fields actually exist or not, it is intriguing to consider that remarkable breakthroughs in science as well as other fields occur after a certain level of accumulated learning has reached a certain peak. Scientists have worked independently of one another throughout the world on the same type of research. Only after a quantum level of learning has occurred in the field (hundredth monkey syndrome) do breakthroughs occur. There have also been studies reported (Atwater, 1996) regarding the presence of formative fields of energy during zygote formation of salamanders. The presence of unique formative fields of energy would appear to have its own motif and design. While the possibilities are intriguing, the common theme in nature-nurture is that the formative impact of motif is universally present in the uniqueness of each individual. Motif transforms internal and external formative features through selection and congruent alignment evolving the unique self.

ESSENCE AND EXISTENCE: THE CREATIVE MOMENT

The nature-nurture dialectic gives rise to the age-old question of which came first, the chicken or the egg. Is there an innate essence within human beings that preexists their birth and destines their future existence? Does environment shape and form human beings with its presses and pulls, determining existing behavior thereby inculcating essential character traits to the individual? Finally, is there some watered down version of both views resulting in the interactionist, co-determination perspective combining genetics and environmental influence? These questions can be addressed by a closer examination of what motifs are and how they function.

Motifs can first be delineated by what they are not. Reviewing the concept of platonic ideal forms preexisting the individual, motifs are not preexisting, set forms. They are formative, which means they are design structures that are capable of taking on almost infinite variant forms within the same family of patterned interactions. This family of patterned forms can be asymmetrical (not identical) to one another yet congruent (allometric transformations). The result is rich diversity within the unique individual.

Motifs seem to have an entelechy (life purpose, as an acorn grows into an oak tree). However, motifs are not predestined in the Aristotelian cause-and-effect sense. Individuals are not simple acorns to be watered into oak trees (though there are some nuts out there who seem to think this way).

Motifs are not just some convenient way of describing environmental shaping through reinforcement schedules. If that were true, all introverts could become late night talk show celebrities and host Barnum and Bailey's Circus. No one denies the ability of behavioral intervention, but what is reinforcing to one person may be totally meaningless to another. This implies some individuality operating.

To understand motifs and contribute meaningfully to the nature-nurture dialectic requires dealing with the concept of uniqueness. The conception of the human zygote by the male sperm fertilizing the female egg results not in a chicken or an egg but in germination of a new unique formativeness. The joining of male and female formativeness germinates into a unique motif effused within and outside of the zygote's DNA structure. DNA itself does not direct what human beings will be, only what needs to be done to get them to what they will be.

The propagation and unfolding of formative possibilities of being require the congruent internal and external selectivity referred to earlier. It is in the creative moment-to-moment unfolding of this constructive congruence that manifests one formative derivation of motif after another.

Whether an individual is destined to be a nuclear scientist or the new chief executive of Microsoft, replacing Bill Gates, depends on the moment-to-moment creative congruent of motif. The motif is manifest in the creative moment, selecting, harmonizing and manifesting unique variant forms of its almost infinite formativeness. Like the unfolding, ever expanding universe, the individual's motif is constantly striving for diversity in its multifaceted uniqueness. While retaining its idiosyncratic intricacy of a family of interacting patterned designs, the unique specificity of each moment-to-moment transformation is a creation of a new facet of motif. The chicken-and-egg issue of nature and nurture is nested in the transformative uniqueness of self.

The motif will harmonize the moment-to-moment interplay of genetic and biopsychosocial facets in whatever way best creates that individual's uniqueness at that point in time. Whether an act of selfishness or of charity, it is the individual's unique, complex motif that presses for creative manifestation within the context of internal and external possibilities for congruence. Rather than selectively targeting isolated traits or characteristics (introversion/extroversion, aggressiveness/avoidance, etc.), it may be more meaningful to recontextualize the nature/nurture question in the light of individual uniqueness. There are no purely introverted or extroverted individuals in all contexts at all times. Indeed, characteristics that are labeled introversion may emerge for the same individual in a one-to-one setting but recede in a crowd scene of a hundred or more. In addition, the degree of extroversion and introversion has been known to vary over time. Interestingly, President Woodrow Wilson was an introvert in one-to-one settings. He needed his wife to relay messages to his cabinet members on a first-hand basis. Yet, Wilson was quite extroverted in his ability to speak to hundreds and thousands of people during his whistle-stop campaign for president in 1914.

Researchers need to isolate trait characteristics in order to make studies possible. Yet, they invariably reify hybrid composites of unique character trait blends into stereotyped, one-dimensional absolute natures in which to fit their subjects. The dynamics of the nature/nurture dialectic may be more meaningfully comprehended by refocusing on issues through the idiosyncratic lens of individualized motifs. The composite complexity of unique, individualized characteristics may then be grasped.

Chapter Four

Motifs: Neuro-Muscular-Skeletal Designs and Personality Temperament

The motif manifests its unique characteristic formativeness systematically throughout the psychobiology of the individual. Motifs are synergistically and harmoniously effused throughout multiple levels of the individual. They are idiosyncratically representative of the individual's physiology, body structure and personality temperament. This chapter presents numerous models of how the human being's holistic congruence of motif has been conceptualized for thousands of years. In multiple ways, they all point to a holistic, mind/body resonance of formative congruence of motif in themas and design structures. It is but a small step to respect the individuation (Jung, 1971) of resonant motifs.

It is important to comprehend that motif's formativeness develops from high symmetry and minimal differentiation at conception to low symmetry and high differentiation (high asymmetry) in maturation. Here, symmetry is defined as perfection in balance of identical shapes and/or designs. Differentiation is that diversity of the single celled zygote into specialized areas that interface into synergized systems but are complementary rather than identical in design. For example, the circular zygote, no matter how it rotates, maintains an identical design. The development of the zygote into multicelled areas that begin defining major human systems marks out asymmetrical designs. They are like objects on a mobile counter balancing one another with complementary designs. Since the mobile has order and design, but with varying shapes and designs, its asymmetry increases with differentiation. The motif of the human organism manifests similar resonant features. When one system (mind/brain) is "pulled" or stimulated, reverberations resonate through the body mobile.

The motif of and within the zygote moves through symmetry at the time and moment of conception instantly proceeding towards symmetrical and asymmetrical differentiation. As this process continues, the holistic idiosyncratic motif is ever refining its nuances, facets or shades of juxtapositioning. Motif is not a set structure but rather a unique set of organizational structuring principles. Its holistic characterization is manifest in multifaceted nuances that, when synergistically emerging together, hint at the nature of inherent motif. These comprehensions are important to grasp as the models of motif infusion to be presented illustrate not a set characteristic for the individual but rather a signature of characteristics echoed and reflected in the many shades and nuances of the motif's psychophysical reality.

MOTIFS AND MODELS

The ancient Greeks (Hardie, 1968) construed the universe and the inherent nature of human beings to be composed of four separate properties: earth, water, fire and air. Aristotle identified these innate properties as a ratio of opposites within the human personality. Hippocrates, called the "father of medicine," delineated inherent personality temperaments as distinct body fluids or humors. These four humors — choleric (impulsive, irritable), melancholic (moody, contemplative), phlegmatic (calm, slow-paced) and sanguine (optimistic, energetic) — reflected innate temperaments found in both personality and biochemistry. While these are depicted as types of innateness (or stereotypes) they depict efforts over two thousand years ago to identify inherent, holistic organizing principles of human beings.

In contemporary times, Carl Jung (1971) researched his own character types making further efforts to differentiate innate, human characteristics. This resulted in his depiction that each person has a dominant function (thinking or feeling, sensing or intuition) and attitude (introverted or extroverted, perceiver or judger). Jung realized that each person was moving towards individuation of a core self, which indicates that differentiation of innate characteristics was built into his theory of personality.

Utilizing Jung's theoretical foundations, the Myers-Briggs Type Indicator was developed as a way of assessing the individual's dominant function and attitude (Myers and Briggs, 1977). This inventory refines measurements of function and attitude into sixteen different combinations, clustering into four groups. Efforts to differentiate and individualize the specific combinations and degree along each type dimension are demonstrated. Inherent, unconscious type specifications are delineated by the inventory. However, measurements are restricted to the four function and attitude types. Individuation is limited to sixteen combinations though refinements of measures along those type dimensions are given. There are almost six billion unique human beings in the world. It seems unlikely that all of the billions of people on the earth could comprehensively be represented into sixteen categories and their refinements. More refined and unique measures of individuality and its nuanced complexity would seem to be in order here, but more will be said about that later.

As was presented in the previous chapter, the DNA molecule utilizes only four bases of nucleotides (adenine, guanine, cytosine and thymine) as building blocks to its genome sequencing. Yet, with only these four components the vast range of human complexity is constructed. Notice that there is somewhat of a paradox here. The infinite complexity of human uniqueness is composed in striking simplicity through a limited number of parts. This is similar to linguistics where a vast number of words and phrases are composed of only a finite number of letters in the alphabet.

While models of inherent human characteristics present essential components as building blocks, it is the architecture and design that creates characteristic features out of these component parts. As will become progressively apparent, the inherent complexity of human beings is a function of articulate design structures of components, not the components themselves. The vast complexity of human uniqueness is a function of the motif's archetexture that determines how the "bricks and mortar" will be constructed and designed.

Inherent characteristics have been correlated to blood types. Individuals can be grouped into one of four categories of personality traits depending on which blood type they are. Those with type A blood tend to be cautious, hard working and attentive to detail. Those with type B gravitate toward being liberal, innovative and free spirited. Type AB blood types correlate with sociability and negotiation in relationships, and type O blood types tend to be hard driving, leaders and task focused (Nomi and Besher, 1982). As mentioned earlier, these are generalized groupings of inherent characteristics correlated with specific blood types. One might hypothesize that as the complexity of the blood chemistry was more closely examined on an individual basis, individualization on the aforementioned traits would become more apparent.

Inherent correlation of temperament and biochemistry has also been discovered in personalities prone to high and low stress. Friedman (1978) found that profiles of high stress people whom he called type A were much more disturbed and activated by high stress than their counterparts whom he labeled type B with their calmer, more poised temperaments. He found corresponding differences in their biochemistry. Type A personalities activate their sympathetic nervous system flight-or-fight response with high concentrations of cortisol and epinephrine. Type B's utilized their parasympathetic nervous system eliciting relaxation responses. Relaxation and pleasure hormones such as endorphins and seratonin are more likely to be present under these conditions.

Further research by Dr. Roger Sperry (1985) found that distinctive behavioral patterns are expressed through unique structures of the brain. He indicated that each person's brain is different at birth with unique neural networks. These hard-wired neural network distinctions influence the unique talents and capabilities of each individual. His split brain experiments indicated differential thinking patterns in the left and right hemispheres of the cerebral cortex. Left hemisphere thinking is conducive to logical analytical processes. The right hemisphere accesses innovative, nonlinear and nonverbal thinking.

However, these divisions are not quite so cut and dry. Because of brain plasticity and redundancy, the vast complexity of the brain's neural networks can reorganize under certain conditions of brain damage to either hemisphere. Neural network reformation may occur under such conditions where one hemisphere may supplant functions lost in the other. Each individual's mind/brain structure is as unique as one's innate temperament. As one transforms and evolves, the other correspondingly changes.

Researchers have demonstrated a strong relationship between mind and body regarding personality and physical body structure. Abravanel and King's (1985) research studies demonstrate a relationship between body design structure and inherent personality characteristics. For example, individuals whose weight distribution is primarily in their stomach area are called the adrenal body type. These people are focused, determined and competent. A second body type, whose weight is primarily in the upper midriff region, is called the thyroid body type. These individuals are diverse, clever and dynamic in personality. The third body structure type is the pituitary type where one's weight is evenly distributed. This type tends to be confident, exposing his or her own point of view and exuding strength. The final body structure type has a bottom weighted design, called the gonadal type. These have characteristics of helpfulness, caring and draw people into their lives.

Corresponding relationships between mind and body dimensions have also been discovered involving facial design structures. Mar (1974) revealed four facial designs associated with distinctive personality characteristics. Triangular shaped faces involve hypersensitive, judgment oriented, self-motivated, intellectualized traits. Oblong faces are related to visionary, relaxed, now-oriented traits. Round facial shapes are related to outgoing, socially adept, comforting traits. Square shaped faces are task oriented, assertive and intensely involved in their goal achievement.

A key point to highlight in such psychophysiological typing is that rarely do individuals have geometrically perfect shaped faces. For example, I have never met another human being whose face is a perfect triangle, oblong, round, or square. Certainly individuals approximate these shapes, but their unique design variations are as distinct as their particular blend of corresponding personality characteristics.

Similar psychophysiological manifestations are presenting in handwriting types. Mendel (1947) found that the way a person writes reflects the way thoughts and emotions in that person's brain are connected. The stylist rhythm in script is a manifestation of internal cognitive rhythmic processes. He found that cursive forms with upward curves, which he labeled arcade style, were associated with a conservative, form-oriented, cautious individualism. He found under curving line styles, called garland, associated with relaxed, easygoing, feeling-oriented character traits. Angular styles were associated with firm, sharply defined, determined decision makers. Finally, the thread style was associated with freewheeling, now-oriented, creative, amorphous formative traits.

As mentioned previously, perfect forms are the ideal, not the real state of affairs. Individual writing styles tend towards certain featured styles but rarely are there perfect curves, angles or threads present. The variability and fluctuations are as unique as the combination of traits associated to these features.

The motif can be viewed as manifesting itself through design structures in body types, handwriting styles and facial features. For example, the gonadal body type (bottom weight), round facial designs and garland handwriting styles all associate with caring, comforting, feeling, peace-oriented traits. Intriguingly, there is present in the design structure of all three psychophysiological manifestations a motif of full-bottomed roundness and circularity.

Design structures with corresponding temperaments of nurturance and care exude a bottom-weighted curve and circularity not unlike a cradle. The cradling, caring motif of nurturing is quite apparent. Such geometric formativeness is present both physiologically and temperamentally. The full-bodied nurturing abundance of caregivers is characteristic of giving, nurturing people. They both literally and figuratively manifest design structures of a curved, rounded, cradled quality which smacks of a mother symbolically cradling and rocking a baby in her arms in a slow-swinging, under-curved shaped motion. The full-bottomed shape reminiscent of the nurturer is symbolic of the mass of nurturance they have to give. The deeper the curve and bottom weight, the more intense the nurturing.

The uniqueness of such a motif is expressed in the individualistic shapes and temperaments in which each person may nurture. One person may tend to be more intense and focused than another and may manifest deeper curves and heavier bottom weightiness. Another individual may be less nurturing, combining with a more judged perspective and expressing a shallower undercurve and less bottom weight. The combination is quite unique and each person's design structure both physiologically and temperamentally will maintain a corresponding, unique congruence.

Contrast the nurturing motif with that of the square shaped facial design, pituitary body type (evenly distributed weight) and angular handwriting. These physiological characteristics correspond to a highly purpose-oriented, striving achiever. A boxed-in, squared off (for competition), pointed, angular (style of writing) design structure and assertiveness both literally (physiologically) and figuratively (temperamentally) are congruent manifestations of each other. These unique individual variations and combinations of varying degrees and intensities of these types of manifestations indicate the person's motif.

The adrenal body type (stomach weight), the triangular shaped face and arcade handwriting (umbrella shaped curve) are physiological manifestations of cautious, conservative, intellectual, and stable temperamental characteristics. The adrenal type (stomach weight) is high on the body, the triangle peaks at the top and the arcade style arches upward. Such formativeness literally and figuratively suggests being above it all, aloof, and striving and being superior under the umbrella of protective conservatism. The design structures have a sense of heightened "aboveness" and singular conservative intellectualism (peaking triangle). There is a "pointedness" to this temperament as well as heightened (aboveness) sensitivity to criticism and imprecision. There, emphasis on judgment (right and wrong) suggests perfectionism. Intriguingly, the triangle is the most perfect formative structure. It is also the design of the scales of justice with the pendulum hanging from the peak point of the triangle. The congruent resonance between physiological and temperamental formativeness becomes more complex when individualized across dimensions.

The thyroid body type (midriff weight) with its oblong face design and thread writing style involves temperaments of high spiritedness, long-term vision and now-oriented creativity. The oblongness of the face, the thread-like handwriting and midriff weight suggest extendedness, free streams of thought (linear/threadlike writing), an indifference to fixed form and a center (midriff weight) from which radiates creative, energetic lines (threads of creative thoughts and sensations) of innovative associations. Again, notice the literal and figural congruent correspondence of physiological formedness and temperamental manifestations. The oblong face (extended) is surprisingly congruent with temperaments of far-sighted (or extended) vision as is extensive innovativeness (thread-like writing) almost totally unrestrained by form. Notice that formative features of extendedness, linear, stream-like forms with little fixed shape effuse and pervade different levels of handwriting, body shape and facial design. Yet, they vary subtly in their expressions at each level. These design forms are organizing principles throughout the organism and recur in varying formativeness.

Motif's design structures are inherently effused at multiple levels of the individual's physiology and personality. While examples of design structures are highlighted, it is important to realize that they are much more complex and detailed in manifestations than is presented in this chapter. Other examples of effused design structures occur in the other described types as well. Again, let it be emphasized that types are only ideal prototypes lacking in the richness of individual uniqueness which is where the real motif emerges.

These design forms of motif capture unique qualities and characteristics of each typed category. Imagine if, instead of a typed category, an individual had varying degrees and intensities of multiple categorical types overlapping and intersecting in his or her own unique tapestry. The rich and unique qualities and characteristics effused through such an individual would be quite intricate and reflect a distinct signature. This is the nature of motif with its unique signature of design structures.

There are others such as Dr. William Sheldon (in Cooper, 1992) who have discovered further psychophysiological groupings. Sheldon delineated three body types based on the embryonic predominance most present in the individual. These types include ectoderm, mesoderm and endoderm. Whichever of these tissues is most present early on will give rise to design structures that exert major influence in that individual's body. For example, the ectomorph is a body structure with a tall, bony thinness. It is small framed with sharp features. The second body structure type proposed by Sheldon is the mesomorph which has a compact, broad, muscular build. The third type is the endomorph which is a rounded type with relatively short limbs and a digestive tract larger than the nervous or musculoskeletal system.

These types correspond to the glandular types. The ectomorph is consistent with the thyroid design of long, lanky and restless. The mesomorph correlates with the adrenal type with its solid, driven warmth. The combination of ectomorph/endomorph corresponds to the pituitary gland with characteristics of detachment, roundness and dreaminess. Finally, the endomorph/mesomorph combination relates to the gonadal gland for women with slenderness above the waist and more body fat below. These women tend to be warm, outgoing, people-oriented and are referred to as the ovarian type. If typological characteristics are enfused at multiple levels of temperament and psychophysiology, then it must follow that, as individuals are unique, there are unique types or motifs effused at multiple levels of each person.

Researchers at Johns Hopkins University (Barker, 1992) propose that everyone is born with a primary gland of influence. Such a gland affects biochemical and metabolic levels of functioning as well as energy use involving selective utilization of macronutrients (air, water, carbohydrates, fats, vitamins and minerals). Each individual has a unique way of utilizing macronutrients because of unique motifs operating at each individual's biochemical and psychophysiological levels. Each person has a unique metabolism reflective of his or her own motif. Individuals frequently desire foods that stimulate their unique metabolism and predominant gland combination.

Ayurvedic medicine from India acknowledges that specific inherited traits come in groups. Asian skin and hair come with brown eyes. Solid musculature comes with heavy bones and dense connective tissue. These inherited trait composites become enhanced in their unique specificity when viewed on an individual, case-by-case basis and manifest specific design structures of motif. For example, while Asian skin and hair come with brown eyes, the individual Asian person has his or her own unique eye structure and size with shades of differences. Each Asian person is uniquely tailored (as in design structure) to manifest his or her own personal characterization of motif despite generalized grouping.

Indian medicine also characterizes three general energy types underlying everyone's energy patterns or *doshas*. They are: (1) *vatta*, which regulates movement; (2) *pitta*, which controls metabolism; and (3) *kapha*, which oversees structure. In Ayurvedic medicine all three doshas need to harmonize together in maintaining balance in the individual.

The need for balance involving metabolism, biochemistry and psychophysical functions and congruence suggests a mind/body alignment. Indian medicine involves recognizing that all matter (including human beings) is composed mostly of vibrating energy waves (note the superstring theory presented in Chapter Two). In this case, energy wave vibration is operating between subatomic particles (quantum units) forming energy fields with their own morphism. Fields of energy have a formativeness or morphism that requires a balance between energy itself and particles of matter (everyday reality, as we know it).

Each individual has a tendency towards one of these three types of energy patterns or doshas. While all three work together, the unique integrated combination of the three tends to favor one more than the other. However, the degree and variance of such an emphasis is quite unique. The field of an individual's energy forms a unique pattern of waves that has its own design structure or motif.

Balance in the individual involves aligning not only a harmonic balance between the three doshas but alignment with the unique dosha or motif of the individual's energy field. Doshas are the meeting point of mind and body (energy and matter). Balancing the individual's energy field with his or her unique formative wave pattern results in harmony of his or her unique mind and body synergy.

These doshas (vatta, pitta and kapha) correspond to glandular and body physiology. The vatta energy pattern relates to thyroid gland and ectomorphism. It further can be grouped with the pituitary gland in its more streamlined version. Pitta energy patterns correspond to the adrenal gland and mesomorph body structure. The kapha dosha or energy pattern is consistent with the endomorph body structure and the ovarian gland.

The three systems of body structure, doshas and glands exhibit a congruence in general type characteristics. These groupings affect what type of exercise and diets would be best suited to each type. Paul Pearsall (1999) refers to the body code of how characteristic types have different nutritional and exercise needs. Such typology affects, among other things, how different appetites may or may not satiate our metabolic rate. The affect on weight gain or loss can be quite significant. Pearsall indicates classifications of strong (the adrenal/warrior and ovarian/nurturer) and sleek (thyroid/communicator and pituitary/visionary). Each classification has its different type of exercise and diet. The strong requires high motion exercise and a low-protein diet. The sleek requires the opposite combination, which would be low motion exercise and a high-protein diet.

While groupings and classifications such as the aforementioned are helpful in pointing us in the right directions, these fall short in healing the specific individual. As has been previously noted, none of these types exists in a pure, ideal form. The unique design of each individual's body structure, metabolic rate, brain circuitry, facial shape and hormonal/glandular emphasis possesses intricate nuances and refined degrees of the type generalizations. This involves more than just fine tuning one's measurements in terms of degree of overlap of type categories.

The uniqueness of an individual's psychophysical design structure is more than an additive measure of potential type opposites (ectomorph and endomorph). Rather, it involves generating a synergistic new formativeness that is more than simply an addition of features. For example, an individual who has a facial design somewhere between triangular and square would not simply present some modified version of a squared triangular shape. That person's facial design would create a completely new design pattern or structure requiring a unique configuration and classification of geometric forms. That individual would be in a unique class as each person indeed has a uniquely shaped facial design.

While there is a tendency to strive to group and categorize, this process is actually abstracting isolated and simplified characteristics which loses the whole of the unique individual for the sum of its analyzed parts. What these models and theories demonstrate is that human beings do have properties of inherent designs that are consistent throughout their psychophysical levels. Yet, these models fall short of demonstrating more than a loose appreciation of how unique and in a class by themselves individuals truly are.

Individuals are not organized by ideal forms as Plato suggested nor are they a blank slate or tabula rasa. It appears that human beings have open-ended, formative organizing principles capable of almost infinite variance in characteristic manifestations. Noting that the mind/body system is capable of high levels of plasticity and redundancy, vast ranges of manifestations are made possible to each individual. With their inherent, unique capabilities and design structures, almost infinite variance of such design formativeness is quite possible.

The mind/body connection manifests an intricate array of communication channels to facilitate communication and resonance of its motif's design structures. These channels primarily involve three major systems in the human being: (1) autonomic, (2) endocrine, and (3) immune. These systems are pathways through which changes in the brain's cerebral cortex are translated (transduced) to the organ, tissue and cellular levels. In this way homeodynamic balance can be maintained.

The mind/body connection translates formative information converting it from mental (energy) to physiological expression. For example, if an individual visualizes a calm, relaxing scene of basking in the sun at some luxurious resort, his or her body physiology will manifest vital signs indicative of someone at rest and joyful. The endocrine system will be stimulated to secrete hormones known as enkephalins and endorphins. The autonomic system will be signaled to produce the relaxation response and the immune system will be strengthened through an increase in white blood cells. These white blood cells are utilized by the body to ward off infectious antigens threatening the body. The process of converting mental energy to physical energy requires transduction from one mode to another. The limbic hypothalamic system located in the midbrain plays a key role in this process (Rossi, 1986).

The design structures of motif are manifest in the pathways connecting mind and body. Every brain (and its concomitant neural circuits) is unique and reshaped through learning. As has been illustrated earlier in this chapter, each body physiology and therefore its connection to the brain manifests congruent uniqueness. Therefore, when messages are sent from the mind/brain (mental functions moving through neural circuitry) to body physiology, their transduction from one medium to another utilizes pathways that are also uniquely congruent. The mind/body connection, while utilizing universal biological structures, is uniquely organized for each individual. The body needs to maintain regulation of its homeodynamic states. It needs to rely on organizing incoming information from internal states and the external environment to maintain this homeodynamic. Individuals utilize their unique design structures to organize information in their own idiosyncratic manner.

While every individual has a limbic hypothalamic system, each has its unique structural design. The limbic-hypothalamus has substructures which include the amygdala and hippocampus. In some individuals the amygdala has a design structure resulting in a lower threshold which culminates in more susceptibility to flight or fight responses during times of stress. In others, their hippocampus is designed in such a way as to offer calmer, warmer and soothing responses to offset the amygdala.

The frontal lobes in the cerebral cortex organize incoming information from the activating part of the brain (reticular activating system) as well as from the limbic hypothalamic system. The behavior of the organism is regulated by how these frontal lobes organize, form and transduce messages to the body.

It has been found by psychophysiologists such as Achterberg (1985) that mind/body changes can be effected through a visualized "body image." The frontal limbic system is where the organization of this visual "body image" is constructed. The actual design structures present in these neural networks affects the constructed organization of such visualization and therefore affects body physiology.

An individual who experiences his or her motif as a somewhat nurturing, cradling, lower body weight and roundedness may find perceptions and cognitions congruent with these characteristics. For example, his or her frontal lobes may tend towards organizing perceptions applying a criteria of fullness (rounded), deep-seatedness (low, underneath), warmth, and moving feelings (slow rocking or cradling). The frontal lobes are uniquely designed according to that person's motif and will engage in symbolic organization of characteristic features into conceptual form. The frontal lobes utilize the right brain as well as the limbic-hypothalamic system in organizing symbolic features and characteristic designs into constructed ideas (Wickramasekera, 1985). In this way, idiosyncratic design structures of motif are transduced from mind to body or body to mind.

The psychophysiological congruence of mind/body pathways can be accessed from any direction. This would follow as motifs are effused through multilevels of the individual. Tapping the uniqueness of the individual from blood chemistry to facial design leads to reverberations of alignment throughout the system.

ASYMMETRICAL MOTIFS

Thus far it may appear that the mind/body resonance motifs are symmetrical or identical in design. Remember that motifs involve an organizing set of principles that manifest unique characterizations of the self but exhibit a vast range of variance. The motif's signature varies with each expression though it retains organizing characteristic elements. As such, the unique ordering function of motif is not identical with each manifestation but similar in form. The similarity represents organizing functions that result in asymmetrical design structures.

The mind/body system represents such asymmetrical formativeness. Roger Sperry (1964) conducted split brain studies revealing a right and left hemisphere specialization in the brain. The functions of right brain (imagination, analog, nonverbal, etc.) and left brain (logical, digital, verbal, etc.) are complementary to each other. They represent a balanced asymmetrical design structure. Even the growth of the hemispheres of the cerebral cortex at birth is asymmetrical. Robert Ornstein (1997) found that the frontal lobes mature early in human development in concert with the biological needs of what is happening at that time. He found a delay in the left hemisphere development near the sylvan fissure (area related to language). Here, the neural network complexity of interconnections occurs later in the left hemisphere than in the right hemisphere.

The criteria involved in the timing of asymmetrical growth hinge on which hemisphere competency is needed to deal with the moment-to-moment task development at hand and when. The right hemisphere is needed for spatial ability in the child to find his or her mother and control of limb movement to become hard-wired in. The left hemisphere matures at a time when the baby is exposed to language and learning of more refined motor movements in infancy. The maturation of the right hemisphere in the fetus assists in its responsiveness to the mother's low frequency noises, heartbeat and rumbling sounds. The right hemisphere is initially more responsive to light when it needs to negotiate vague images conveyed by relatively low frequencies which also affects auditory stimuli and its perception.

The asymmetry of an individual's brain is not only evident in its anatomical structure of right and left hemisphere differentiation, but this asymmetry also is unique to an individual's brain and like no others. Edelman (1992) describes how each human being's brain has unique enfolding gyruses and manifests varying degrees of dominance in left and right hemisphere differentiation. Note the generalization that males tend to be left-brain oriented (logical) whereas women tend to be less specialized utilizing the brain holistically. Yet, there are males who are less differentiated in hemisphere dominance than some women are. Each individual needs to be viewed as manifesting a unique brain structure and signature of electrical activity all his or her own.

The effects of brain differentiation and uniqueness of design structure are blatantly clear in the mental illness of schizophrenia. Julian Jaynes (in Ramachandran & Blakeslee, 1998) relates how schizophrenia could be a regression to more primitive states of consciousness (the bicameral mind) in which the left and right hemispheres are less differentiated. In this situation, individuals with minimal hemisphere differentiation are more prone to psychosis. The failure to establish hemisphere dominance impairs the interaction between hemispheres. Symptoms such as auditory hallucinations (hearing voices) result as the lack of dominance impairs orientation and referencing of stimuli. It is suggested that this condition inhibits awareness. The left brain transmits cognitions, intentions, emotions and so on to and from the right hemisphere. Lack of differentiation confuses left hemisphere communication creating the delusion that external forces are operating when in fact it is the right hemisphere responding. Delusions such as thought insertion, passivity and withdrawal are possible. These findings are supported by the National Child Development Study (Ramachandran & Blakeslee, 1998).

When the design structures within the individual begin to become impaired and disintegrate to lower levels of regression, there is a loss of organizational design structure and asymmetry. The individual's unique brain structure requires some degree of asymmetrical differentiation and hemisphere dominance, or dysfunction may occur. Regression of the design structure of motif prevents functional performance and illustrates the importance of design structures in the health of human beings. The impact of these findings will be explored in a future chapter on motif and health issues. For now, suffice it to say that the asymmetrical motif is effused in the psychophysiology of the human being. The degree of organization inherent in motifs is critical in maintaining homeodynamic balance.

THE TRANSDUCTION OF FORMATIVENESS

The psychophysiology of mind/body connections has referred primarily to physical manifestations of formativeness (face, body, blood type, handwriting, brain structure, etc.). Throughout these levels, a unique congruence of temperament and physiology has been illustrated. At this point, formativeness will be presented as a uniqueness of energy design manifest through imagination, language, movement and cognition. The visualization of a relaxing scene and its impact on the body has already been described. What is now highlighted is that the effectiveness of imagery is not only on its content but also on how its very design structure sends reverberations (like a dropped pebble creating ripples in a pond) through psychophysiological levels. For example, if an individual desires to rest and relax, he or she may recall a pleasant memory of past activity (swimming in a beautiful, cool, sunlit lake). What may trigger the basic relaxation response is not the content of the image (swimming in a lake) but the motif of having a bright light shining while one is cool and drifting. Motifs are design oriented, which can involve sensory as well as abstract structures.

If the design structure of the individual is involved in imagery, reverberation will be transduced through the mind/body system, and relaxation will occur. For example, a particular design structure may involve a central, bright light radiating down upon a wide open area that is circular, at the bottom of the imagined picture, and fullness of dense heat is present. The design structure therefore involves a top-down dimension widening at the bottom in a circular form with a dense quality filling the space (in this case heat or warmth). Certainly the individual may have a pleasant memory that helps him or her relax. However, the person may not realize how important the inherent design structure is as an integral scaffolding supporting the particular image. Without this embedded, structural design the imagined scene may be quite ineffective. The individual at that point may experience difficulty in achieving a mind/body resonant harmony of rest and relaxation.

Motifs involve design structures which embody information in the transduction process. When information is transduced from the mind to the body (or reciprocally) the procedure involves a congruence of formativeness. The psychophysiological process is quite complicated but the operating principle involves a resonance between, for example, the design structure of a mental image and its concomitant physiological matrix. The design image of a humorous incident will reverberate into congruent physiologically designed responses of laughter and nonverbal expressiveness. It is the formativeness features of the image's design that is transduced into physiological design form as a patterned response.

The very word "information" can be viewed as to "in-form" data or messages. To place messages into a characteristic form is a coding process. For example, when humorous images are constructed juxtaposing incongruent expectations, shock effects of surprising outcomes generate physiological shock waves throughout the person's adrenal glands, resulting in a rush of pleasure hormones (enkephalins and norepinephrine) as well as laughter. It is well known that what one person finds humorous may be boring to another. The subtle design structures embedded in imagery need to approximate that of the individual's (subtle contrasts of opposite expectations versus more blatant slapstick contrasts, etc.) to be transduced into physiological congruent design structures that elicit humorous responses.

Information involves how data and stimuli are arranged and organized into a design structure. To "in-form" someone or to be "in-formed" involves the arranging and designing of data into a meaningful form (organized into a shape or design) that is congruent with the individual's motif. It is these formative design structures that articulate unique configurations of motif that convey meaningful "in-form-ation" throughout the psychophysiological levels.

The mind/brain of an individual has its own unique structural design. As the brain is part of the larger biochemical body (endocrine, central nervous immune system, muscular skeletal, etc.) its unique design structure is asymmetrical and therefore resonant with the rest of the enfused body motif. Such resonant uniqueness of enfused mind/body motifs facilitates psychophysiological interaction.

There is evidence that the mind/body system has innate capacities to form (or in-form) figures, shapes and designs in responding to the environment. Etcoff (1999), a Harvard psychologist, demonstrated through infant studies on attraction that observed facial symmetry increased infants' attention time and positive nonverbal expressions. Individuals have an inherent capacity for design structures that utilize perceptual cognitions, which can reverberate into physiological manifestations. A recently published book, *The Mozart Effect* (Campbell, 1997) also refers to the individual as a multilevel designed human instrument responding to different types of musical rhythms producing mind and body altering effects. For example, Baroque music has a particular rhythm that referred to as iambic pentameter. The structural form of this rhythmic design has been found to increase mental performance in learning as well as relaxation.

It goes without saying that, while design structuring is an innate capacity, each individual responds to different musical vibrations and frequencies with a fine-tuning as a unique instrument. Henry David Thoreau in *Walden Pond* wrote that each person must march to the beat (unique rhythmic design) of his or her own drum.

Steve Halpern (1978) and Jonathan Goldman (1996) refer to the human being as a human instrument of music. In discussing harmonies in music, they indicate that a harmonic can be created on the piano by striking a low "C" note, which when sustained will resonate with higher "C" notes thereby creating overtones or harmonies. Each higher "C" in the next octave (eight notes between one "C" to the next) vibrates at higher multiple ratios than the one before it (first harmonic two times as fast, second harmonic three times as fast, and so on). It has been presented by Halpern (1978) that as the pitch ascends the musical scale, evoked images (on metal disks with metal filings) would manifest organic shapes (pentagonal stars of sea urchins, hexagonal cells of honeycombs, etc.). Organic designs emerge out of inorganic material.

The motif can be seen in harmonic ratios of the organization of the human being. As one moves up the levels of organization from the cellular to the mind/brain, increasing organic patterns of complexity emerge. Motifs are not set forms but rather are formative (that which generates form varieties, design structures, etc.). As a result, the diversity and refinements of motif will increase with higher levels of the human organization. At the same time, similar to harmonies, the increasing complexity of design structures manifested at higher levels of organization will resonate as overtones to those preceding.

Reverberations throughout the mind/body system are not unlike harmonic overtones resonating throughout the human instrument. A key distinction here is that individual motif of the human instrument determines the archetexture of multifaceted design structures. Therefore, unique, formative vibrational energies will resonate throughout the mind/body system manifesting idiosyncratic "harmonics" of growth and development in the individual.

There is a perpetuating dynamic at work here. The motif operates as an architectural instrument unique unto itself. As growth chords are "struck" (developmental stages), unique facets of the human instrument generate unique vibrations (patterned forms of growth processes, e.g., neuro-hormonal, muscular/skeletal). These psychophysical changes in turn manifest increased refinement and differentiation of unique motifs, which in turn generate ever more intricate "vibrational" energies in the mind/body system.

Research by Rauscher and colleagues (1997) demonstrates that listening to classical music such as Mozart facilitates symmetry processes involved with higher brain functions. The ordering effects of listening to music involves increased concentration, ability to make intuitive leaps and so on. Formative abilities were found to increase for those musical listeners. Organizing energy patterns can both generate and be generated by mind/body design structures. Human beings can learn to access their own self-generative formativeness through alignment with their unique motifs.

The effects of mind/body interactions on the health and well-being of the individual were expressed by one of Freud's early students, Wilhelm Reich. Reich (1949) perceived how neurosis could occur in the body especially in cases of trauma. He believed that reorganization of body experience could have a concomitant reorganizing effect on psychological health. Reorganizing effects of mind/body alterations will transduce and reverberate throughout the levels if they are congruent with the individual's unique motif. This can be seen in many cases where alterations of one person's imagery are quite ineffective for another. For example, the hypnotic suggestion of being burnt will produce blisters on some individuals but not others. The brain cannot distinguish between subjective and objective reality. If the formative structure of the hypnotic image suggested is not congruent with one's motif, no psychophysical manifestation will occur as in the previous situation on relaxation.

Cognition-like thoughts and images are biochemical products of the brain, which, as has been described earlier, has its own unique organization. It stands to reason that the brain's unique organizational design produces cognitions with their own distinctive design structure. Whatever the brain organizes will be transduced into body manifestation. This involves the muscular skeletal system, which can manifest reorganization in the body. If there is hypnotic suggestion for an individual to move his foot, the brain can organize this image if the structure is congruent with its unique motif. Once organized, the image affects the motor centers of the cerebral cortex and the foot will move. This may feel like an involuntary experience to the individual. Yet, it was experienced as a result of congruence of imagery structure with that of the brain's unique motif. Such congruence with unique motifs is the very essence of establishing rapport with the individual, his or her brain structure and psychophysical manifestations.

An example of such congruence is reported by Rossi (1986) describing the recovery and then relapse of a cancer patient. The patient was first informed that a new, experimental drug had proven highly effective in the treatment of cancer. His recovery was remarkable. When he was later told that further testing of the drug had demonstrated its ineffectiveness, the patient's condition worsened and he later died. As the brain cannot tell reality from imagery, the self-suggestion was obviously congruent to his own unique brain structure and was quite effectively transduced to the body's biochemistry resulting in death. Indeed, thoughts and images are things that when congruently structured with one's unique brain design become physically manifest. Such is the capability of mind/body transduction of organizing design structures of motif.

Robert Masters (1994) indicates that language patterns can effect changes in the mind/body system if the movements to occur are described in such a way that the mind is compelled to create cognitions which trigger changes in the motor cortex of the brain. Whether conscious or unconscious, these trigger effects in the motor cortex initiate muscular body activity.

The structure of language can be utilized to effect multiple changes in heart rate, breathing, skin color, temperature and so on. The psychophysical alterations are practically endless. However, the congruence of unique motifs in design structures is essential for all successful transductions to occur. Bandler and Grinder (1975) have described the importance of pacing and leading the individual in how they utilize language patterns to structure change. Utilizing the work of Milton Erickson, Virginia Satir and Fritz Perls, Bandler and Grinder focus a great deal of effort on tailoring their change interventions utilizing the individuality of the client. They describe how focusing on the unique sensory experience of the individual assists movement into an altered state of consciousness. They then utilize these alterations to effect imagery and cognitive changes that will in turn manifest helpful, physiological changes (relaxation, feeling comfort, powerful feelings of confidence, etc.).

Such an approach acknowledges the reciprocal mind/body interaction. Mental imagery can effect physiological changes and these changes can further influence future mental images. This dimension of mind/body mutuality points to an important reality. That is, change and effect can occur at any point along the mind/body continuum. Mind and body are not black and white, separate entities. The use of such terms is only a convenient way of addressing a much more complex state of affairs. Mental functions of awareness, memory, learning, cognition and so on are possible from the neural network signals present in the central nervous system. The CNS includes the brain and the peripheral and autonomic nervous system as well. These neural networks are biological and as such are parts of the body. There is a fine line between where mindfulness begins and where it ends.

In initiating psychophysiological changes and alterations, language patterns uniquely structured to pace and lead the unique experience of the individual must also address individual self-awareness levels. The individual's awareness of the subtleties of his or her own experience constitutes a movement of attention from one sense to another. In expanding and opening an individual to fully utilize his or her unique motifs, awareness of one's complexity needs to increase. Such awareness can be assisted through a movement of attending to a variety of sensory experiences to open the channels to all incoming information.

Awareness and utilization of motifs require the individual to be able to process multiple levels of complexity regarding personal experience. Many individuals are limited and blocked in awareness in one or more of their sensory systems (visual, auditory, kinesthetic, olfactory, gustatory). Sense awareness is important to access psychophysiological congruence and one's own unique motif.

To achieve expanded levels of sense awareness, Masters (1994) advocates the use of language patterns that move the individual's attention from one sense to another until integration has occurred. As self-awareness of sensory systems increases, there is an alteration of consciousness that integrates the complexity of sensory structure into its own unique design structure. In addition, such integration culminates in an altered consciousness that is congruent with psychophysical sensory integration.

MOTIFS AND ALIGNMENT

The depiction of mind/body as a continuum of psychophysical functions and processes emphasizes the need for congruence of unique design structures within the individual. When congruence has been achieved, the mind/body system can be considered aligned within itself. The need for alignment is important to maintain homeodynamic functions both biochemically and psychosocially. Mental and biophysiological processes are mutually supportive as the individual's unique motif is reverberating through the system.

Alignment is not a fixed state but rather a dynamic process involving constant adjustment and feedback loops. For example, an individual may feel pressured into getting a job task completed in a hurried manner and ignore physical signs of stress, not going at his or her own pace. Integrated awareness of one's own motif occurs through mind/body signaling. When your car is about to run out of gas, a red light may go on signaling you to stop. Similarly, an aware individual can attend to when the stress creates a short temper and he or she "sees red" in emotional anger. Adjustments to realign are then in order.

What facilitates this realignment is the gyroscopic guidance system of unique motifs. There is a rhythm, pace and way of doing things that is uniquely characteristic of the individual. Attending to what makes one a unique individual can assist in the psychophysiological feedback loop of mind/body communication. The design structures of motif function as indicators of when this psychophysiology is out of alignment. Knowing one's unique complexity with full awareness allows clear attention to telltale signs of when alignment is less than satisfactory. Masters suggests using: (1) movement work (motion, kinesthetic and tactile exercises combined with imagery); (2) image work (utilizing visual, tactile, kinesthetic images); (3) language patterns involving psychophysical changes; and (4) altered states of consciousness (used to facilitate the processes of the latter). While these exercises are effective, the unique application of them individually is what maximizes their effectiveness.

Notice that these procedures involve a movement in sensory awareness from one sense to another. The way in which each person's movement of attentiveness (slow, detail-to-detail specific sensory experience or rapid, more generalized sensory groupings, etc.) reflects features in their design structure. When congruence of external suggestions and internal motif exists, the individual is likely to enter a state of flow. In this focused state, there is a merger of individual absorption with the task at hand (Csikszentmihalyi, 1990). Such psychophysical congruence can create optimal performance in individual functioning.

It is the idiosyncratic confluence of attention style, task orientation (witness the flowing absorption of a professional tennis player) and movement all resonating to the individual's unique motif. It is important to emphasize that while alignment of mind/body focused activity may seem almost perfect as in cases of high performance, there is a homeodynamic process in effect. Moment-to-moment experiences and growth require constant adjustment to changes and challenges as a result of a constant state of flux. A person needs to self-pace and attend to conditions of when and where environmental demands in work, love or friendship may require new adjustments but in a manner congruent with their motif.

As a result, alignment is somewhat of an asymmetrical process. Constant adjustments to time, place and personal demands require a flow-like movement in motif. The design structure of an individual's attention style (panoramic, detailed, narrow, rigid, etc.), his/her shifting sensory experience and moment to moment environment challenge involves a becoming process. One is never perfectly aligned but rather moves in one's style of formativeness somewhat asymmetrically congruent with oneself and tasks at hand. The becoming process of motif is an unfolding asymmetry moving towards alignment but never quite perfectly aligned. The closer one gets, the higher one's capacity to utilize one's innate talents and abilities. The more one resonates and acts in motif, the more one's innate capacities differentiate and grow.

Articulation of motif for the individual involves a highly unique, flowing configuration that, as described previously, is effused throughout one's psychophysiology. The unique configurations of motif are refined, idiosyncratic signatures manifesting their novelty in numerous ways with familiar characteristic features. These organizing motifs are guiding principles of psychophysiological balance and performance.

Chapter Five

Motif of Individuality: Archeidentity and Archetypes

Human nature is sometimes best represented not by describing all of humankind but by describing a specific man or woman. Yet historically efforts at comprehending human behavior have centered upon categorizing individuals in terms of typological classifications. The previous chapter presented some of these models of classification. While models go a long way towards laying foundations of understanding human behavior, they fall short of grasping the fine complexities that identify unique, human individuality.

Interestingly, Swiss psychologist and one of Sigmund Freud's students Dr. Carl Jung (1971) described the need for human beings to mature into their own individuation. Yet, he advocated innate, archetypal characteristic polarities (introversion-extroversion, Yin-Yang, etc.) which each person incorporates into their character to varying degrees. Jung indicated the existence of a collective unconscious from which the self draws intuitively as a universal resource of knowledge and creativity. He suggested that each individual has symbolic archetypal qualities drawn from the collective unconscious which are inherent in one's character. While Jung depicted that each person needs to individuate his or her own sense of self, he presented the construct of archetypes as ways of construing the core essence of self. It is a curious paradox that Jung, who clearly grasped the need for the self's individuation, would propose typological classifications involving the self.

Jung realized that in the individual's dreams, symbols and character types are a balancing of archetypal polarities which was at the heart of the self's mental health. His focus of balancing Yin and Yang (female and male energies) points to a unique integration of polarity types for each individual. Unfortunately, more emphasis is placed during assessments of individuals on type classification and diagnosis than on grasping the fine complexities of an individual's unique design of balance and interplay of polarities. Such a focus accesses meta-level (one step above) cognition recognizing the formative design of the individual in this balance of interplay. It is at this level that the formative design structures of self reveal themselves in the proportionality of character trait composition.

Integration is not a set point of polar opposite character traits. It is dynamic fluctuation of the individual's self regulated by the proportionality of varying character trait contributions. The complexity of multiple character trait contributions (introversion-extroversion, thinking, feeling, etc.) becomes a formative composition and expression of individual uniqueness.

The motif of such a composite expresses its own proportionality of character trait contributions in a synergistic, not additive, manner. That is, the balancing of multiple character trait contributions results in a construction of a third entity of unique synthesis of polar trait duality. An individual's way of synthesizing composite integration of multiple character traits is the formative manifestation of motif.

Synthesis can be experienced in the linguistics of language. For example, the word "me" has two separate sounds, the "m" sound and the long "e" sound. There is a totally different sound experienced when these letters are expressed separately and when they are expressed together. The "me" sound integrates the "m" and long "e" sounds synthesizing a new integrated ("me") sound unique to the two letters sounded separately. The "me" is a new composite, as both letters are sounded together in a flowing oneness of steps (no interval between sounds). It is in the flow of oneness where the unique composite integrated sound of self emerges.

In a similar fashion, synthesis of character trait contributions creates unique integration of "sound" compositions which orchestrate individual uniqueness with motif as the harmonic conductor. The new synthesis is a manifestation of the self motif. Unfortunately, many assessments of an individual grasp at his or her complexity through refined classifications in typology while still insisting on fitting that individual into a type. Even Jung released typecasting to the creative integration of the self tapping into the universal self of collective unconscious.

The highly regarded and utilized Myers-Briggs Type Inventory (MBTI) is an example of refined type casting (Thomson, 1998). Based upon Jungian type dimensions, the MBTI utilizes four polar dimensions capable of sixteen combinations. These four are: (1) introversion-extroversion, (2) thinking-feeling, (3) intuition-sensation and (4) perceiving-judging. Introversion is defined as withdrawal from social interaction whereas extroversion is its opposite, seeking interaction with others. The thinking dimension is defined as organizing experience with concepts and thoughts analysis, whereas its polar opposite, feeling, organizes experience utilizing emotional evaluations. The intuitive dimension is defined as a preference for direct experiences where other possibilities are imagined. The sensation polarity is defined as one where individuals have direct experiences that are right in front of them. The perceiving dimension refers to a way of functioning in the outside world preferring to have direct experiences (intuition or feeling), whereas judging types prefer to organize their experience (thinking or emotional evaluation).

These four dimensions can create sixteen combination forms as seen on the following chart:

ISTJ	ISFJ	ISTP	ISFP
INFJ	INTJ	INFP	INTP
ESTJ	ESFJ	ESTP	ESFP
ENJF	ENTJ	ENFP	ENTP

Each of these sixteen combination type forms has what are called dominant and secondary characteristics. In addition, each type combination is further refined into what are called brain-sidedness, alternatives, double agents, tertiary and inferior levels. These refinements have psychophysical correlates.

It has been found in position-emission topography (PET) scans that each of the four dimensional polarities is a functional capability with its own particular brain neural circuitry (Thomson, 1998). For example, the front of the left side of the brain has circuits for extroversion and thinking, extroversion and feeling, introversion and sensation, and introversion and intuition. The front of the right side of the brain has circuits for extroversion and intuition, extroversion and sensation, introversion and feeling, and introversion and thinking.

The left side of the brain utilizes circuits for judgers which include functions such as concept formation, general abstract thinking, use of words and numbers, and seeking precise conclusions. The right side of the brain utilizes circuits for event orientedness, concreteness, specificity, pattern and image utilization and evolving problem resolutions in an appropriately contextualized setting. These attributes of the brain's right side are designed to address how perceivers directly experience their world.

As Thomson (1998) indicates, potentiation of inherent functional capabilities in the here and now is a time consuming process. Selectivity operates in the interaction of self and environment potentiating differential functional capabilities (extroversion, thinking, etc.) as emerging dominant over others left underdeveloped. The preference of one set of functions and attitudes over another emerges as the figure of personality within the background of developed potential.

Typing, no matter how refined, is therefore descriptive, not predictive, of the nature of human beings as unique individuals. Typing is not the reality of the unique individual but rather the selected innate characteristics one has learned to emphasize and develop. There are qualities within the selection process affecting the kinds of choices and integration of various characteristic type dimensions. These qualities are operative in the formative organization principles utilized by the individual that affect the selection process of which characteristic type dimensions are to be developed.

While environment exerts its force on which traits may be more desirable in one setting than in another, it is the individual's unique motif that operates at metaselective levels in-forming the overall process, as was demonstrated in the previous chapter. As a foundation for this understanding, it is important to return to the type refinement levels mentioned earlier.

The MBTI structures its depiction of an individual's type at various levels from the most to the least dominant (dominant, secondary, alternatives, double agents, tertiary and inferior). These various levels depict the gradations of preferred dominant type characteristics. The ENTP type (extroverted, intuitive, thinking and perceiving) would be presented on these levels as:

Dominant – extraversion with intuition
Secondary – introversion with thinking
Right brain – extroversion with sensation
Alternatives – introversion with feeling
Left brain – extroversion with thinking
Double agents – introverted with intuitive
Tertiary – extroverted with feeling
Inferior – introverted with sensation

The contributions from the various type characteristics decrease from the upper to lower levels. The result is a much more complex picture of the individual than being stereotyped into a set category. However, such gradation points to an inherent difficulty with type casting efforts. As each individual is a unique complex motif, accurate representations of the individual can only be approximated in such a process but never actually achieved. It is only when the precise, proportional qualities of the individual's vast range of characteristics are assessed at the micro level that access to the unique individual can ever be achieved. Individual assessment is as much an art as it is a science.

As mentioned previously, typecasting only describes, not predicts. In order to access the individuality of a human being, the focus requires one of uniqueness rather than categorization no matter how refined the typing process. It is interesting that as more and more levels are differentiated and characteristic variables added to the classification process, the ultimate end would culminate in a complexity of proportionality. It would manifest a unique "categorization" in which the only member that would fit is that very individual under scrutiny.

While PET scans have found neurological correlates for general trait functions, individual personality temperaments with their own motifs have highly distinguished scans known as evoked potential signatures. Each individual's neurological circuitry is as uniquely wired, generating its own electrical, evoked potential signature, as his or her personality.

The individuality of motif is manifest not as a static state but in dynamic flow of unique movement and organizing principles. The physical structure of a human being is never static but rather constantly renewing itself at what appears to be a consistent rate of change. This is only an appearance to the naked eye as multiple rates of change in growth and development of body organs and tissue occur differentially as indicated in previous chapters.

The life of an individual organism is its homeodynamic flow of energy and movement orchestrated by its organizing principles of motif. The point is that flow is a key concept in the manifestation of unique individuality physiologically and psychosocially as well. The motif of individual temperaments flows through a proportional integration of various characteristic dimensions creating uniqueness. In addition, such a proportional integration of character traits (introversion-extroversion, thinking-feeling, etc.) may fluctuate over time with growth and development. Also, multiple traits are involved far beyond what any single personality test can measure (dominance – submission, optimism – pessimism, etc.).

Such a vast range of numerous character traits with varying degrees of contribution generate a complexity of wholeness in the proportional integration of self. This complexity cannot be reduced to a set formula of proportional mix of traits as the individual is evolving at varying rates of development. It is akin to attempting the measurement of Picasso's art as it developed from his blue period to his cubist designs.

In the development and growth of unique motifs, the flow of movement generates a unique third-level characteristic conventionally known as chaos. As the unique motif of the individual's temperament evolves, it has its own logic (psycho-logical) that appears "chaotic" to the outside observer. As the Heisenber uncertainty principle indicates, one can never be totally objective (one is part of what one measures) to what is being measured (Wolinsky and Ryan, 1991). Whether one is measuring the location or speed of an object, the very act of measurement influences the results.

As will be presented, individuals are truly one-of-a-kind characters in their own class. They manifest unique, flowing motifs that present what appears to be a chaotic quality in their growth and development. Just as placing sounds of letters together creates unique, heretofore unheard phonemes, the flowing integration of uniquely proportioned character traits evolves into new features previously not present in the parts alone. The emergence of unique "sounds" in the individual can emerge in a surprising, seemingly chaotic way. This is the creative leap where the whole is generated as the parts come together forming that third quality of something more than its parts. The development of the internet is a classic example of holistic evolution which continually surprises and seems to grow in diverse, chaotic ways yet with a unique formativeness all its own.

When someone says that such and such a person is a "real character," it is that unpredictable, unique, seemingly chaotic quality of individual motif emerging in its own way. The surprising, unique, chaotically unpredictable nature of individuality can challenge a scientific categorization process. It is much easier to seek broad dimensions within which to categorize. Yet no matter how refined the distinctions may be, the uniqueness of flowing motif has its own "character," if you will, which emerges in its own chaotic leap of integrated life form.

To say that the majority of adults in America are extroverted says nothing about who each of these adults actually is. While it may serve a psychosocial purpose to see how one compares with a group norm, it is deceptive to imagine that such normative measures access the identity of each individual. Idiosyncratic tests of a projective nature (thematic apperception and Rorschach tests) generate individual profiles along dimensions of degree of integration and personality organization. While measurements of individual life themes and ways of organizing and structuring experience emerge, identification of unique complexities of flow and inherent artistry rarely occur. Usually such approaches deal with the degree to which an individual can integrate and organize his or her experience through measuring projection, not articulating in freeform association his or her own, unique experiences of optional performance. A test may measure how an individual organizes himself or herself. Motif is the inherent principle by which the self constructs and organizes.

This leads to a fundamental distinction between personality and character temperaments. Personality is the way in which one copes and adapts in one's lifestyle and can change over time. Character structure deals with core inherent temperaments that remain relatively stable but can evolve or mature over time. The unique character structure needs to evolve in its own "characteristic" way (surprising and chaotic as it may appear). The point at which character structure is aligned with personality creates a sense of flow and unique transformative experiences. It is to this congruence that idiosyncratic growth and uniqueness need to emerge.

The capacity to align the personality or ego structure of the individual with the inherent organizing principles of motif is what Jung (1971) referred to in the individuation process. Behind the persona or mask of the individual is the uniqueness pressing for unity and manifestation of the whole selfhood. A great deal of emphasis is placed on measuring personality and character traits. Yet, such efforts may fall remarkably short of accessing unique, organizing motifs pressing for emergence.

The proportionality of character trait contributions to an individual's temperament can manifest the design structure as unique integration. The integration is not static as mentioned previously but rather is in a unique state of flow. As such, this unique, flowing integration is the substrate of personality structure and evolves over time through maturation and differentiation. Case examples will be presented later.

Congruence of character trait proportionality progresses from childhood to adulthood in much the same way psychophysiological proportions persist in body structure, handwriting and facial design. Growth, enlargement and expansion occur in all these areas, yet the proportions remain roughly consistent. This can be seen in reunions of old classmates. You may meet a classmate whom you have not seen in thirty-five years yet be able to "see" the younger student of years ago in the older man standing before you. The proportions of temperament and psychophysiology may remain roughly consistent enough to perceive the motif's manifestation and allow recognition.

Understanding that core organizing principles of motif form the substrata of personality can go a long way towards clarifying issues of generational transmittance of traits. In the previous chapter, the point was made that there are no genes for specific traits. Rather, general dispositions are present that increase the probability that certain traits and behaviors later in life may develop (alcoholism, violent behavior, sociopathy, etc.). Focusing on the inherent motif of an individual as a prelude towards dealing with any specific trait emergence could go a long way towards prevention and redirection of potential risk or endangerment.

Instead of focusing on a particular trait (acting out), it might be as valuable or even more valuable to align with and harness an individual's motif assisting its healthy utilization. Before that can happen, there needs to be an acknowledgment that motifs are present and operative. I do not believe in what's called a "bad seed" but rather in an unidentified and stereotyped labeling that misjudges individuals at critical early age time periods.

Recognition of the presence of motifs could alert responsible adults on how to attend and supportively utilize inherent organizing self-principles of the child. If this is achieved during the formative child rearing years, perhaps many of the aberrant behaviors we are witnessing in today's educational and social settings could be averted.

It is important to understand that every human being has inherent organizing principles of motif. This is not contingent on social or educational development. While the motif's degree of manifestation and maturation certainly depends on appropriate psychosocial development, its presence is an inherent, life giving formative design structure. The individual could not exist physically much less psychologically without it.

Comparative contrasts can be made between Jungian archetypes and what are termed archeidentities. The latter refers to the unique individuality of identity that permeates multiple levels of the human being. This identity is the manifestation of motif. While archetypes refer to universal qualities (masculine/feminine), archeidentities are concerned with the unique design integration of these qualities. As such, archeidentities are unique to each person and not universal in content quality. They are universal in the larger sense that each individual is a unique archeidentity unto himself or herself. Table 5.1 demonstrates comparative features between archeidentities and archetypes. Throughout these comparisons is the construct of formativeness, which is in unfolding, evolutionary flow. The motif is a fertile garden with vast, characteristic ranges of assorted flowers arranging and growing themselves in ever expansive, ground breaking design patterns. As long as it connects with the larger ecosystem of earth, wind, warmth and rain, its holistic characteristics will grow themselves through formative alignment with inherent motifs.

Life is formative and flowing. An individual's life is the unique, idiosyncratic manifestation of this life principle. Accessing the unique, formative flow of the individual's motif unlocks his or her life principles to flower and blossom with dynamic brilliance.

Tending to one's garden involves cultivating useful habits that etch in characteristic qualities of one's motif. Knowing which habits enhance one's motif's manifestation involves aligning and attending to one's sense of self. Such aligning efforts require self-attending and self-listening skills, many times nurtured through meditative and self-observation experiences. Feedback from mentoring people in our lives can also provide critical self-knowledge and discernment of healthy habit formation for character manifestation.

Table 5.1
Comparative Features

Archeidentities	Archetypes
• Particularized schematics.	• Generalized themes.
• Complexity of qualities.	• Simplicity of a quality.
• Asymmetrical formativeness.	• Symmetrical, set forms.
• Configuration expressed in novel detail.	• Configuration expressed in stereotyped generalization.
• Motif of design is characteristically variable preserving its signature.	• Mode of design is characteristically preset and invariant in preserving its signature.
• Unique formulativeness of multiple types.	• Typical formulation of single types.
• Expansive to qualities and characteristics undiscovered and not included on bipolar continuums of type dimensions.	• Restrictive to qualities and characteristics known and included on bipolar continuum.

The formative flow of motif is unique for each individual's archeidentity. When rigidity and fixation set in for whatever reason (genetic mutation, *inutero* imbalances and toxicity, severe dysfunctional early childhood experiences, etc.) the formative flow of motif can be unduly restrictive. Distortion in one's beliefs of self-identity and self-other relationships can impair healthy utilization of one's resources. In severe cases, fixation and rigidity can lead to psychopathology and even what is termed evil behavior. The Hitler character has many trappings of such severity. Hitler's fanatical obsession with omnipotence and authoritarianism speaks volumes about his fixation and rigidity. He had no capacity to integrate character traits of dominance/submission, power/helplessness, self-absorption/other absorption, egocentric systonic/other dystonic and so on. For whatever reason hypothesized (bad seed, genetic mutation, abusive childhood, anti-Christ, all of the above), it is clear that he was of a rigid, preset, authoritarian character structure. His fixation on rigid character constructs of power, control, egocentricity and the like was paradoxically responsible for his rise and fall. The face of evil invokes such rigidity and single-minded obsessiveness. While such attributes may be valuable at times, they fail in the long run to honor the life principle of formative flow in evolutionary growth. They become the seeds (bad seeds in that sense) of their own destruction.

THE PSYCHOID ARCHETYPE

In discussing and reviewing archetypes and archeidentities, it is important to relate Jung's conceptualization as it relates to integration and synthesis. While he may not have addressed the idiosyncratic uniqueness as a motif directly, his following conceptualization serves as the forerunner to taking this next step in the articulation of formative, flowing motifs.

Jung (Aziz, 1989) later in his theory of archetypes referred to the psychoid archetype which was the progressive synthesis of instinct and spirit. To Jung, instinct was the innate pattern of human behavior, and spirit was the innate pattern of meaning that was ascribed to life events. He understood archetype as the progressive synthesis on a continuum of dichotomous opposites.

Such a conceptualization of archetypes approaches the construct of motif as an archeidentity. However, while they both deal with construction of synthesis, the motif goes further towards articulating uniqueness and artistic formativeness determining characteristics of individuality. Jung's focus on archetypes of a psychoid nature is ambiguous about the precise process and criteria of individuation as resulting in a merger into individual wholeness. Yet individuality is an expression of uniqueness by implicit definition. For all his work on individuation and the synthesis process of the psychoid archetype, little mention is given of the fundamental principle of individuation, which is the idiosyncratic characteristic that makes a human being individual and unique in his or her own way.

In addition, Jung's archetypal constructs involve synthesis on a continuum of polar opposites resulting in the individual emerging. The construct of motifs operates on implicit presuppositions, which indicate that the individual is never not a unique whole. The synthesis that emerges is in resonance with inherent formativeness of motif already present. The uniqueness of the individual is inherently present before synthesis occurs and actually serves as an organizing and guiding principle in the synthesizing process.

This is not meant as a critique of Jung but rather as a context in which to set the next stage for further theoretical development. The idiosyncratic nature of the individual is a unique "category" or "archetype," if you will, that can only type cast one person because only that individual "fits" that class. This begs the question of archetypes when referring to individuals as resulting in paradoxical effects of class and member. In the case of unique motifs, class and members of that class are identical.

Jung also described the archetype as not being strictly intrapsychic but also constituting a psychophysical continuum of meaning unrestricted by space and time. As such, archetype is active in nature and behavior as well as in psyche. His principle of synchronicity emerged from archetypes.

Synchronicity refers to the meaningful parallel of internal and external events (dreams and day-to-day events) not causally related but manifesting a kind of orderedness. Synchronistic events are causal, involving an ordering principle transcending space and time.

The construct of motif as an organizing principle in hierarchy of multilevel dimensions reflects Jung's synchronicity principle for the individual. Motifs are unique organizing principles that operate through the psychophysical organism of the human being. The ironic parallels in body shape, handwriting, brain circuitry and so on with character traits and temperaments are but a few expressions of the individual's mind/body synchronization. It also is similar to motif's manifestation in nature/nurture issues as selectivity of motif in environmental situations reflects and parallels the attributes and characteristics of the individual. When reference is made to the idiosyncratic nature of the individual, a form of synchronicity is operative. The individual's uniqueness is expressed in myriad ways both within the mind/body psychobiochemistry and the external psychosociophysical reality at large. Synchronization occurs uniquely for an individual as a result of inherent, formative motifs and their selective attraction for multidimensional resonant forms.

It may be no surprise that an individual with a robust and outgoing temperament, who is optimistic in outlook, may attract and selectively draw into his or her life people, opportunities and events that enhance such an outlook. This person may have children quite similar and/or polar opposite with complementary qualities. In social settings, he or she may gravitate to and draw attention from high profile segments of society (business opportunities, radio and television producers, modeling agencies, etc.). Yet the same person may have other dimensions of motif such as nuances for characteristics larger than ego or self needs. In such cases, what may seem like surprising, unlikely contacts with such figures as priests or rabbis may eventually occur, reflecting deeper dimensions of the individual. Jung's synchronicity is inherent in the idiosyncratic dimension of individual uniqueness. Uncovering the inherent motif of the individual reveals the uniqueness, which synchronically selects and proliferates its organizing principles through his or her lifestyle.

The causal events in a person's life can reflect the illogic of unique organizing motifs of the individual. The strange and odd coincidental happenings in one's dream life and in one's awakened, everyday life may seem mind boggling and defy logic (for example, Jung dreamed of Winston Churchill the night before he read about him in the newspaper, reflecting the content of Jung's dream). Only by grasping the unique motif of Carl Jung and his perspectives on psychology, universal self and religion could such coincidental experiences even begin to become coherent. The uniqueness of organizing motif exerts its own electromagnetic force field. The human body is electrical in nature (the central nervous system, cardiovascular rhythms, etc.) and as such generates magnetic fields as evidenced by magnetic resonance imaging and other measurements.

These fields are reflective of the unique organizing motifs of the individual, and they influence and are influenced by the larger ecology at hand. It has been said that animals and birds can detect seismic tremors of earthquakes prior to their occurrence because of shifts in magnetic fields. Even some highly sensitive individuals have been said to be able to sense the impending occurrence of earthquakes. When Tokyo experienced an earthquake of a 7.2 Richter scale magnitude, some individuals tried to warn the government before it happened but went unheard.

Through the refined articulation of the individual's motif, many features of a compelling nature emerge as hidden resources and enriching dimensions. Jung's attention to the psychophysiology is grounded in his construct of archetypes. He focused upon the extension of archetypes unconstrained by space or time. Such transcendence of spatial and temporal frames suggests the veritable unlimited capabilities of the individual when grounded in his or her own unique archetype or, more accurately, archeidentity. When the individual is well grounded in his or her unique, formative flowing motif, the combinations and permutations may be almost incalculable. Notice that the individual's brain has more synaptic combinations (nerve connections) than there are atoms in the known universe (Rossi, 1986). Accessing a potential of such magnitude requires utilization of refined levels of motif articulation. God, if you will, is definitely in the details.

INNATENESS REVISITED

The innate nature of archeidentity in organizing motifs needs to highlight what is unique in the individual. The innateness of the individual's characteristic uniqueness involves dynamics of flow. It is this unique movement of formative flow that is characteristically innate to each individual. It is this characteristic motif of unique nuances of flow in the self-organizing capacities that constitutes the integrity of self. The unique formative flow of the individual is the design function that allows individuality. The human genome would require ten trillion base pairs to provide the necessary information for the human phenotype (formativeness) which is far beyond its structural capacity (Elman et al., 1996). Intriguingly, the genome of the human being and the chimpanzee share 98.4 percent of the same genotype yet their phenotypes could not be more distinct (Elman et al., 1996). The environment need only provide subtle nudges to nurture useful self-organization of the individual. Elman et al., (1996) refers to morphogens within the human being (chemical gradients and global regulators) as instrumental in phenotypic development. He suggests three ways innate characteristic formativeness may be present: (1) representation of symbols, (2) architectural constraints, and (3) timing also known as chronobiology (cycles such as circadian and ultradian rhythms).

As neither genetics nor its interaction with environment can totally account for the expression of the human phenotype (outward physical and functional formativeness), there is a third force. This third force is morphogenic in nature. The morphogenic nature of a human being requires formativeness in the organizing principles of his or her own individual development. It is the motif of unique characteristics in individual formativeness that constitutes an innate archeidentity. The manifestation of archeidentity occurs through flow. Csikszentmihalyi (1990) has written extensively on flow experiences, which facilitate optimal performance states. Flow has the quality of focused, absorbed concentration which the mind and body coordinate together on some task or skill-related activity (tennis, chess, writing, etc.). Flow involves not only mind/body functioning but also life sustaining biochemistry on the cellular/organ level.

Life is in constant states of homeodynamic flux (flow). States of being and becoming involve a characteristic flow that moves in an idiosyncratic motif. There can be no formativeness without flow, and flow dynamics of change require formativeness in which to move. Notice the flow of a river. It has both whirlpools idiosyncratically positioned while simultaneously currents are moving through the twists and bends of the riverbanks. Each whirlpool and current is idiosyncratic as the flow both designs and is designed through interaction with the river's formative banks. The river as a whole formative flow interacts with its larger environment thereby establishing its characteristic position in the larger ecology.

The human being is a formative, flowing motif serving as a vessel or vehicle for evolutionary growth in the larger ecological environment. The form and function of human motifs interlace together in a hierarchy (multidimensional systems). Elman et al. (1996) indicates that archetextural constraints along with timing can serve as morphogenic influences in growth and development. Intriguingly, the description of the human being as a formative, flowing motif of form and function is indicative of how architects describe design processes of building and construction. The archeidentity is the formative flowing motif that interacts both within itself and the larger environment. When observing an individual in his or her unique flowing motif, one perceives it as intelligence and beauty that is artistic in both form and function. Witness a Michael Jordan in flight or a world class chess master's brilliance in perceiving multiple sequences of moves before they have even happened on the board.

Analyzing a motif in a reductionistic effort of testing and dissection is similar to analyzing a motion picture. When turned off, each cell of the movie is a separate frame, which is fixed and stationary. Research scientists trying to find the innate "movie" of individual identity by looking for it in each separate "cell frame" (character traits) are missing the forest for the trees. How does one stop the motion to discover it, and how does trying to discover it eventually interrupt the movement of motif? It is like trying to catch quicksilver – always elusive yet ever present. This is the Heisenberg uncertainty principle operating in the human world of being. One does not have to go to the quantum level of subatomic particles to observe that, in trying to measure the speed and position of a moving object (human being), the very process of measurement itself interrupts and creates uncertainty as to where the object is and is going.

The motif moves and flows following its own innate characteristic constraints. It is formative and evolving, both shaping and reshaped through selective self and environmental interactions. To capture the presence and operation of motif requires capturing its flowing, dynamic qualities. To demonstrate this case, studies will be presented later in the chapter. Before this can happen, it is important to fully understand the distinction between archetypes utilized in assisting individuals in their lives and their archeidentity which manifests unique flowing motifs with their own balance and alignment.

EGO STATES AND ARCHE-IDENTITIES

Jung indicated that the archetype was not limited to one conscious state. As the individual self cannot be localized into any one set ego-consciousness, the unique archeidentity permeates but transcends these states. Rossi (1986) indicates that an individual anchors events in his or her life through what he calls state dependent learning. Learning, memory and behavior are associated with a contextualized ego state of consciousness located in a set place and time. These events could be reaccessed through appropriately recontextualizing the scene, time and place of occurrence. These states are specific and particularized, split off from the whole of awareness. The archeidentity of motif is the background from which these figural events emerge. While the contextualized events may be special unto themselves (a precise childhood memory or holiday family gathering), single events are not in themselves unique expressions of motif. However, the way events are constructed in shape, design, sequence, rhythm and schematics accesses the skeletal motif embedded within.

Alfred Adler (one of Freud's students) once had an early recollection of having walked past a graveyard as a child. While the content specifically dealt with life and death, the structural design dealt with downward (burial) and upward (afterlife striving) movement (Ansbacher and Ansbacher, 1956). Indeed, Adler's motif incorporated inferiority and superiority compensatory strings which involved the schematic of vertical, up and down life movement. The particular ego-state an individual is in is reflective of only a particular but silent dimension of unique motif. Formative motifs are dynamic movements that are not localized to any one part or level of the mind/body system. Motifs are the individual's unique dynamic background potentials. They are manifest holographically (are holistic at all levels) and serve as an unfolding, morphogenic guidance in the individuation process.

Because motifs are archeidentities, they can never be fully manifested in a fixed, local (time and space) ego state. The "I" of the individual is therefore aligned with Jung's construct of self, which encompasses all ego-states and is part of the larger eternal universal self. The motif is the formative uniqueness of the individual self and draws upon numerous archetypal patterns. These may be universal themes of dismemberment, renewal, wholeness, self-realization, Godman, hero, mandala (cross), initiatory ordeals and rites of passage, great mother death/rebirth, wise old man, hostile brothers, hero birth, trickster figure, spiritual ascent and descent, or masculine (yang) and feminine (yin) energy. While all of these character qualities and more impinge upon the individual, it is the idiosyncratic, unique characteristic of motif that serves as the archetextural guide orchestrating the harmonic nuances among such archetypal qualities. It is the guiding characteristic of the character traits that arches over all the rest as the conductor motif.

The question of where consciousness is located in terms of mind/body systems is resolved in that as in quantum mechanics and Jung's eternal self, nonlocalization is its realm. As motifs are hierarchical (multidimensional), formative motifs are unconstrained from any part of the mind/body system. As such, consciousness resides throughout the individual's formative manifestations, not simply in ego-consciousness of everyday life. This will be more fully explored in future chapters. At this point, it is valuable to point out that as motifs are not localized in any one or more ego-states, they serve as an inner guidance of what may be called the awakened life. It is oftentimes asserted that people are in dream or trance-like states only to "awake" during the daylight. This presumes that the daytime state of being awake is the real reality.

However, the numerous roles played out as doctor, nurse, butcher, baker, husband, wife, adolescent, male, female and so on are all states of defined con-

sciousness (or trances). These are no more real or unreal than dreams and fantasies one may have in the wee hours of the morning. It is critical for one's mental
health to be able to know the differences between these states.

Many people become confused as to who they are and what their purpose in
life is all about. This is more likely to occur in nodal times of change (adoles-
cent/midlife crisis, etc.). The ensuing role and ego-state confusion can be so
complicated with seemingly discrepant information that individuals may be
temporarily immobilized. At times like these, aligning with unique, inherent
core anchors of motif can provide a stabilizing, comprehensive sense of who we
are.

As motifs are formative and evolving, accessing them can help us reach the
roots of our unique history. In identifying what makes us special and comprehending persistent, evolving design structures in our life development, we can
now sense and choose how and where we as unique individuals can take the next
step in our unfolding lives. The next section will illustrate motifs in action.

MOTIFS IN ACTION: CASE PRESENTATION

Motifs are dynamic movements within and throughout a person's life development. They may appear in the form of metaphors, analogies and symbols.
However, motifs transcend such expressions as they are more than simply useful
ways of characterizing behavior. Motifs are organizing principles which, as will
be seen in the following cases, serve as an infrastructure upon which complex
ramifications of individual change and evolution emerge. A metaphor may relate
to a person's situation or event in the past, present or future. Motif permeates the
individual's time line, expressing developmental, idiosyncratic formativeness.
The case to be presented operates with such a distinction between motifs and
metaphors and thereby strives for comprehensive life change processes within
and beyond a problem solving orientation.

This case involves a fifty-two-year-old divorced air traffic controller. He is
struggling with the loss of a significant other relationship, which had lasted for
seven years. He has been experiencing severe mood swings of a manic-
depressive nature, is on medication and is being seen by both a psychologist and
a psychiatrist.

He describes his position at work as quite enjoyable in the way he can line
planes up for landing, coordinate the sequence of planes in an orderly step-wise
process of movement and experience a sense of control over his environment.
He also enjoys aviation and experiences real freedom while flying as a pilot.

He recognizes a pattern in his relationships as one of controlling how each
partner should act and feel in order to have a perfect relationship. There are key
design structures operating in the motif of his life structure. First, he positively
responds to up and down movement that is cyclic in nature. Note his penchant
for guiding planes down in perfect (or near perfect) sequential order while assisting others in clearing for takeoff. In addition, he enjoys being an observer at
a distance, facilitating the movement of other objects. He also enjoys the ordering process of sequencing events. The coming and going of events in and out of

his life is also present. There is also the visual element of watching/observing as a way of enjoying the flowing movement but preserving his sense (though somewhat constricted) of control. He further feels (kinesthetic) freedom when he flies his own plane though he still is at the controls. He represents himself as someone who is engrossed with streams of movement. There may be planes streaming by, thoughts rapidly passing through his mind, people coming in and out of his life including partner after partner. Notice the parallel between planes that he lands and his landing a partner, as well as planes that take off and partners that take off on him.

His motif also has what might be called a derivative design structure quality to it. He can describe an event, be it landing an airplane or a partner, or an experience on one of his three jobs, and derive further multiple examples from each, creating massive details from which further derivations would occur. He often achieves this through using analogy statements of " . . . and it's like . . . such and such." For example, he would discuss the complicated number of variables regarding how one plane might land and all that entails. He then would derive further details by comparing it to other events, stating " . . . and it's like the workings of a car transmission." Such constant parallels and further explicit details are a deductive procedure creating multiple levels of information. He can "build down," if you will, ever-deeper levels of detailed analogies but is unable to "build up" or be inductive in his logic structure. This is because he is so weighed down by data he cannot integrate and "come up" with a bird's eye perspective. In short, he becomes overinvolved and lost in the myriad details of his own cycles. He cannot re-cycle and induce construct-oriented cognition, which only perpetuates his feelings of helplessness and loss of control.

While the aforementioned dynamics are part of his motif's design structure, they are restricted and rigidly bound into an archetypal form of perfectionism and order. He has seen (visual mode) numerous relationships come and go without expanding his learning about his motif. He enjoys flying, being the master at the controls of a perfectly ordered stream of events. Yet his effort to control his life and those events streaming through it creates conflict within his own motif of freedom in flight. His motif requires a release of control of events to allow their cyclic movement. This includes his own movement as a participant in a creative stream of spiraling, cyclic movements.

He indicates that his partners essentially have had trouble with his efforts to order his and their lives which is why they seemed to be "taking off" on him. His mood swings of mania (multiple jobs — he had three at one time, rarely sleeping) and depression (crying, difficulty concentrating, intense negative thinking coupled with feelings of abandonment) reflect his up-and-down design structure becoming pathologized.

The alignment needed is for him, in addition to his ongoing treatment, to evolve his motif in a more differentiated form. The conflict with his own motif is that the joy and pleasure he has with the up and down, sequential movement of coming and going involves a fixation at that level. He has not grasped that while planes can come and go, they can also return in cyclic fashion. While he understands this in terms of his work and mood swings, he becomes fixated in his relationships. By preventing his relationships from being in the process of flow, he interrupts his own cyclic motif and thereby turns dynamic partners of flow into controlled objects of affection. In preventing each partner from coming and going as needed eventually to return, he controls their behavior so that they do not feel free to fly their own "flight plan" which would most likely return them to him.

By opening to his motif of a sequential, up-and-down streaming flow of events, he establishes a more meaningful sense of control. He achieves this through writing a letter to his former partner, opening and releasing the grief he feels by her loss and committing to leave the "door open" if she decides to return. In this way, he can gain closure (complete his cycle of coming and going and possible return by becoming a participant, not a strict observer) regarding the loss as well as complete the grieving process. He has to participate in his own motif through releasing cognitive and emotional material expressed in his own behavior. As such, he is able to become the unique motif of flowing sequential movement that he is so good at facilitating in his work.

His motif's penchant for derivativeness is now able to integrate and "build up" (completing is cyclic flow of vertical movement) massive detailed tiers of information into meaningful constructs. His inductive movement from details to design is a structural development of expanding his cyclic motif more fully and completely. The release of personal grief in a framework congruent with his motif allows alignment with necessary idiosyncratic characteristics. This enables him to feel whole about his loss.

His motif is a formative, flow cycle of coming, going and returning movements. He needs to learn how to complete his own cyclic motif and genuinely participate in his own feeling of being free to fly through personal and professional life experiences. As he learns to trust in his own motif of being open to a natural, sequential ordering of his life events (rather than superimpose one), a leveling off of his mood swings occur. The peaks and valleys become more rounded and stabilized.

An additional facet of his motif is that each time he processes through these cycles, there is something new to be learned and he feels more comfortable. There is an asymmetrical feature to his repetitive cycles as with each passage unique features emerge (new partners, learnings, facets, self-understandings, etc.) which enhance a maturing and evolution of unique self.

It is interesting to note that his psychophysiology is consistent with his motif. He is tall and thin; he moves, talks and thinks quickly and has a high-energy temperament with an angular facial design. Yet there are idiosyncratic nuances of a weighted midriff and rounded facial element and long, thoughtful pauses. As his comfort level with his own motif becomes more stabilized, his thoughts are more fluid and balanced in tempo, and he is able to plan for more sequential contingencies in both his personal and his professional life.

This case demonstrates the value of accessing the individual's formativeness as a way of gaining unique information about him. The unique information of individuality is coded in the form of form. Black (1969) refers to the form of form which contains essential information of living organisms. He indicates that life arises from information that is innate in biological form. He hypothesizes that mind/body systems are basically transformations of information in the form of form. Rossi (1986) suggests image, archetype (archeidentity), symbol and right-brained consciousness can be understood as a theory of information inherent in form. He further suggests that what is unique, odd, strange or idiosyncratic can be core qualities of individuality.

These researchers are suggesting the critical nature of unique formativeness as striking at the core of individuality. The motif's formativeness holds essential information systems out of which new patterns of self-evolution may emerge. Accessing the individual's unique motif accesses individuality throughout the mind/body system.

The following chapter will illustrate how harmonizing and aligning with one's motif cannot only enhance one's general sense of well-being but also increase levels of personal performance. Issues of tapping inherent resources will illustrate how to develop brilliance inherent in formative motifs.

Chapter Six

Motifs: Developing the Capacity for Brilliance

The archeidentity of each human being is embedded within a unique, formative unfolding motif with an inherent brilliance all its own. The design structures of a motif's architecture reflect a formative intelligence novel in their creative manifestations. Brilliance is the natural capacity innate in each human being to perform and/or fashion products at a uniquely intelligent level of excellence. Brilliance in behavior or performance and fashioning of products reflects improvisation and innovation. Individuals' uniqueness endows them with their own novel forms of what they are capable of doing quite well. It comes as no surprise that novelty and improvisation in brilliant expressions of excellence in performance and/or making of products are reflective of the inherent novelty of the individual. Whether in a great composer such as Mozart or a magnanimous scientist such as Einstein, brilliance manifests itself in the excellence of ingenious and uniquely innovative trans-formativeness in their respective fields.

The remarkably intelligent design that structures innovations is indicative of the individual's unique motif. Einstein reflected innately designed talents for symbolic, mathematical manipulation and relativistic frames of reference. Mozart manifested innately designed talents for harmonic and chord syntax structures. Each manifests brilliance in symbolic (numbers and notes) reorganization of their respective fields generating brilliant design structures of a novel intelligence unique in their time.

It is important to emphasize that individuals do not have to be as impactive as a Mozart or an Einstein to manifest brilliance in their lives. Someone mechanically minded (predisposing design structures for manipulation with spatial objects) who can take the rust-frozen engines of lawn mowers and motorcycles and restore them to excellent condition reflects a unique design intelligence in the brilliance of his or her work.

Brilliance emerges from the novel expression of an individual's unique motif and is a manifestation of that person's unique intelligence of design. Black

(1969) indicates that information content is inherent in an improbable (unique) life form. This means that an individual's unique, formative motif holds intelligent, informational content.

Rossi (1986) indicates that the essence of individuality is the unique, idiosyncratic expression of self. Uniqueness involves new and novel responsiveness by which a person's individuality processes information in formative ways. The mind is evolution's most sophisticated design-structuring medium in giving, receiving and transducing (translating from one medium to another as in mind/body) information. Transduction of information (in this case brilliance) occurs, preserving the unique design form of an individual's motif. Ordering of information is preserved in corresponding design structures in communications between mind/brain/body interactions. Healing utilizes similar ordering preservations as will be discussed in the following chapter. Whether as a mental image and/or body restabilization, formativeness in form and order are preserved, as in a Mozart sonata whether on sheet music or performed.

Brilliance involves an ingenious reordering of information, which already exists in some formative order. When novel stimuli challenge an individual, his or her own uniqueness provides innovative redesign and reordering properties. This is the manifestation of brilliance. Such brilliance of unique, innovative motifs is a form of intelligent design structuring.

Intelligence in design involves sophisticated ways of reorganizing information. The neural circuitry of the brain enables neural cell assemblies to etch in spatio-temporal patterns of nerve impulses (Hebb, 1949) which can enhance novel behaviors. Design structures involve intelligence in how to organize and integrate information in unique, syntactical ways.

Design structures involved in syntax as well as other organizing processes can be seen in spatio-temporal brain patterns of language and movement. Calvin (1996) indicates that conscious, short-term memory can only contain seven, plus or minus two, bits of data at any given time. This forces the brain to efficiently and effectively chunk or organize information into meaningful, hierarchical organizational structures for ready access. Calvin concludes that biological structures are involved in preexisting universal grammar. He proposes that the brain is inherently wired for tree-like structures needed for syntax in language. Such a universal grammar program is actually a metaprogram providing ways in which specific grammar rules in any given language can be learned.

The design structures of linguistic syntax are more extensive and complex than conventional word ordering or positioning aspects. Their use conveys a mental model to the listener. The use of tree structures (actually they are upside-down tree designs) deals with sentence phrase design. For example, subordinate clauses in rhymes are contained or packed within larger ones. Notice the rhyme in "The House That Jack Built" with subordinate phrases packed with larger phrases such as: "This is the farmer sowing the corn/that kept the cock/that crowed in the morning." Bickerton (1990) refers to nesting of phrases embedded within phrases as Chinese boxes, stacked one inside another. These are not serial constructions but enfolded, embedded ones. Note the parallel design structure of these linguistic "trees" nested within the enfolding DNA protein molecules. The design structures utilize similar principles of embeddedness, which is characteristic of embedded motifs at multilevels. It is curious that embeddedness is a feature of enfolding levels or tiers recurring throughout the self's organization. From DNA proteins to the cerebral cortex, enfolded design structures illustrate a configuration where they turn in on themselves. This involves a selfreflectiveness and possible source of one's consciousness.

Edelman and Tononi (2000) describe how consciousness arises from the interactiveness of numerous brain regions reflecting uniqueness of the individual. They present the emergence of consciousness from sequenced, ordered arrangements in the brain's circuitry. Neural pathways self-reflect in mutual interactions in the thalamicortical core region of the brain. This core involves twoway signaling between neurons (messages proceed forward and backward within the core region).

Conscious thought involves a set of relationships between neurons with a meaning that goes beyond (but includes) energy and matter. The realm of consciousness is created through the unique ordering motif of the brain, body and social world where meaning is consciously made. The totality of psychosocial formativeness evokes consciousness of meaning. Edelman and Tononi (2000) describe how thought is a process founded on deep brain structure mechanisms, which include nonrepresentative memory (unconsciousness), value constraints and activation of cortical regions such as basal ganglia, hippocampus and cerebellum. They indicate unique ordering of the brain for consciousness to emerge, defining this mechanism as the dynamic core hypothesis. The hypothesis states that neuronal activity contributes to consciousness only if it is involved with a cluster of functioning neurons that possess the properties of strong, mutual interactions in sets of these neurons extended over hundreds of milliseconds.

Sustaining consciousness requires complexity (differentiation of nerve clusters) of core composition that is in a state of evolution. There are parallel, oneway loops coming from the core through the cortical regions incorporating the external world stimuli and returning back to the core. Unique, symbolic parallel ordering of motifs can emerge in the core resonant with these external, communication loops. The need for evolving complexity, self-reflectiveness and parallel (symbolic ordering of correlations) information loops all point to the functional properties of formative motifs as a basis for individual consciousness. The ordering and design of unique brain motifs (neural pathways of distinctive complexity) sustain meaning and consciousness for the self. Edelman and Tononi (2000) utilize an apt metaphor to describe the motif of the brain/mind as a diverse group of specialists all learning to communicate with each other. Such communication requires complex orchestration of formative motifs.

Linguistic structures involve argument designs (e.g., what role each word plays in a sentence: verb, noun, adjective, etc.). This is a further ordering paradigm that universal grammar structures facilitate. The child learns mental grammar by listening to language. Deaf children learn by observing sign language. They learn how to order and sequence word role usage.

Studies at the University of Chicago (Golden-Meadow, 1999) strongly suggest that nonverbal gestural language may be the precursor to speech. Deaf children from both China and the United States invented gestural sign language more sophisticated than that of the language of speech. Even more intriguing, their inventions resembled each other's more than those of their parents. The nonverbal communication of gesturing taps into the same brain structures for grammar as does speech. Brain imaging studies indicate Broca's and Wernicke's brain structures (related to producing and comprehending language) are activated when sign language is involved.

Elizabeth Bates (1999) at the University of California, San Diego suggests that gestures (nonverbal symbols) share a common neuro substrate. Such a substrate indicates a hard-wired-in neurological structure in brain/mind complex for communication in symbols, patterns, shapes and coding which is precisely what motifs incorporate into their unique design structure. Indeed, the presence of design structures in nonverbal communication constitutes up to 93 percent of the overall meaning of spoken language in conversation. Removing the spoken word reveals the critical, underlying role complex design structures of motif play in nonverbal, gestural patterns of communication.

The stringing together of words creates unique meaning. The access of innate linguistic structures through learning syntax and word positioning aspects of grammar augments intelligence and brilliant improvisations. Combining gesturing with word usage (which actually is fundamentally learned in prenatal experiences as described in Pearce's *The Magical Child*) is a more sophisticated way of harmonizing and integrating movement with word usage.

The paradox of communication is that we string together meaningless phonemes (syllable sounds) to create meaningful language messages. This is actually the result of design structures organizing sound structures into form structures of sound. Novel communications involve storing spatio-temporal patterns of sentences in appropriate brain circuits. There patterned designs serve as metapatterns, describing patterns of patterns which assist in improvisational communicating.

The critical importance of formativeness in communication can be seen in the neural deficits of dyslexia (a learning disability in reading comprehension). Researchers such as Berninger and Richards (1999) have discerned that dyslexics struggle with connecting phoneme sounds of letters with word symbols. For example, the word "cat" consists of three phonemes; "kuh," "aah," and "tuh." The dyslexic hears only the complete sounds of "cat" but is unable to break down the formative components of the word into phonemes. As this is the first step in reading, dyslexics experience poor performance in this area.

The difficulty dyslexics have with rhyming tasks utilizing phoneme sounds points to the essential role of formativeness in constructing communication symbols to deal with novel situations. The finding that dyslexics could be suffering from inefficient brain pathways (Wernicke's area and the angular gyrus in the parietal lobe) has prompted efforts towards reeducation. Positive reading performance has been reported at the Lindamood Phoneme sequencing program, encouraging students to identify how sounds feel while being verbalized. For example, "p" is a "lip popper" as the lips begin together but then "pop" apart (Berninger and Richards, 1999). Such movement choreographed with phoneme word sounds emphasizes formativeness and sensory connections. The possibility of developing alternative spatio-temporal pathways is currently being explored.

The formative capacity for stringing together sounds, movements, word associations, story telling and even musical notes into a melody represent core faculty brain organization. These core faculties are able to bundle multiple functions such as language and movement in generating multiple spatio-temporal patterns in neural cell assemblies. The bundling or grouping of functions can be viewed in language organized with music, dance and/or planning activities. This allows for greater diversity in generating complex interrelated design structures capable of novel adaptations. In this way, the motif of the brain/mind is ever evolving, differentiating variant design structures in a unique mosaic of formativeness.

The intelligent design structures of bundling multiple functions together enhance the generation of diverse, solution-oriented improvisations. The larger the number of redundant variant designs generated, the higher the probability that one of the variant forms will be the best fit for the novel situation at hand. It is not unlike the universe with its billions and billions of stars and galaxies. Such a vast redundancy of celestial forms virtually guarantees that some form of life will exist somewhere out there.

The cortical regions are specialized throughout the brain (Ojemann, 1983). Large areas of specialization enhance the possibilities of novel sequences of various kinds (hand, mouth movements, mimicry and narration). Craik (1943) describes how the central nervous system is capable of modeling or paralleling environmental events with a matching small-scale internal representation. From this internal model, variant, alternative actions can be played out, sorting for the best fit.

Simulation of factual situations and generation of alternative coping devices weed out all but the most effective. Creativity and intelligence involve playing mental games (formative exercises of alternative solutions) that "shape up," so to speak, the intelligent design structures. In this way, a Darwinian evolution of a better brain "shapes up" (design structure) brilliant expressions of improvisational capabilities.

The linguistic structure of the brain utilizes universal grammar preexistent in the brain to facilitate syntax, word-role positioning, analogue associations and argumentation. These functions involve formative ordering in one way or another. Stringing words together to make sentences is essentially a formative operation. Complex communication systems are created by further stringing, requiring complexity in design structures. The patterns of patterns of communication resonate with internal brain structures. The knowledge of syntactical sequencing, chunking and sentence structuring develops powerful predictive designs from which creative, novel responses can be generated.

The spatio-temporal patterns of linguistic design structures have a firing sequence that operates synchronously as in a musical chord or melody. One can map the firing sequence of cell assemblies (Hebb, 1949) of neurons containing these spatio-temporal patterns on a musical keyboard. Thus, correlating a one-to-one relationship between a particular neuron cell assembly (circuit of nerves) to musical notes on a scale allows patterns to be heard as a melody. Lewis Thomas (1979) describes listening to Bach as a way of listening to the human mind. There truly are formative resonant patterns embedded throughout the mind/body brilliance of expression.

THE SYMBOLIC BRAIN

The brain is the most highly developed (and formative) structure in the process of evolution. Terrence Deacon in *The Symbolic Species* (1993) indicates that the ability to manipulate and integrate symbols is what distinguishes humans from animals. Intriguingly, he suggests that language development is evolution's "horse" pulling the "cart" of the brain in manifesting the ability to manipulate meaningfulness in symbolic terms (words are symbols in themselves). This capacity to connect action with internal representations is the operation of developing meaningful symbols.

Deacon indicates that the inner layers and columns of the cerebral cortex contain many levels enfolded upon themselves. It is in this domain where complex symbolization and integrative transformative reorganization may take place. I do not believe it is any coincidence that similar levels of enfolding occur in the DNA molecule where there exist tier levels forming multiple layers. These enfolded layers are themselves archetextural structurals capable of generating multipurpose programs and patterns reflective of motif's design structures.

Hebb (1949) describes how neural cell assemblies are capable of generating multiple spatio-temporal patterns that compete for neural pathway expression. Brilliance becomes manifest when these multiple patterns interact competitively for best "fit," resulting in novel expression of performance and/or product fashion. Motif is the capacity to generate symbolic, integrative design structures. Motifs are capable of intelligent, organized patterns of brilliant, novel expressions. The example of a teenager able to solve complex puzzles such as Rubik's Cube in a short period of time compared to the frustration of many adults in solving it indicates novelty and innovation free of set ways of thinking. When accessing formative motifs, creative and innovative problem solving and achievements can reach a level of brilliance.

For example, in learning to execute movement of a precise nature (shooting basketballs, darts, etc.), multiple variant patterns are generated that may facilitate accurate performance. When a critical mass has been reached (number of variant spatio-temporal patterns generated reflect resonance with ideal form of movement for accuracy), then action is initiated. This is demonstrated when basketball players are asked to visualize shooting free throws using mental imagery and remarkably improve their accuracy.

Some individuals will achieve this outcome more successfully than others depending on their unique design structures generating an appropriate range of variant spatio-temporal design patterns. This is the property of motif to generate multiple design structures. As one's signature may vary, unique characteristics remain consistent. Variant forms of ordering are a characteristic of motifs and parallel variant spatio-temporal patterns generated in neural cell assemblies.

This parallel of ordering is what Black (1969) describes in his depiction of information content inherent in improbable (meaning unique and unlikely to occur by chance) form (design structuring of motifs).

In discussing brilliance and how it is a functional manifestation of motif, it is important to understand intelligence in its broadest context. Intelligence has typically been defined for the past fifty years as a measure of IQ (intelligence quotient). This is a composite score based on normative data that standardized levels of intelligence depicting normal and deviant ranges of IQ measures. The original instrument for this was the Stanford-Binet intelligence test.

Alfred Binet invented the first tests of intelligence in the early 1900s. His tests focused upon verbal memory, verbal reasoning, numerical reasoning, appreciation of logical sequences and ability to indicate problem solving in daily tasks. In 1912, Wilhelm Stern presented the concept on measuring such tests of intelligence with an index he termed intelligence quotient or IQ. This was actually a ratio of one's mental age compared to one's chronological years.

There were criticisms of this testing approach on the basis of cultural bias and superficiality. Yet, IQ scores demonstrated their predictive value of success in school and therefore were considered valid measures of what was construed as intelligence. Intelligence at that time was defined in a somewhat circular logic as whatever IQ tests measured. Thus, intelligence was primarily defined in terms of logical-mathematical and verbal constructs. These were primarily academic abilities and therefore quite predictive of academic success.

Such a narrow view of intelligence leaves out capacities of performance in terms of dealing with practical issues of living. How do individuals use what they know in ways that are needed to function intelligently in various life settings (work, love, friendship, etc.)? These forms of intelligence are quite often neglected in testing and assessments. Steinberg (1985) found that there are differential levels of functioning between adaption to novel conditions and success with standard IQ test type problems.

With this discrepancy in mind as well as construing the mind/brain system as modular (brain evolving with a number of separate organs or information processing neural components), Howard Gardner (1993a) developed his theory of multiple intelligences. He defines intelligence not as a single "g" factor but rather as a variety of different potentials (as in brain differentiated with modulation of discrete, separate areas of specialized function). He utilizes a biopsychological potential definition of intelligence as the ability to process information that can be activated in a cultural setting to solve problems or create products that are of value in a culture (Gardner, 1993). Intelligences are neural potentials that depend on cultural activation, opportunities and personal and family decisions.

Gardner suggests there may be as many as eight or nine intelligence potentials. Gardner initially associated core faculties of intelligence with sensory modalities. These involved potential, possible candidates as visual intelligence and tactile intelligence.

The design structures of motifs involve sensory structures reflected in neural circuitry, body physiology and immune system design (shaping and honing of antibodies to antigens) which reflect an organizing and unique formativeness within the individual. Gardner's theory of multiple intelligences utilizing sensory modalities (which are uniquely designed for each individual) parallels unique sensory structures of design embedded throughout the organizational levels of the individual. Gardner indicates that each person's intelligence profile is unique as to his or her combination of sensory potentials of processing information. The unique intelligence profile of each individual in terms of different combinations of potential structures clearly reflects formative design structure profiles one would expect of motifs. The multiple intelligences Gardner (1999) describes are: (1) linguistic, (2) logical-mathematical, (3) musical, (4) body-kinesthetic, (5) spatial, (6) naturalist, (7) interpersonal, (8) intrapersonal, (9) spiritual and (10) existential. These intelligence potentials are symbolic systems with corresponding neural substrates in the layers and columns of the cerebral cortex. Each system is considered to operate on its own, intact, not requiring the assistance of neural substrates from the other symbolic systems. Each symbolic system of the ten intelligence potentials has its own rules and principles of organization. In addition, they are autonomous in that they can operate without being told to do so. Their activation or triggering can occur simply by the presence of selective forms of information and/or events internally or externally being present.

Such qualities of selectivity and organizing principles responding to discrete forms of information and/or events are precisely those qualities operative in architectural motifs. As the design structure of motifs select for equivalent forms in the internal or external environment (shape of a mental image or way a social scene may be seen), they are triggered through resonance of shape and design in the matching of unique design structures with the form of the information presented.

Cognitive scientists refer to Gardner's intelligence potentials as "cognitively impenetrable" or self-contained systems. This implies that such potentials are distinctive from one another. In addition, Gardner describes how each individual has a unique combination of these intelligence potentials as they may overlap with one another and with varying degrees of intensity.

What emerges from all this is that the distinctively unique, symbolic organizational principles with their own neural substrates resonate and display properties of motif's design structures. The symbolic formative organizing principles of intelligence potentials uniquely overlap and operate on a nature/nurture selectivity (resonance for distinctive form design). As such, they provide substantial correlation that design structures of organizing motifs are a genuine presence in each individual.

As individuals have their own unique profile of intelligence potential, they therefore operate with unique abilities to manifest their own brilliance. The organizing abilities in intelligence potentials reflect operative motifs in design structures. As such, the unique, creative capacity to generate highly intelligent systems of symbolic reorganization within the domain of that individual's organizing motif capacity reflects the distinctive, natural brilliance of that individual. Each individual is endowed with his or her own principles of inherent organizational capabilities known as motifs. As intelligence systems are essentially distinctive sets of organizing principles, they reflect the motif's ability to generate and integrate distinctive higher ordering of improvisational achievements. These may be product formation and/or performance achievement. The natural brilliance every person possesses involves the unique organizing potential of motifs which are manifest in unique intelligence profiles.

There is some difference, however, between Gardner's criteria for intelligence and how motif is utilized. Not only does he employ criteria of requiring neurobiological "cognitive impenetrability" and symbolic organizational systems, but to qualify for being a discrete candidate as an intelligence potential it must be valued by the culture and solve relevant problems. This last criterion does not necessarily apply to motifs. As motifs reflect the unique, idiosyncratic organizational principles inherent in the individual, they are not dependent on the immediate culture. Lack of cultural compatibility can, however, adversely affect manifestation of motifs. The cultural value may or may not provide incentives for the individual's talent to manifest itself but that does not mean that the intelligence potential is not present. For example, Bill Gates may not have prospered in the nineteenth century but that does not mean his potential to succeed is not present, only that it has been activated or triggered by a selectively relevant and timely formative experience. Perhaps Gates would have dominated the gold rush to California and been even more successful if there were no Internal Revenue Service to prevent his monopoly.

Closer inspection of Gardner's multiple intelligences may shed even more light on the nature/nurture issue of utilizing culture as a criterion definition for intelligence. In reviewing his multiple intelligences, he utilizes the following definitions:

- Musical — Certain parts of the brain needed in role of production and perception of music (right hemisphere). Has a symbol system of notation and universal facility seen in all cultures.
- Bodily-Kinesthetic — Localized in motor cortex, each hemisphere dominant, body movement control on contra-lateral side. Advantage to species of a culture and a universe.
- Logical-Mathematical — Capacity to analyze problems using logic, perform mathematical operations, and utilize the scientific method of inquiry.
- Linguistic — Capacity to utilize language, spoken and written forms, and accomplish objectives through language manipulation.
- Spatial — Capacity for recognition and manipulation of patterns of space as well as limited areas.
- Interpersonal — Capacity to comprehend purpose, meaning, motivations of others demonstrating effective working relationships.
- Intrapersonal — Capacity to understand self and personal motions demonstrating a working self-model.
- Naturalist — Expertise in the ability to classify and recognize vast numbers of species. Pattern recognition is involved accessing natural forms (bird-like or tree-like).
- Spiritual — The potential to deal with cosmic possibilities and controversies driven by powerful, personal, painful or aesthetic experiences.

- Existential — Capacity to delineate one's sense of self in the greater scheme of the universe and to others.

As mentioned earlier, not one intelligence potential ever exists in solely pure form. For example, psychologists demonstrate a combination of linguistic and logical intelligence potentials. The varying degrees that one is present more than another may emphasize whether one becomes a writer and/or researcher in the field. The varying profiles are as unique as the individuals who may be assessed. If the culture ever reorganized itself to no longer value the intelligence potentials of psychologists, it does not mean that these capacities are not present (though it does mean psychologists might go the way of the dinosaur).

These intelligences are not founded simply on sensory systems but rather on neurobiological substrates in the brain that utilize the sensory systems in one of its multifunctional ways. For example, musical intelligence uses the auditory sense, as does linguistic intelligence, but the sounds go to different parts of the brain as part of the symbolic representation of that particular intelligence potential.

The organizational structure of the brain is designed both at the modular and holistic levels. This will be described shortly. The capacity of such an organizational structure is to utilize the aforementioned intelligence potentials to generate an inherent natural brilliance unique to that particular person in question. The unique capacity of the individual to generate creative improvisations that fashion a product and/or perform exceptionally well will be seen to manifest the creative brilliance inherent in the motif's formative intelligence profile.

BRILLIANCE IN CORTICAL DESIGN STRUCTURES

The cortical regions of the brain are designed through an orchestrated refinement of localized structures or modules. Refined design structures are required for complex task completion. Complex tasks require input from numerous cortical regions each making its refined characteristic contribution. For example, Gardner (1993a) describes freehand drawing requiring left hemisphere structures for detail and right hemisphere structures for achieving mastery of object shape and form. Brain refinements of localized, specific functions vary with the level of task complexity. The more complex the task, the more refined localization design structures are required. Specificity of function correlates with finer cortex design structure localizations.

Refinements in design can be seen in language functions. The frontal lobe (Broca) of the cortex is utilized in grammar selection. Yet, comprehension is adversely affected by temporal lobe damage. The distinctive characteristics of intelligence and cognitive function are correlated to particular areas of the brain which are morphologically distinct (Gardner, 1993a). Aspects of vision (contours, direction and depth) as well as auditory functions (frequency and temporal interactions) demonstrate high correlations of function and form.

Intriguingly, architects utilize the concept of form following function and how function may result from form. Indeed, the archetexture of the cerebral cortex utilizes archetextural principles to an ever-increasing level of artistically distinct specificity to achieve complex task achievement. The brilliance of such design structuring and function is even more apparent in what follows.

The cerebral cortex is highly specialized in its modular organization through the utilization of unique design structures known as columns. These columns are cylindrical entities found in the inner layers of the cortex and are formations composed of neurons. Hubel and Wiesel (1982) describe them as a form of organizational "chunk" or unit. In the visual part of the cortex, they are representative of its organization.

Column formations found in the frontal lobe support functions of abstract thinking. In this context, there is less topographical mapping (not as modularized or specialized in function) of information flow. Column formations process multisensory information (stimulation and location receptors in the skin). Columns in the frontal lobes process temporal and spatial, here-and-now information.

As information (sensory stimuli, internal neuron interactions and motor neuron excitation) increases, the topographical neural "map" becomes less precise. Massive information shifts neural mapping towards plasticity and reorganization. Such functions are actually integrative in nature.

Columns are fundamental units of organization that support integrative functions. It is the structural design of the column that integrates neural mapping reorganization. The formativeness of columns serves as an organizing feature informing (shaping and designing in motif-like functions) neural information processing.

This becomes even more intriguing in the way columns themselves are grouped and designed in even more complex structures. Such complexity reflects ingenious (brilliant) ordering dynamics. For example, columns are a similar size within and between species. Various species of monkeys may have cortexes with different numbers of columns and varying cortex sizes, yet the actual dimensions of the columns themselves remain the same. The critical factor is not in the size of the column but rather in the arrangement of varying numbers of columns. Organizational design or motif becomes essential in the integrative reorganization of higher order abstraction manifested in creative brilliance.

Columns themselves are composite design structures. That is, they are most likely to emerge into formation when a maximum number (critical mass criteria) of axions are diverted in a unique way. Columns are holistic formations that come together in unique design arrangements facilitating higher brain/mind ordering functions.

The archetexture of the brain is altered with varying numbers of columns in unique arrangements and layers. Kendel (1982) indicates that structural organization of the brain involves preexisting, neural pathway connections that can be strengthened or diminished. Various forms of learning, classical conditioning, habituation and so on selectively strengthen or diminish subsets of potential repertoires of capabilities. These preexisting, formative connections are the built-in scaffolding (motifs) of the brain, honed and pruned through interaction effects of selection. Environmental factors and learning opportunities are selected and

selective (mutuality of preexisting structural formations and environmental influences) to varying degrees effecting preexisting pathways culminating in
unique, behavioral expressions. These unique behaviors will be both contextualized for the requirements of the environment and idiosyncratic manifestations of
unique, personal motifs. These new behaviors can serve as creative forms of
brilliant improvisations.

Motifs can be compared to what biochemists term polymers which operate
as fractals. Polymers are long, chained, carbon-based molecules of biomers
(two-chained molecules). The DNA proteins are examples of large or macropolymers. Fractals, on the other hand, are geometric, mathematical form structures that repeat themselves in self-similar but variant ways. Fractals express the
degree of dimension of an object or topographical landscape (Grosberg and
Khokhlov, 1997). For example, there are three dimensions in space (height,
width and depth) and one dimension in time.

As fractals are self-replicating patterns, their perpetuation is a self-similar
but never exact duplication. Snowflakes are examples of self-similar patterns
replicating but with slight variations in each specific replication. Snowflakes are
self-similar as each flake has a subtle variation from the others creating a similar
but variant difference.

Sepensinki triangles, which have smaller triangles within triangles (like
Chinese boxes within boxes), are another example of fractals. There are slight
variations of pattern designs (circles, squares and spaces) within each group of
triangles at various levels of organization. This causes their density of pattern to
vary between greater and lesser degrees. This means that their dimensionality is
not exactly two or three but somewhere in between. In addition, the graphic display of a landscape illustrates repetitive patterns of hills and valleys characteristic of that terrain but with variance in height and depth. There are self-similar
design structures repeating themselves at multiple levels of dimensions but with
slight variances of heights and depths. As such they are never exactly one-, two-,
three- or four-dimensional. The uneven landscape represents unique characteristics of self-similar but slightly variant patterns of hills and valleys. They do not
fit a nice, neat form but rather something unique. Sometimes their dimensionality is close to two (length and width) and at other times close to three (length,
width and height). The varying of dimension is fractional which is why such
fractional dimensions are called fractals.

The DNA proteins seem to coil and configure in unique repetitious, self-
similar patterns. They exhibit fractal-like design dynamics. The extended chain-
ing of polymer proteins creates nets or gels of crisscrossing patterns. Such formations have been found to facilitate rapid increase in metabolic rates.

It has been found that in prebiologic protein (before the onset of reproduction) such macropolymers of protein were randomly configured. As life evolved,
polymers began to order themselves through formativeness exhibiting deviations
(variant forms) in unique configurations. The astonishing finding was that these
unique configurations (motifs) served as permanent fingerprints in fractal replication. The chained evolution of essential building blocks of life forms involved

unique fingerprints of organization in the DNA polymers. They exhibit fractal-like qualities of self-similar but variant patterns.

These findings are highly consistent with the formativeness of unique motif configuration imbued throughout the multilevel organizational structure. The inherence for unique improvisational brilliance within each individual exists in the very essence of motif's design structure. Life itself requires unique, design form improvisation in evolving ever-brilliant adaptations and solutions to an ever-changing world.

DEVELOPMENTS IN SYMBOLIC AND LINGUISTIC IMPROVISATIONS

The capacity to improvise is invoked when dealing with the question of what to do next. Savage-Rumbaugh and Lewin (1994) suggest that life poses this quandary of how one is to structure, organize and proceed on a moment-to-moment basis. Questions such as these are likely to present themselves throughout nodal points of life transitions where routine patterns of behavior no longer are adaptive. Examples of these points can be one's first day of formal education, adolescence, marriage, parenthood and so on. In addition, questions of what career to choose, style of living, changes brought on by aging, death and values alteration all re-surface the "what to do next" question. Even what to do on one's vacation, weekend or any other sudden increase in time and/or diminishing of structured activity can reignite such a concern.

Piaget (1979) indicates that how well one answers these types of questions is reflective of one's intelligence potential for improvisation. Brilliance is the capacity to synchronize self archeidentity of motif within one's psychosocial cultural context maximizing optimum complexity of self-potential expression. A clear example of this is the brilliant collaboration of Richard Rodgers and Oscar Hammerstein in their numerous musical scores. Their unique design potential is clearly manifest through musical and linguistic intelligence in the social/cultural contextualized field of entertainment.

Calvin (1996) describes such brilliance of intelligence potential as the ability to invent something on the fly. It is the cutting edge of moment-to-moment interaction of how the self constructs and creates his or her own experience in the contextualized present moment (or movement). This involves a new combinational principle of reorganization. Calvin suggests this can be as simple a situation as what to buy while grocery shopping or what leftovers to munch on late at night. It may also involve saying something never expressed before (as in poetry) or inventing new recipes.

The "sweet spot" as Calvin calls it is the creative moment-to-moment flow of improvisations (not unlike a jazz musician), ordering and reordering meaningful (to one's self-motif/design structuring) symbols in such a way as to create new meanings and/or products. Such intelligence potentials are utilized in a manner and fashion consistent with one's motif and design structures. Indeed, the arrangement, syntax (sequential ordering) and design's organization are self-reflective of the self's archidentity of motif. The signature of self-creation in this moment-to-moment sweet spot is symbolic (utilizes the self's symbols) of motif's design structures.

These design structures are reflective in column arrangements of the cerebral cortex just presented as well as in the individual's overall brain organization. The intelligence potential of each individual's capacity to improvise creative organizations in the here-and-now sweet spot varies with the individual's brain organization. The ability to do what one has never done before requires a synchronization of self-expression that emerges through cerebral competition. That is, novel ways of ordering and designing words, imagery, conceptual ideas, constructs, metaphors, categories and so on compete with one another for a "goodness of fit" regarding the self needs of the situation at hand. This is a complex process as will soon become evident.

There is an unfolding of the individual in creating improvisations in this sweet spot. One is going from the known (where one is) to the unknown (where and what one wants to have and/or be). The juxtaposition of the known and unknown is called the familiar surprise and reflects the cutting edge, moment-to-moment encounter. It presents the individual with a boundary distinguishing a familiar, settled way of living from a new frontier of possibilities. The individual's consciousness needs to sort through and select from multiple, competing patterns of novelty in eliciting the precise fit.

Motifs generate numerous design structures that exhibit similar but different orderings (each time I sign my name is a variant form of the fundamental characteristics that make my signature a unique motif). In generating multiple novel improvisations to adequately "fit" the needs of the moment-to-moment sweet spot, numerous variant design possibilities are generated. They may all be characteristic of my mode of operating but quite variant in specific possibilities.

The brain operates on a millisecond-to-minutes time scale of consciousness. It generates numerous neural firing patterns (spatio-temporal firings) which are variants of certain cerebral patterns in the brain's cortex. Each of these variant copies (or design structures of motif) compete and are evaluated in light of a goodness of fit for the situation at hand. There is a biasing on how well these spatio-temporal patterns resonate (goodness of fit) with what is already present in the "bumps and ruts" of the brain's cortex (Calvin, 1996). Being able to select an appropriate, witty reply, the next move in a chess game, and so on all reflect a "good guess" or harmony of making the appropriate selection. The degree of goodness of fit reflects the self's optimal level of functioning. Brilliance is the optimal response most resonant with the motif of the individual that meets the needs of the next contextualized moment.

Calvin indicates the core faculties are present (preexisting potentials for linguistics and movements coming from same formative structures). Brain regions are multifunctional serving as broad based core faculties out of which differential abilities like language and movement talents emerge. These are distinctive for each individual reflecting unique motif potentials operating. The operation of core faculties as generalized distinctive potentials out of which specialized abilities emerge, correlating with new motifs, are innate, unique sets of characteristics out of which specialized design structures emerge.

The design structure variant that "wins" the competition for goodness of fit (wittiest reply, for example) is the one with the biggest chorus (reflects the optimal averaged, best-fit pattern among all other variants). This will etch in the brain's "bumps and grooves" an alteration in the spatio-temporal neural design pattern. Strengthening and deepening such etchings tend to preserve and bias future such design structuring. There is a pruning and honing of the neural pathways through such competition and utilization.

Calvin (1996) refers to such design alterations as shifting mosaics which can enhance similar (though variant) intelligence candidates (spatio-temporal patterns). These mosaics, in neural circuitry, shape and design are motifs' future commands for novel movements.

Motifs, therefore, operate in and through shaping and design mosaics of neural patterns, which are evolutionary. They can discover new orders (refinements and differentiations) of formativeness. Spatio-temporal neural patterns evolve variant (mutations at times) forms, which enhance and support novel and improvisational orderings. In this way, motifs are capable of evolutionary emergence through variance and competitive resonance selection.

Calvin describes the effect of flattening the cerebral cortex and how it would resemble a mosaic, dynamic patchwork quilt. These patches would never be at rest as dynamic patches of mosaic move, shift boundaries and fade, recreating whole new arrangements. Spatio-temporal patterns in these mosaics represent a kind of cerebral code in schema (design structure) form. They represent sensory, movement and imaginative metaphor schemas. They can resonate with similar, long-term memories and associations but with variants for change. This may involve divergent thinking and a willingness to suspend conventional thinking in the creative, improvised moment-to-moment experience. The quilt-like patchwork of the flattened cortex displays topographical reorganizing features paralleling fractals. Self-similar yet variant cortical display patterns of spatio-temporal patchworks are but another illustration of how motifs are imbued in multilevels of the organism.

Intelligence involves a patchwork of know-how and know-what mosaic regions of the brain (Calvin, 1996). Finding new, underlying order solutions, creative harmonies and so on involves intelligently taking the next formative, evolutionary step in some symbolic system. Intelligence is the formativeness of motif to differentiate in multifaceted, biopsychosocial levels. Motifs may differentiate to ever-increasing multifaceted levels of refinements (remember the tasks of Rubik's Cube and multialignments needed simultaneously).

Such task refinements are correspondingly required of the cerebral cortex. Not only surface area but column number and arrangement orders correspondingly differentiate in both specialization and orchestration of simultaneous multialignments. The surface area (bumps and folds of cortex) increasingly sculpts its own complex formativeness to accommodate the novelty of the "sweet spot." Such cortical changes in mosaic design structures imply a functional intelligence of flexibility and creativity able to transcend the bonds of instinct and generate novel solutions. Motifs are reflected in intelligence through divergent, creative design structures (spatio-temporal patterns). They are not so much goal oriented as resource oriented increasing the probability of the individual's successful adaptation.

There is a tendency towards some confusion and chaos in generating brilliant improvisations in novel situations. The ability to step outside the box (as in connecting all points in a nine-dot configuration without lifting your pen) involves creative reordering, breaking with the expected strategies. Seeking novel solutions involves novel unique combinations capable of multialignments. The motif's capacity for creative, similar but different design structures capable of recombinant variation with distinctive characteristics offers unique solutions to complex tasks. Such is the essence of one's natural brilliance. Ways of tolerating confusion and ambivalence (ordered chaos) will be presented later. For now, it is important to recognize that motifs potentiate at both the cortical and behavioral levels in enhancing neural mosaic designs supporting recombinant strategies in dealing with task resolution.

THE PARADOX IN MOTIF

The need for novel solutions surfaces most readily when one's life events, perceptions, attitudes or behaviors are at odds with learned expectations. Many times individuals will learn from parental and peer influences what kind of person they are and how they should behave. For example, someone raised by high achieving parents in an upper-middle income community may come to learn that he or she too should be a high level achiever. That person may come to believe that he or she is meant to make his or her mark on the world rising to the top of his or her field.

However, there may be a rude awakening when that same person with these learned expectations of self experiences negative attitudes and poor motivation in achievement. Experiencing contrast in what one has learned to be and do with what one actually is and does can result in dissonance and existential crisis of meaning. Encounters with antiexpectation events are provocative to the individual's coping ability.

At such nodal points of contrast and change, the individual is challenged to discover different perspectives and coping mechanisms that bring his or her destabilized system back in balance. The need for novel solutions in attitude and behavior now emerges. The individual now needs to explore, compare, challenge and evaluate variant ways of reorganizing symbolic meanings in his or her life in ways that can restabilize homeodynamic balance.

The capacity to generate variant design structures (spatio-temporal patterns) comparing and contrasting the best fit candidate can be accessed utilizing motif as a resource. Self-redefinition and challenging learned beliefs and expectations require unique resources of motif with which to anchor the individual while searching and selecting for appropriate novel solutions.

The discovery of disparate events and personal revelations from expected norms has the paradoxical effect of motivating and inspiring (concomitant with confusion and shock) utilization of innate, organizing motifs for resilience. Indeed, the very existence of organizing motifs becomes quite apparent when conventional ways of perceiving unexpected life events emerge. For example, when Victor Frankl, a Nazi prisoner of war, in 1941 visualized himself giving a lecture twenty-five years into the future about survival in concentration camps, he was utilizing innate, organizing resources for resilience in adaptation.

The innate capacity for infinite appropriateness of response adaptation is in the streamlined, design ordering systems of mind-body connections. When unexpected discrepancies threaten to destabilize the human system (whether internally or externally) higher ordering design structures of motif are called into action. This may involve adjusting to extremely harsh environments of shifting temperature or assaults on one's self-esteem and concept. Whatever sudden, shocking surprise emerges, the structure of interacting body networks efficiently maintains individual, homeodynamic balance (Eliott, 1999). She refers to such perfect ordering of body systems as the shape of intelligence.

Whether dealing with a traumatic shock or confused bout of discrepant information (regarding self of others) it is the higher ordering of the mind/brain design that cybernetically orchestrates novel responses. The natural brilliance of the mind/brain design lies in its integrative and interpretive capacities. Brown (in Gardner, 1993) describes the functioning of individuals as integrated wholes. Dealing with novel conditions effectively and efficiently requires mind/brain activities capable of handling multiple sources of interacting information. Integration of such information flow involves appraisal and response selection. What this means is that the mind/brain needs to utilize patterned activities (Gardner, 1993a), not individual ones. These patterned activities (spatiotemporal patterns) are capable of multialignments of numerous mind/brain functions necessary in relating the massive detailed environmental variations to those of the human organism. The motif is the architect of these design patterns, which orders and extracts selective information informing novel adaptations. The process of deciding which of the leftovers in the refrigerator to eat involves matching the available food tastes with what that individual's unique tastes are at that point in time. Just sorting out whether one wants a salad, turkey sandwich, or nothing at all involves more ingenuity than one might imagine. I suppose if one realized all the brain power involved in such decisions, one might just lose one's appetite. Of course, that would be a novel solution in resolving what to do next and perhaps a brilliant one if seeking to lose weight.

INNATE BRILLIANCE

The innate capacity for brilliance can be illustrated in how the mind/brain system can create formative synthesis from physical sensations. Brown (1980) presents how the mind can create form perceptions and concept complexity by abstracting meaning from sensory stimuli. The case of Helen Keller is a clear illustration of abstracting meaningful form from multiple sensations. She was a blind and deaf mute who could only feel sensations. Her instructor assisted her in associating the experience of water running through her hands with the formation of hand symbols. From such breakthroughs, she was quickly able to develop into an intellectual genius. The innate organizing abilities of formativeness allowed her to comprehend the rules of syntax. Learnings such as these supported her mastery of the essential structure of language. Brown (1980) suggests that children grasp rules of language innately but this has not been recognized.

The fascinating case of Helen Keller illustrates how innate intelligence potentials reflect natural brilliance when formativeness of motifs is accessed. The symbolic, formative capacities of each individual's unique motif are nurtured through an environment of shapes, designs, structures, syntax and so on which activates inherent organizing capacities. There is indeed a shape and design structure of intelligence uniquely manifest through each individual's motif.

The intellectual genius of Helen Keller was activated through the hand shapes and symbols of sign language resonating with preexistent intelligent designs of motif. What may have enhanced her unique shape of intelligence was that the senses of sight and sound were not available to her. As a consequence, she could not distract from her own organizing potentials of intelligence which almost "forced" her to develop her innate formative, organizing motif. As such development requires time, concentration and mental discipline, her sensory limits actually delineated her channels towards brilliance.

Brown (1980) suggests that intelligence can operate at the unconscious level. Individuals who are deemed schizophrenic, paranoid, multiple personalities and such have a great deal of mental activity invested in psychological disturbances while at the same time have an observing "I" that functions with awareness of their surrounding reality. The unconscious ability of the mind/brain system to organize responses in meaningful, unique ways is demonstrated in the complex psychophysiological adjustments, which maintain delicate homeodynamic balance.

Claxton (2000) discusses a facet of innate, unconscious design structures in terms of subliminal perception. This is perception without consciousness. Claxton presents studies in which blind individuals unable to see pictures placed in front of them are able to imagine relevant associations. For example, mysterious ideas and images would come floating into the subjects' minds related to the visually presented but unseen pictures. In another study, subjects were presented with the suggestion of "eat more cookies" after "seeing" the subliminal message flashed "mommy is leaving" vs. "mommy is loaning it." Those subjects exposed to the "mommy is leaving" flashed subliminal message ate more cookies but didn't know why. Claxton describes implications for eating disorders.

Brilliance can operate at multiple levels of awareness where either consciously and/or unconsciously one is seeking to solve something. Many times there is a period of pondering the question and a multitude of related facets. The process of creative problem solving may also involve a period of incubation where complexities of novel problems present with no clear solutions in sight. A classic example of this is the scientist who was puzzled over discrepant information regarding the chemical structure of carbon-based molecules. It was only after he had a symbolic (formative) dream that the answer became clear. When he awoke, he remembered dreaming of the head of one snake engulfing the tail of the other, forming a ring. He realized the brilliant answer to a novel situation that the structure of carbon molecules could be circular or ring-like instead of linear. Its discovery now serves as a key foundation in comprehending the organic chemistry of human beings. Symbolic formativeness resonates throughout one's unique motif and serves as powerful resources in creative and intelligent innovations.

The resourcefulness of motifs reflects the symbolic formativeness of the mind/brain's evolution. Brown (in Gardner, 1993a) suggests that innate intelligence (unique to the individual) evolves in creative flashes. That is, when human beings evolved from animals, they developed higher cognitive capacities to organize and utilize symbolic thought forms. Brown suggests that "mind" may be a second creative flash of human evolution beyond cognate biological structures. Here, the functioning of the brain generates interactive systems, which emerge as formative mental patterns (or motifs) with unique capacities for existing independently of its biological brain-structure. Dossey (1999) also ascribes to such a thesis that when mind/brain formative patterns emerge, mind can exist as an independent entity.

The organizing features of mind involve a different set of ordering properties than that of the physiological brain. Brown (1980) indicates that brain functions involve translation of physiologically related data. Mind ordering properties are concerned with symbolically intangible and individually acknowledged events, ideas and abstractions. Brown indicates that such ordering incorporates capacities for new creations and those intelligence potentials are an expression of the "creative flash." Intriguingly, the transformative capacity to generate new creative intelligence forms is characteristic of motifs in generating variant design structures.

The transformative capacities of motifs to generate multiple variant design structures are precisely what evolving, complex organisms require. Generating powerful designs of intelligence potentials (musical, linguistic, etc.) are essential for organisms to adapt to novel problem-solving conditions. The new creations of improvised, intelligent responses to novel problems are reflective of the cutting edge evolutionary nature of motifs.

Evolution of new creations is not a matter of finding new materials to work with (atoms, electrons, protons, etc.). Evolution is the living process of ordering, designing and refining creative new life forms (formativeness). In this perspective, the unique artistic motif of an individual represents evolution's improvised response in each person's motif.

SURPRISED BRILLIANCE

The innate potential of motif, as mentioned previously, may be manifest in unconscious and/or subliminal perceptive experiences. The emergence of such brilliance in motifs may be clearly viewed in idiot savants and individuals in traumatic conditions. In both these conditions the intelligence potential seems to just happen without necessarily a conscious awareness of making or willing it. Idiot savants show marked deficiencies in personality, self-care, social relationships, academics and so on, yet may display genius by playing like a concert pianist. They usually have one highly developed area of intelligence in which they can perform brilliantly. Their innate, organizing motif for some reason remained intact in that area of their functioning yet was retarded in development in other areas of potentiation.

Traumatized individuals, whether suffering severe abuse or neglect in early childhood or later years, seem to have developed ingenious coping methods. They serve as brilliant improvisations in dealing with horrendous conditions. Some individuals develop mind-altered states of going out of body, engaging in intricate symbolic fantasy trips. Others become absorbed in fixations and idealizations living in a future time having discovered some great truth of the universe. New creative orderings in mental function can invoke hypnotic-like altered states to facilitate transformative changes.

While some may argue that these are coping mechanisms, the sheer creativity and brilliance of adaptation in working within the abusive context displays innate intelligence design structures. We have all heard stories of parents who experience the shock of seeing their child pinned under a car as a result of an accident. We all marvel at a 5'2", 105-pound female empowered to lift that car to free her child. Certainly there is the fight-flight response activated with the concomitant of adrenaline to supercharge her system. However, the altered state of reorganized higher brain center functioning accesses belief and thought forms of what is possible and necessary. Many times individuals under stress discover enormous talents and activities that they feel "forced" to use, whether recovering from grief and loss, job separation or any other distress. When survival is at stake, innate action potentials of motif are activated. I can remember one client of mine describing how in his junior year of high school football, he realized his need to make the varsity. One day at practice towards the end of the season he was playing second string. He felt he had nothing to lose and suddenly exploded during scrimmage with perfectly timed charges and forearm thrusts. Such maneuvers were so well timed and powerfully executed that they literally lifted three-hundred-pound linemen off the ground. All year he had been struggling, playing hard to no avail. Then suddenly, he stated that something seemed to take him over. His excellent play resulted not only in making the first string, but a full four-year scholarship to college.

Motifs may or may not be consciously chosen and manifest. Their brilliance can emerge in the most unforeseen but sychronistic fashion. It is not unlike the synchronicity to which Carl Jung referred. The perfection of timing and intervention in resolving novel problem situations or in answering the question of what comes next is the new creation of motif. The mind/body symbolism and concomitant literal manifestation of motif reflect the unique ordering of design structures imbued through multiple levels of organization. Motif can clearly be perceived in the design structuring incorporated in linguistics.

As each individual profiles unique intelligence potentials, creative, improvisational solutions to novel problems will be idiosyncratic to that person's motif. The idiot savant's musical intelligence may be capable of remarkable innovations in chord syntax while depleted of most other resources. Creative improvisations on the piano may be characteristic of how answering the novel question of "what do I do next?" is accomplished for that particular person. Traumatized individuals (Victor Frankl in a Nazi concentration camp) may utilize other ingenious ways characteristic of their unique motif (linguistic and creative imagery projection into the future).

Eric Berne (1972) wrote an interesting book, *What Do You Say After You Say Hello?*, dealing with this very question of how individuals structure transactions and life scripts. People sometimes create fictional goals (Ansbacher and Ansbacher, 1956) for what they believe their life should be (perfectionist, high achiever, nurturer, etc.). These goals are subjective, symbolic cognitive/emotionalized constructs based upon early childhood experiences and learning. Reflecting on Elman's (1999) commentary stated earlier, the child's beliefs about self, the world, objects, relationships and time are formed by the age of five and are impenetrable (remain unchanged) to formal education. This reminds me of an old adage that as the twig is bent so grows the tree.

However, there is a fatal error in this line of reasoning. While it is true that early childhood experiences can leave a permanent impact upon the child, it presumes that the zero to five developmental environment is all formative. The unique preexisting cognitive structures of the individual exert their own organizing potentials. Self-selectivity (biases and unique slants in the self's interactive experiences) manifests unique characteristics even in the wake of formative childhood experiences. The old adage can be improvisingly altered to read "the twig is bent on becoming its own tree." There is determination of the unique organizing principles of motif to find its way (life always finds a way of expressing itself) through environmental experiences to manifest some version of itself. Individuals experience stress and dis-ease when this version is significantly deviant from healthy alignment of core motifs. The fictional goals would need to be challenged in a restructuring and reorganizational way generating new improvisations to the novel questions of living. Formal education does not provide such relearning experiences. It does not access core motifs that can regenerate unique improvisations in course correcting for deviance.

The motif has enormous capacity for improvisation as it can generate almost infinite variant design structures seeking a "best fit" evolution, which has been previously discussed. These design structures are capable of symbolic formativeness. The cerebral cortex with its column design multiarrangements is constructed in enfolding arrays where symbolic forms of intelligence can be generated. Improvisational responses can be most readily generated from formative symbols capable of assuming multiple nuances and meanings. For example, an individual's fictional goals are symbolic design structures of belief that themselves can have multiple nuance frames of meaning. In addition, the root stem of motif from which they were abstracted and are cognitive as living metaphors can also be accessed and regrown into new cognitions. An individual with fictional goals of perfection who has developed multiple problems of poor self-esteem, anxiety and judgmentalism with poor interpersonal relationships needs to reformulate his or her symbolic fictional constructs. In psychotherapy, perfectionism can be cognitively (or affectively in many cases) reframed and reexperienced as being in process of becoming (perfecting rather than having to be perfect). It can also be constrained to limited areas of a person's life (only be perfect in gardening) so as to resymbolize perfectionism in more relativistic rather than absolute frames of reference.

The ability to reconceptualize and reconstruct is constrained to the unique intelligence potential of the individual's motif. A musician may symbolically work out these issues in designing chords and tones, tapping special meanings. Intriguing research by Rauscher et al. (1997) at the University of Irvine, California demonstrates enhancement of cognitive reasoning among preschoolers. By playing Mozart and other classical pieces of music, improvement in concentration, intuitive leaps and even athletic performance was demonstrated. Such findings illustrate the ordering and symbolic generative capacities of tapping into only this one formative resource. Discovering ways in which an individual's environment can resonate and enhance other innate motif capacities within the individual can greatly enhance his or her natural brilliance.

Such resonance enhancement in symbolic formativeness can be seen not only in music but in the intricate linguistic capacities. The masterpieces of William Shakespeare are unrivaled in the literary world. The symbolic formativeness in his classic soliloquy "To be or not to be" would seem to present the ultimate level in dealing with the novel question "What do I do next?" His capacity to capture multiple human conditions in a poetically concise prose-like motif represents natural brilliance honed and pruned to artistic refinement. Parallel to such intricate literary formations is Albert Einstein's theory of relativity ($E=MC^2$). Utilizing the oxymoron phrase "simpleton/genius" turns back on itself in realizing that brilliance involves comprehensive symbolic formulations manifest in concise and precise expressions.

Brilliance is evident when watching a chess master like Bobby Fischer with his genius for strategic and logical dexterity. Each move achieves multiple tasks (positioning, defending, strategic play, deception, etc.) with efficiency and precision. Be it a short or long chess game, each move follows step by step in precise sequence and design. The culmination is the complex, effective reorganization of individual pieces into a holistic, choreographed movement to achieve checkmate.

The unfolding, precise movement of each piece shapes and is shaped by what the opponent does. Yet, the chess player is bent on utilizing innate, strategic, syntactical moves to exert his or her characteristic, formative motif in play. In chess, the game ends with checkmate; in life, the game has no real end as motif continues "long after we have shuffled off our mortal coil" (William Shakespeare, 1987). Even after our physical death, our motif can be carried on (reformulated) in our offspring, the next generation. They take what they symbolically need to incorporate into their own motif at a new creative flash of evolutionary artistry.

The motif of brilliance is unique and is manifest in the uniqueness of the individual. Accessing the "real you" in you is the most challenging and wonderful expression of brilliance possible. The unique artistry of individual uniqueness goes beyond a particular style of dress or talent. It has to do with the unique, formative and symbolic ways an individual manifests that quality (or multifaceted sets of interacting qualities characteristic of one's motif) of being oneself. This is a much-bandied-about phrase. Yet, to be one's self is to be (or not to be) exerting the sense either felt and/or intuited of the "I"-ness both within and without. Time and space prevent full treatment of domain but the "I" is innate to the consciousness of characteristic, organizing motifs. Accessing one connects to the other.

Intriguingly, the design structure of columns in the layers of the cerebral cortex reflects the "I" design. The way these columns or "I" shapes are arranged and organized reflects unique configurations occurring at multi-tiered layers throughout the cortex. The enfolding of multi-tiered layers involves unique columnar "I" arrangements. It is the complex organization of columnar "I"s that can manifest inherent "I"-ness of the unique individual self. While not always conscious, the enfolding multi-tiers of columnar organization exert its unique configuring principles throughout the individual. Yet the "I"-ness is not localized only here but in the enfoldments of DNA and through multi-levels. The "I"-ness of self is imbued in the formativeness of motif at all levels.

The inherent brilliance of the self's unique organizing principles may manifest itself in surprising, novel and unexpected ways. Many times, ingenious, unwitting flashes of brilliance (dreams of snakes eating each other's tails leading to the benzene ring discovery in organic life forms) may go unrecognized. Learning how to tap into and utilize surprising, intuitive, unexpected flashes of brilliance is learning how to access the unique formative creations of an individual's idiosyncratic motif.

THE EINSTEIN FACTOR

The access of one's unique motif of brilliance involves a form of self-reflexives. As has been mentioned previously, the organizational levels of the individual reflect an enfolding of tier levels from the DNA protein level to the cortical layers. A sense of consciousness involves an unfolding of multiple layers of one's design structure of awareness. Consciousness is awareness of one's self. The deeper one's awareness of what one is aware of the greater the consciousness and unfolding of complexity.

This principle can be found in Wenger and Pol's work (1996) on the utilization of self-expression and feedback to enhance intelligence and brilliant levels of functioning. Essentially this process involves eliciting one's own self-expression and feedback on such expressions. For example, Stephen Hawking (the eminent English physicist paralyzed except for his eyelid) expresses himself through computerized connections and receives immediate feedback on what he signals. He then utilizes feedback on self-expressions to refine and differentiate concepts and ideas in his writing and again receives more immediate feedback on those modified self-expressions. This looping, self-expression feedback flow generates increased consciousness of unconscious self-manifestations. It is hypothesized that this "Einstein factor" (named after Albert Einstein who was famous for thought experiments which provided for such loops in perception/cognition) may have kept Hawking alive for the last thirty years.

Describing a perception and/or observation out loud provides an external focus (tape recording, writing, talking to another person). The feedback from such external focusing draws upon ever-larger portions of the person's unconscious resources in that and related areas. Unconscious resources are manifestations of formative flowing motifs. The more concentration on the self-expressed design structures occurs, the more expansive articulation of their complex motifs emerge.

Emergence of such formative motifs from self-looping communication occurred in the case of English inventor Michael Faraday (Wenger and Pol, 1996). Faraday wrote on the theory of electromagnetic force fields and lines of energy emitted from them. His writings were in the motif of streams of consciousness (lines of words strung together with no beginning or ending sentence structure). His streams were wild and poetic. The formativeness of his writings resonated with those of his inner design structures. Electromagnetic fields entranced him so much that as he received more and more self-looping feedback, his poetic streams became more and more expansive and articulate. His writings began to focus on the strength and persistence of the rainbow's form (design structuring) in the midst of the waterfall's torrent. The formations in his writings (the mode or motif of utilizing streams of consciousness are his method or vehicle of expression) resonated with inner thought, constructing designs of electromagnetic fields. These fields exert lines of force throughout the randomness of space (sunspots exploding on the surface follow electromagnetic lines of force in their bursts of energy).

The lack of a clear pattern in Faraday's writings reflects the inner brilliance of formative streams of consciousness (which is a patterning of another kind). There is a need to suspend, as Faraday did, logical understanding, simply acknowledging thoughts, ideas, associations and so on which may come, externalize them, and attend to immediate feedback on them. In such a process, further development and articulation of ideas, behaviors, improvisations, action plans and so on can emerge. If the required concentration on one's unique, self-expressiveness and feedback loops is maintained, the individual's unique design structures of motif can emerge and differentiate. Unique improvisation candidate solutions to novel problem issues can then be generated. From the variant, solution-oriented design structures generated, the appropriate improvisational form can now be selected.

Many times brilliance in self-expression and improvisation occurs more by accident or chance rather than planning. Mozart heard the music in his head and simply wrote it down. Yet this was not planned as a deliberate act. There is an old adage that necessity is the mother of invention. When our survival and welfare are at stake, when what we expect is juxtaposed with what we experience, we develop self-looping consciousness as a coping adaptation.

Brilliance may be evolutionarily hard-wired in as a way of dealing with the way change occurs (and may threaten) in our lives (Watzlawick, Weakland and Fisch, 1974). Any change to the homeodynamic flow of the organism (extreme temperatures, nutritional deficits, divorce, tax audit, etc.) creates stress. Perception is directed to discrepant experiences of what we expect or hope for contrasted or juxtaposed with what we experience. The comparisons and contrasts in our life experience require a high quality of attention and perception. The novel situation generates unexpected challenges requiring unique solutions improvised from available resources. New perspectives and paradigms become essential tools of adaptation.

The innate perceptual attentiveness to discrepancy is a powerful coping response alerting the individual to the emerging needs of a new situation. To adapt and evolve one's linguistic capabilities and structures enable one to generate new perspectives and survival-oriented paradigms. The capacity of linguistic structures to generate new paradigms and perspectives is anchored in multiple formativeness of how they can string symbols (words, sentences, etc.) together in unique syntactical design sequences. Take for example the literal/figurative juxtapositioning in linguistic formativeness. Words are both phoneme sounds and meaningful symbols (associations of people, places, things, parts of speech, etc.). In addition, words can have concrete (literal) meanings or be utilized in a metaphorical (the formative use of the word form) or figurative manner. For example, one could say the tree is *bent*. The literal or concrete meaning indicates the tree is not straight but crooked. To say that one is *bent* on achieving a goal utilizes a metaphorical or figurative manner of speech. It employs the idea of nonstraightness and angularity to connote a bias or set tendency to move in some unique way.

The contrasting features of literalness and figurativeness generate alternative, variant design structures that can serve as improvisational solutions. For example, the biblical story of Solomon and the two women who were disputing over whom the real mother was is a classic juxtaposition of literal/figural interplay. As both women were arguing over the child between them, Solomon proclaimed that he would have the child physically cut in half (literally split between them). At that moment, the genuine mother released her hold on the child (figuratively no longer split or fighting over the child) to protect him. Solomon then proclaimed her the real mother. The wisdom of Solomon was a brilliant utilization of the literal/figurative interplay on what it meant to split or share the child. By exaggerating one linguistic form (literal) the counterbalance of a meaningful figurative solution of releasing the child to keep him safe emerged as a new, improvised formative solution.

Such contrasting linguistic formativeness represents multiple tiers or levels of both symbolic meanings and corresponding neurological enfoldments. The resonance of formative design structures is uniquely different for each person. Novel problem situations generate unexpected challenges which invoke juxtapositioning formativeness uniquely structured and available for each individual.

The novelty of new moment-to-moment challenges presents a fractional mix of both known and unknown elements. Embedded in the familiar aspects of a problem (parents fighting over a child) is the unknown (how or what indicates true parenthood). Intriguingly, the embedded juxtapositions in contrasting levels such as literal/figurative represent evolutionary structures that can generate formative, adaptive improvisations. There is a resymbolization of the linguistic syntax such that now perspectives and paradigms can be achieved. They are artistic design structure variants selected as improvisational solutions to solve multidimensional difficulties.

Wernicke's brain part is responsible for associating sounds to letters as well as picture representations. These preexisting linguistic structures are capable of reformulation (resymbolization) when invoking the formativeness of multilevels or tiers. Juxtapositions in word/sound/meanings at literal and figurative levels are potent resources in generating vast numbers of variant design structures from individuals, mostly culminating in select, brilliant improvisations.

The hypnotic language patterns of Milton Erickson (1980b), known as the father of modern day hypnosis, demonstrate how multiple meanings and juxtapositions can be generated. The tapping of central juxtapositions of conscious/unconscious processes parallels the contrasting nature of novel conditions (known/unknown). Even Freud's writing of jokes suggests that puns, jokes and slips of the tongue reflect this kind of interplay.

Notice that any given word can be developed by the unique motif of the individual to manifest that person's inner motif. For example, take the word "flower." One could change the phoneme (sounding) of the word to accentuate it as "flow-er." A completely new form emerges. "Flower" of course means a plant blossom. However, "flow-er" could be constructed to mean one who flows or moves easily. Contrasting different sound or phoneme patterns generates emerging formative changes. These formative changes reflect the unique design structures of the individual's inherent motif. The mind/brain can hold simultaneous symbolic constructions such as this one. These are juxtapositions that create multiple, formative possibilities. Ongoing feedback loops affect these design structures in ever refining, complex fashions.

Generation of variant design structures occurs through contrasting juxtapositions reflecting a part/whole dialectical tension. Life is always unfolding (as are the multileveled tiers in the individual's motif). There is an unfinishedness of part/wholeness interplay. There is always some part dealing with a wholeness (cell/tissue, organ/organism, brain/mind, individual/family, etc.).

Juxtapositions liberate and generate multiple variant design structures as they transform fixed things or forms into the flow of formative possibilities. We are solid but liquid, ego but self, particle but wave. While individuals identify various roles played in life, they are the author and creator of a whole style of life (Ansbacher and Ansbacher, 1956).

To cope with the novelty in life is to cope with what's novel or unique within our own life. We deal with life and we are life. The brilliance with which we uniquely develop who we are is the degree of formative motif we choose to self-express while attending to its feedback. The individual is designed to deal brilliantly with life because he or she is life with all its fractal beauty "bent" on becoming more of what it already is. The fractionation of (part/whole interplay) juxtapositioning is in the individual both being/becoming. Creative brilliance is the interpoint between the being of unique motif becoming the artist in refined design.

The complexity of improvisations generated by motifs in juxtaposition reflects a refined artistry. It is important to note that the greater the refinement and complexity of a unique improvisation, the more asymmetrical its formativeness. For example, as evolution evolves higher level complex adaptations, the more asymmetrical are the structural formations. Pribum (in Ramachandran and Blakeslee, 1998) has found that healthy brains are designed with greater right and left complexity and differentiation, and are thus asymmetrical. There is either a right or left hemisphere dominance (asymmetry). Higher ordering and specialization are reflected in the asymmetrical formativeness of motif development.

Indeed, the greater the development and growth of the individual, the more diverse, asymmetrical and unique one becomes. Einstein's brilliant improvisation regarding the space-time continuum is manifest in $E=MC^2$. Such a formulation is not in balance with conventional physics and as a consequence is asymmetrical. Many brilliant innovations occur early in a young scientist's life as he or she still in the "formative" years (both literally and figuratively). However, artists may not fully develop their innate talents until after years of honing and pruning (not unlike the cortical neural networks become more sophisticated over time).

The point of asymmetry and brilliance is that they tend to characterize one another. The individual's uniqueness is the motif's manifestation of one's idiosyncratic complexity unlike any other person's. In this way, motifs are asymmetrical in their uniqueness and exhibit brilliance through the wide range of variant design structures from which select improvisations can be chosen. Brilliance is the asymmetry of intelligent motifs manifest in the formative resonance of being and becoming one's self.

A final note on brilliance is that innate genius is holistic, involving multimodal (language, movement, meditative reflection, breathing, exercise, rhythm, visualization, chanting, etc.) dimensions of an individual. The intricate uniqueness of each individual motif utilizes its own particular profile of these modalities. Each profile is idiosyncratic, synergizing varying intensities of modalities in manifesting brilliance. Indeed, the very process of discerning the unique integration of multiple cognitive, affective and sensory/behavioral modalities is an act of brilliance. Such an act is the very medium by which brilliance can now be uniquely enhanced through its own motif.

Chapter Seven

Healing Motifs

The need for brilliance in improvisation is nowhere better illustrated than in the healing process. Maintaining health requires moment-to-moment adaptations of homeodynamic stabilization to a wide range of potential invaders and disruptions. Foreign intruders such as bacteria, viruses and environmental toxins threaten and challenge adaptive capabilities of the individual's regulatory systems. These include the decision-making capabilities of the frontal lobes of the brain as well as the hypothalamus in the limbic system of the midbrain regulating temperature, respiration, cardiovascular, heart rhythm, digestion and emotional dynamics. Health is a multifaceted concept involving multiple levels of the organism (cellular to psychosocial functioning) which requires up-to-the-moment improvisational adaptations to maintain the dynamic organizational constitution of the individual.

Central to health and healing is the body's immune system which maintains defense and resistance to the foreign intruders that threaten stability. The immune system is diverse and spread throughout the organism. It includes lymphocytes (white blood cells), macrophages, natural killer cells, T-cells and B-cells as well as the organs that produce them (thymus gland, spleen, and bone marrow). The immune system produces generalized designs of antibodies that are later honed and specifically shaped to match the configurations of invading antigens that threaten stability of the organism's homeodynamic functions. The immune system utilizes a family motif of generalized design structures from which to develop unique shapes to counteract specific antigens (Edelman and Tononi, 2000). The formative capacity of the immune system generates variant design structures which relate to the health and strength of its resistance to disease (Ornstein & Sobel, 1987).

To function effectively, there needs to be an alignment of mind-body synchronization and harmony to maintain a strong and effective resistance in the immune system. The individuality of the organism must be aligned and congruent at the psychosocial and physiological levels for the organism's integrity to be maintained. Healthy immune system functioning requires that mind/body alignment resonates with the individual's unique, organizing motif. What allows access and accentuation to the uniqueness of each person augments his or her inner healing capabilities. Harmony of mind/body alignment is recognized at its most potent levels when the individual is living, behaving and functioning at his or her most idiosyncratic level. Orchestration of the individual's multiple systems (specialized modules within the brain as well as the other physiological systems) occurs through the organizational complexities of motif.

SYNCHRONIZING MOTIFS

Synchronicity of mind and body requires that the unique integrity of the individual's organizing principles of self are maintained and enhanced. If the individual experiences confusion and overwhelming chaos at psychosocial and/or psychophysiological levels, risk to health can manifest itself in a dysfunctional immune system. Impairment of immune system functioning can either be in the form of suppression or overactive vigilance resulting in self-attack. In the latter case, an overzealous immune system attacks components of the individual's body, misidentifying these parts as foreign invaders or antigens (Ornstein & Sobel, 1987).

Health of the individual involves maintenance and enhancement of his or her idiosyncratic organizational principles that are embodied in unique motifs. These unique motifs are the formative, flowing organizing principles of the individual upon which health and longevity are grounded.

The ability to access and accentuate formative motifs is essential in dealing with such disorganizing features. The capability to anchor and ground oneself in core formative motifs can provide organizing properties to sustain one through such periods. This point will be elaborated later on in this chapter. The organizing properties of formative motifs serve to enhance mind/body synchronicity and harmony.

IMMUNE DESIGNS

Healthy immune system functioning involves design capability of antibodies to match, mirror and thereby eliminate through these properties invading antigens. The individual's unique, idiosyncratic formativeness needs to be maintained to support the functioning of the immune system's design abilities. As has been presented previously, the immune system initially develops prototype design antibodies which later are able to be specifically refined and tailored to match and mirror the vast shapes and forms of invading antigens (bacteria, fungi, viruses, etc.). For the design capability of the immune system to be functioning at optimal levels of performance, the overall formative idiosyncratic organization of the individual must be maintained. As Weil (1995) has described, what happens above the body happens below. There is a parallel of mind/body correlation. This will be expounded up on later in the form beliefs, expectations, and placebo effects. For now, suffice it to say that the immune system's design capability of shaping and tailoring its prototype of antibodies to match, mirror and engage antigen invaders will be enhanced or diminished by the parallelism of overall integrity of mind/body formativeness.

As will be depicted, illness represents a dedifferentiation (Weil, 1995) of organizational integration. The organizational integration of an individual constitutes the degree of wholeness or mind/body harmony achieved. Ornstein and Sobel (1987) discuss how the human brain can be construed as modules of brains within the whole brain. The degree of harmonious orchestration among these brains within the brain can constitute integration within the individual.

The hypothalamus is part of the limbic system as is the amygdala and hippocampus. Sometimes the balance of functions can go awry. The amygdala deals with emotions of anger and fear and the hippocampus can serve to modulate calming, soothing experiences. The hypothalamus coordinates numerous body functions and emotions and has neural pathways to the pituitary gland. This gland is considered the master gland of the body as it orchestrates secretions of neuropeptides, neurotransmitters and neurohormones. The limbic system itself deals with threatening and crisis situations able to initiate the fight or flight response (Ornstein & Sobel, 1987) and can send the body into heightened states of alarm and arousal.

The limbic system is closely connected with the frontal lobes of the cerebral cortex which Ornstein and Sobel depict as the brain within the brain dealing with decision making and emotions. While there is no one part that controls the whole mind/brain/body system, the frontal lobe/limbic system connection comes closest to that function. If orchestration between these two systems is disorganized and confused, imbalances and distortions in thought, body, physiology (e.g., immune system) and behavior can occur.

The mind/body system maintains and enhances healthy organization of the individual as long as it can exercise appropriate stabilization functions. During periods of stress (emotional and/or physiological) the unique organization of the individual is threatened with confusion, disequilibrium and chaos. The mind/body synchronicity is challenged to generate unique, creative and at times brilliant adaptive coping responses to reestablish stability. For example, if the individual is suffering from the stress of loss, pain of arthritis, and dealing with the loneliness of aging, destabilization and dedifferentiation (loss of higher level ordering and refinement in mind/body functioning) threaten the person's organizational stability. When the person's organization is not able to maintain its integrity at high levels of complexity, formativeness is affected at all levels. This includes the immune system's design capability to refine and articulate necessary design structuring in antibodies to ward off specific antigens. Indeed, loss of organizational capacity at one level (psychosocial) affects that at other levels (psychophysiologically) as well.

CORE MOTIFS

The ability to access and accentuate core formative functions of motif can assist in the restabilization of the individual's organizational integrity. This occurs in the inherent capacity of core motifs to generate unique, improvisational design structures to enhance and maintain individuality of organization especially during times of distress. Threats to one's health can be multifaceted requiring the person to generate brilliant improvisational design forms to cope with and adapt to novel problems presented. These may involve lifestyle adjustments tailoring pace of life, relationships, career, nutrition, self-care, exercise and so on to the unique, personalized needs and temperaments of the individual.

WELLNESS REMEMBERED

The appropriate functioning of the psychophysiology of the immune system can be enhanced through such individualization and tailoring of one's lifestyle. When alignment occurs between psychosocial lifestyle functioning and one's core formative motif, remarkable positive changes in health can emerge. Accessing internal healing processes within the individual through such alignment can be seen in what Herbert Benson (1996) calls wellness remembered. He defines wellness remembered as times and experiences in a person's life where what they believed, expected and performed healed them in some way. For example, he describes how a patient's belief in his or her doctor's orders of prescribed treatment is twice as likely to increase his or her survival rate from life-threatening illness. In another case, it was found that when patients have a positive belief in treatment approaches for angina pectoris, they have a 70 to 90 percent recovery rate. When the belief they hold about treatment is negative, their recovery rate drops to 30 to 40 percent.

Such wellness remembered events (formerly known as placebo effects) have been demonstrated to have similar health enhancing effects on such disorders as bronchial asthma, herpes simplex cold sores and duodenal ulcers. Benson illustrates that wellness remembered is a more meaningful term for the placebo effect. The power of belief, faith and expectation has been demonstrated to be twice as effective, as opposed to the one-third effectiveness rating given to placebos.

Intriguingly, the opposite effect, that of nocebos (negative beliefs and expectations, focus on dying rather than living), is equally powerful in influencing worsening of health and recovery. Surgeons hesitate to operate on individuals who believe they are going to die. The psychological effects of beliefs and expectations can be specifically measured. Increases in beta-blockers have been measured as a response to remembered wellness events that are designed to prevent rapid heartbeat.

Benson, who pioneered the discovery of the relaxation response, describes the inner healing potential within the mind/body synchronicity of the individual. The ability to access the innate healing benefits of the relaxation response through imagery and breathing is indicative of how the mind/body system can reorganize and rejuvenate itself. The power of positive belief and expectation activates the body's natural healing and reorganization of individual integrity. The regeneration of tissue and reestablishing regularity of respiration, temperature and cardiovascular functioning are just some of the healing and reorganizing functions that are part of the healing potential within (Ornstein & Sobel, 1987).

Such concepts as wellness remembered, placebo, power of positive belief, thinking, expectancy and so on all access and accentuate the mind/body system's capacity for generating healing. Yet no two individuals heal and reorganize formative functioning in the same way (Weil, 1998). The unique way people individually perceive and construe what is healing for them is highly individualized. Medical treatment is rarely identical for each person with exact dosage of medication and type of intervention. This is no small issue. If the design and form of treatment intervention is not individualized and tailored in just the right way for uniqueness, the patient's recovery could be diminished. Weil (1998) describes the patient as not totally responsible for illness but yet not totally helpless. He advocates that the individual trusts his or her inner guidance in terms of attending and listening to inner body wisdom. This becomes especially valid in terms of types of nutrition, exercise and psychosocial lifestyle (quality of relationships, interests, pace and tempo of task challenge, etc.).

Indeed, many illnesses are a result of deficiency in an essential "vitamin" if you will. This is the vital "vitamin I" of taking care and attending to the "I"-ness or individuality of what makes you the unique person you really are. Benson refers to such self-attentiveness as extended self-care. This is not to suggest that this is the whole picture of what health is all about. Benson refers to health maintenance as a three-legged stool. The first leg involves self-care. The other two include medication and surgical procedures. However, Weil (1998) and others emphasize extended self-care as a primary source of prevention and early intervention.

SELF-CARE AND HARMONY

The concept of self-care goes beyond simply getting a good night's sleep, going on a two week vacation and buying a new set of clothes (not that these aren't helpful). Rarely do individuals know themselves in the most intimate, emotional and physiological ways. It is not uncommon for individuals out at an evening dinner to encounter some confusion as to what they may want to eat from the menu. They may even resort to having the waitress or waiter suggest something, not really knowing or sensing for what they (or their body) have a taste for. Few people know and honor who they are as unique individuals. I have often heard patients in treatment express they don't have time to get eight hours of sleep, grocery shop for fresh vegetables, or practice meditative-type experiences.

IDENTIFICATION DYSFUNCTIONS AND SELF-ATTACK

The immune system functions at its peak when harmony exists between mind and body (Weil, 1998). It can carry out its protective function of flushing out viruses, fungi, bacteria and even some forms of cancer when this harmony exists. Yet the immune system operates as a surveillance, detection and elimination agent of foreign invaders threatening mind/body stability and synchronicity. Its appropriateness of surveillance and detection functioning presumes it can identify the difference between what is safe and/or parts of the body as a whole and what constitutes foreign invaders. Disorders such as lupus, arthritis and allergies are examples of an overreactive immune system misidentifying friend for foe and zealously attacking what it thinks is the enemy.

Interestingly enough just as the immune system is unable to distinguish clear design structures of what is safe and what is threatening, similar issues can be operating at parallel levels in psychosocial experiences. The individual who cannot or will not attend to and take time to learn and identify what are his/her needs, tastes, emotions, priorities and so on is similar to the overreactive immune system. Difficulties of distinguishing self from other design structures are operative at both the psychophysiological level as well as the psychosocial level.

The immune system is the primary defense and protective boundary of what constitutes and essentially defines the unique structural organization of self. Difficulties of distinctive identification at multiple levels of the organism are symptomatic and symbolic of a similar dysfunction at both levels.

SYMPTOM AND SYMBOL

Loss of formativeness in organization can be both symptomatic and symbolic of mind/body disturbances in harmony. What occurs psychophysiologically and what occurs psychosocially are both symptomatic and symbolic of parallels operating at multiple levels of mind/body (Achenburg & Lewis, 1984). Lupus is characterized by a confusing number of symptoms such as joint pains, pleurisy, high fever, and extreme malaise. The immune system in such cases causes interruptions in blood flow to a number of organs (e.g., kidneys and the brain, which can result in organic psychosis). Genetics and individual temperament are involved with immune disorganization. Yet two cases of women suffering from lupus illustrate powerful effects from alteration in beliefs, attitude and change in psychosocial lifestyle. One woman fell in love and got married. The other developed a passionate career endeavor. The symptoms in both cases went into remission, symbolic of the passionately enhanced formative lifestyle changes. The increased, optimal level of organizational functioning at the psychosocial level was paralleled at the psychophysiologically level. While this does not constitute hard scientific data, it does suggest possibilities of maintaining and enhancing high degrees of formative organization uniquely specialized for each individual. At such uniquely individualized degrees of organization the ramifications for healing are quite empowering.

MIND/BRAIN ORGANIZATION AND IMMUNITY

Ornstein and Sobel (1987) assert that the brain is organized to take action, to move, to heal, not to reflect and contemplate abstract thought as an end in itself. Yet to serve this protective and healing purpose, the brain has the organizational capacity to etch in neurological pathways known as schemata. These design structures of neural pathways serve to organize through selective filtering incoming sensory stimuli. What matches or fits these schematic designs is perceptually recognized.

These neurological schematics (the logic of neuronal connections) are affected by innate organizing motifs and their interactive refinement and learning of the environment. The world models that result (usually by the age of five) serve to alert the brain/body safeguards of what is safe and enhancing to the organism and what is threatening. When incoming stimuli do not match such world models, a priority signaling system indicates something wrong in the interactive process. Stress and alarm messages may be initiated. The formative nature of schemata and the resulting world models influence what is perceived as safe or threatening.

The organization of the brain reflects the evolution of its structural design. There are three major stages of brain evolution: (1) reptilian brain stem (fundamental, biological stability such as heart rate, breathing, territorial presence, etc.); (2) mammalian brain (midbrain of the limbic system dealing with blood pressure, homeostasis, emotional responses, flight or fight, etc.); and (3) neo-mammalian brain (involving the cerebral cortex including adaptability, human characteristics, decision making, organizing internal/external world interactions, memory, speech, etc.).

The archetextural (designing) and archeological (evolution) aspects of the brain have developed from relatively simple to highly differentiated levels of complex organization. The further up the evolutionary stage of development (reptilian to neo-mammalian), the greater the uniqueness in design structures and organizational capacity. The neo-mammalian brain is highly differentiated in four specialized lobes (occipital, parietal, frontal and temporal). In addition, the cerebral cortex (thin layer of gray matter) consists of intricate arrangements of columnar design structures. The cortex has highly specialized centers for a variety of functions (math, movement, verbal ability, etc.).

For all of the rational, decision-making abilities, the larger function of its language, perception and judgment faculties is designed for protecting and healing the organism. The signal that arouses the brain's attention is the one that indicates a change in existing states, both physically and mentally (consciousness) (Ornstein & Sobel, 1987). Whether a change in hunger, social relations or any novel problem condition, the innate priority system of the brain adapts responses to correct and heal the condition.

Key to the protective function of the brain's organization is the hypothalamus located in the midbrain of the limbic system. As mentioned before, this brain structure deals with fight or flight responses and is closely connected to the pituitary gland, the master gland of the endocrine system. The perception of threat and/or illness activates a recognition in the brain's signaling system alerting the hypothalamus (known as the brain within the brain) and the frontal lobes of which it is closely connected. Neurochemical messages are sent from hypothalamus to the pituitary gland to initiate what is deemed an appropriate balancing and healing response.

The immune system is closely connected to these brain structures as has been demonstrated by Besedovsky et al. (1977). Emotional states, which involve the hypothalamus, can flood the signaling system and affect the immune system's production and organization (Shavit et al., 1983).

If there is damage to the structural design of the hypothalamus, the immune system can be adversely affected (Ornstein & Sobel, 1987). The thymus gland is responsible for producing T-cells that are involved in surveillance and antibody functioning. Disorganization in the structural design of the hypothalamus can alter production levels of T-cells in the thymus gland, adversely affecting immune system functioning.

Stress signals (perceived instability in one's world model) initiated in the hypothalamus-limbic system can also adversely affect immunity. The brain's perception of threat can signal the pituitary gland to secrete neurohormones (catecholamines, corticosteroids and endorphins). These hormone secretions produce immunosuppressive effects. Both physiological as well as psychological disorganization can lead to immunosuppressive (or overreactive) responses, as in allergies, which create imbalances and vulnerabilities to illness and disease.

Brain organization can also affect immune system functioning at cortical levels. Geschwind and Galaburda (1984) has found that left-handed people have 2.7 times greater thyroid and bowel disturbances than right-handed individuals. Left-handed individuals were found to have higher rates of immune system deficiencies as well as migraine headaches. Left-handed individuals are hypothesized to have reversed or mixed dominance in hemispheric functioning. That is, their language and spatial functions may be reversed (language in right hemisphere, spatial in the left). Such an organization of function could result in lower levels of differentiation especially if mixed dominance (lack of specialization in hemispheres) is present. Renoux and colleagues (1983) describe similar findings of left hemisphere effects on rats' immune systems. There was a decrease of T-cells in their spleens. The qualitative level of formative brain organization has significant effects on immune system functioning and capacity to generate adaptive, healing responses.

MOTIFS OF BELIEF, FAITH AND EXPECTATION

Ornstein and Sobel (1987) describe how the brain can organize for healing responses when patients have belief and faith that transcends common sense reality expectations. They report on the effects in women who unflinchingly have faith and believe in their doctors' treatment decisions, prescribed medication, the caregivers themselves and God's power to heal (if that was His will). Under such powerful frames of reference, the brain generates neurosignatures (unique design structures) of healing, which activate positive physiological reactions and resources for recovery. It is as if cells in the women's bodies behaved in concert (organized motif) with a spiritual confidence that a higher purpose was to be achieved in her life. Such were the effects in women who believed and had faith in their healing through prayer. Having powerful, positive beliefs and expectations in one's attitude and perception of one's capability to deal with illness are significantly correlated with better health. O'Leary (1985) found that arthritic patients improved with positive expectations of recovery and ability to deal with their condition. The perceived ability to control or positively influence illness (self-efficacy) is a critical factor in one's mental orientation. Bandura and colleagues' (1985) studies reveal that strengthening perception of self-efficacy in phobic patients decreases the stress hormone catecholamine. Expectation levels associated with beliefs are a significant variable in dealing with stress. Bresnita (1984) discovered cortisol (stress hormone) levels higher in those that expected stress to be worse than it was.

Ornstein and Sobel (1987) suggest that people are neurologically predisposed to discover the healing effects of faith. Faith is lost when patients allow the illness to define them. The panic of suffering and pain results in a loss of self-esteem when the unique identity of the individual's motif is lost in the pain distraction of the illness. The consequences of lost unique identity are feelings of weakness and increased vulnerability to accidents, prolonged illness and conscious and unconscious dread (Ornstein & Sobel, 1987). Reestablishment of core self and organizing motifs is essential in renewing vigorous health and faith in one's healing capacity.

Motifs of belief and faith are highly unique and individualized for each person. The formative nature of how and what an individual believes and has faith in are determined by multiple factors (spiritual/religious, sociocultural, individual/family, etc.). Yet the way an individual selectively organizes and filters his or her belief and faith is contingent on one's unique motif. While the content will be refined and interactively sorted in one's psychosocial cultural experience, the structure and organization of faith and belief will be highly individualized through one's motif. Witness how two Catholics raised in the same sociocultural setting and individual/family environment may manifest their faith and belief in unique ways. One may abandon formal rituals and rites adapting a highly individualized spirituality of higher power. The other may maintain the more traditional, ritualistic rites of passage. Yet, each may equally be healed by faith and belief.

The power of faith and belief can work in destructive ways as well. Benson (1996) describes how traumatic events can have fatalistic power. For example, one woman lost her hearing when she listened helplessly to the unaided screams of a man beyond her reach. The power of one's unique faith and belief (or lack of it) can build or destroy health.

HYPNOTIC BELIEFS

The power of formative faith and belief accesses hypnotic capacities of trance within individuals. Caprio and Berger (1998) present the concept that patients can make themselves ill through self-hypnosis. Thinking and believing that one is ill is a form of autosuggestion (self-suggestion) capable of inducing illness. For example, if one dwells on small aches and everyday discomforts when first awakening and throughout the morning, by lunch that person could be feeling fatigued, nauseated and spend the rest of the day bedridden. The formative nature of one's beliefs and thoughts are powerfully creative.

Caprio and Berger (1998) indicate that negative beliefs are internal forms of self-hypnosis, which need to be challenged and cleaned out in order to regain control of one's own mind. For example, self-expressions such as, "I am burned out, sick to death, worried to death about my job, etc." are self-hypnotic inductions of negative beliefs. They create destructive illusions around which mind/body interactions organize which can lead to physical dysfunctions.

Lowered resistance in immune system functioning may be due to lack of nonindividuation of uniqueness. When negative, destructive illusions predominate to the exclusion of one's unique identity, problems in mind/body synchronicity emerge. Trance illness or diseases can be generated by developing powerful mind/body beliefs that have far-reaching repercussions. Reestablishing an awakened, core self involves accessing unique configurations of one's self-expressiveness. Only by challenging one's trance-induced illness can inner healing truly emerge. Utilization of core motifs serves a critical role in the awakening process of one's core identity.

HEALTH AND RELATIONSHIPS

The human brain resonates to the social organization of relationships. The form and stability of an individual's social relations can have powerful influences on an individual's health (Ornstein & Sobel, 1987). Strong ties can preserve one's social world and feeling of social organization.

Like strong belief systems, meaningful bonds with others can stabilize both one's self and one's world view (Ornstein & Sobel, 1987) when major changes threaten disruption. Ornstein and Sobel (1987) describe how Japanese immigrants who maintain meaningful contact with their cultural characteristics remain relatively immune to illnesses as compared to those that do not. The ability to depend on friends for support prevents feelings of isolation, panic and indecision in times of confusion and crisis.

These are cultural characteristics which serve as organizing psychosocial motifs. Meaningful bonds involve resonance of unique cultural motifs of which individuals within that culture can resonate. Healthy immune system functioning can be enhanced in the process as evidenced by Japanese immigrants who adhered and preserved unique characteristic features in their roles of work, love and friendship. Preserving cultural heritage invokes the organizing roots of motif supporting blossoming health.

Ornstein and Sobel (1987) describe how formation of social organizations utilizes complexity of talents (language, symbols and communication). The multipurpose functions of social organization itself (family, affiliation needs, communication, etc.) depend upon flexible formativeness of symbolic logos (organizing motifs). Individuals are social animals formatively creating social networks with characteristic features of motif.

Ornstein and Sobel (1987) illustrates that living in a socially disorganized milieu can result in increased deaths resulting from stroke and high blood pressure. Family instability, separation, divorce and so on can orient individuals to disease. Ornstein presents how when unemployment increases by 1 percent there is a 4 percent increase in suicides, 5 to 7 percent more murders and 2 percent more cardiovascular cases.

When a spouse is lost through death, the surviving partner's grieving temporarily weakens the immune system. There is a decreased activity in white blood cell count. Bartrop et al. (1977) found a depression of the immune system in times of serious emotional stress. Separated, divorced and single individuals experience a two to three times greater increase in death rates (Ornstein & Sobel, 1987). Maintaining meaningful social relationships congruent with the individuals' motifs serve to stabilize bereaved partners in times of loss.

John Bowlby (1969) discusses the effect of separating of infants from their primary caregiver. The loss of touch, handling, playing and so on can affect social development of attachment. Separation increases anxiety, depression, withdrawal and despair. Such negative emotions impair the immune system. They are the result of dysfunctional interruptions in establishing meaningful bonds of attachment. Quality attachments require resonation of formative bonds among partners organizing motifs.

EMOTIONS AND HEALTH

The quality of one's emotional life affects and is affected by beliefs and expectations. Emotions involve a subjective evaluation of one's experience. Emotions such as humor, joy, love and affection have been demonstrated to increase calming neurotransmitters (serotonin) in dealing with stress-related disorders (Siegel, 1986; Cousins, 1980). Other emotions such as anxiety, anger, hostility, shame and guilt increase production of stress enhancing hormones (adrenalin). Ornstein and Sobel (1987) reported that stress can cause tumors in rats. Kasl et al. (1979) discovered stress in overachieving cadets and susceptibility to illness. Locke et al. (1984) describes how anxiety and depression among students can reduce natural killer cells in the immune system. Ornstein and Sobel (1987) indicate stress gets into the immune system when overwhelming shock triggers the sympathetic nervous and endocrine systems suppressing immune functioning.

The possibility exists that the feeling self-system of the brain may be in the close-knit connection of the limbic and frontal lobe brain structures. The particular organization of these integrated brain design structures is unique for the self-system of each person. These structures involve decision making and fight or flight stress reactions to novel problem situations. The indecision of whether to fight or flee or the perception of helplessness and hostility activates alarm reactions (Ornstein & Sobel, 1987).

Liberman (in Ornstein & Sobel, 1987) described that while expression of feelings has an overall healthy effect, the most significant prediction of decreased health was the degree of aggressiveness and hostility present in the individual. The lack of expression and acceptance of one's feelings disrupts the individual's ability to cope and ventilate. Fixation and repetitive "stuckness" of blocked, repressed emotional expression increases the perception of stress in the patient.

While incessant ranting and raving are not conducive to reducing stress, a balance needs to be found when to vent and express intense emotions and when to leave things alone. Such decisions involve a unique balance for each person. If the individual is not honoring his or her own natural pace and intensity of emotional expression, disequilibrium (or dis-ease) can result. The individual needs to access the unique set or balance point of "when to hold and when to fold." For some, low intensity may work best while for others great elaboration and flamboyance may be in order. Passivity coupled with a denial and/or refusal to express appropriate (for the unique individual) anger and frustration can result in poor health. Ornstein and Sobel (1987) report on angry outbursts of cancer patients upon receiving news of their diagnosis. Such feistiness and independence correlates with higher recovery rates. The key point to emotions and health is that the degree and intensity of expression need to resonate with the unique character and need situation of each patient.

MUSCLE BUILDING: IMMUNE MOTIFS

The way in which individuals exercise and utilize their unique, emotional motifs can strengthen and enhance immune resistance to illness and disease. Derogatis and colleagues (1979) describe how long-term cancer survivors express a great deal more hostility, anxiety and other negative emotions than those with less survival time. The unique assertiveness allows patients to express and exercise unique features of their personality characteristics. McClelland and associates (1980) express that if power needs (ability to influence people) of patients are chronically thwarted, suppression of the immune system results. Overinhibition (reactivity) leads to a decrease in salivary levels of immunoglobulin A, a sign of immune suppression.

Accessing and exercising unique emotional characteristics can alter and strengthen immune resistance. Kiecolt-Glaser and colleagues (1984) found relaxation training and guided imagery three times weekly enhanced feelings of self-efficacy. This was evidenced by increases in natural killer cells in the immune system. Dillon and associates (1985-86) illustrate how positive emotional states enhance immune functioning. For example, people who watched humorous films of Richard Pryor or altruistic films of Mother Theresa demonstrated signs of increased immune resistance.

Norman Cousin's *Anatomy of an Illness* (1980) relates how women with breast cancer suppress anger and hostility. When they learn to exercise their unique emotional characteristic feelings (venting and getting things off their chest — a form of organ language representing symbol and symptom) there was some reduction in cancer levels. Assertive (the expression of the individual's unique, emotional characteristics) and challenging attitudes assist the patient in being proactive with his or her illness in building immune system "muscle" of resistance.

The immune system can learn (be conditioned) to suppress (Ader & Cohen, 1975) or enhance its surveillance levels and antibody production. The ability of the immune system to specialize antibodies to match and eliminate antigens depends on the individual's mind/body synchronicity of formative motives. When patients believe and/or feel they cannot assert and express their unique emotional states and characteristics, there is suppression of the immune system's ability to function in healing, formative ways.

Ornstein and Sobel (1987) describe how organic diseases are interconnected to multiple dimensions. These include altered beliefs of one's self-concept, relationships to others and social positions in the sociocultural world. These multidimensions all involve formativeness in organization and design. Realigning the individual along these dimensions utilizing formative, inherent motifs of the patient can have powerful, healing effects. Disturbances can occur at multiple levels of genetics, organs systems and so on. Yet synchronicity of formative mind/body motifs can reverberate throughout and beyond these multiple levels for healing.

Key factors in exercising the "muscles" of immune motifs involves the patients' levels of hope, flexibility and self-efficacy. Schmale and Iker (1971) discuss how attitudes of hopefulness are predictive of which patients would develop cervical cancer. Spence (1984) found that hopefulness and lower incidence of cervical cancer are strongly connected. Mason and colleagues (1969) similarly found that patients' presurgical hopefulness and trust were positively correlated with quicker recovery. Optimism and hopefulness enhance the exercise of patients' unique emotional characteristics in the healing process.

Ornstein and Sobel (1987) indicate that not all individuals exposed to the Auto Immune Deficiency (AIDS) virus HTLV-III develop into the full blown illness. While AIDS may ultimately be treated by a major medical breakthrough, the early stages of viral exposure indicate a partial role for formative mind/body synchronicity. One novel approach considered in treating HIV involves utilizing formativeness in reverse. That is, scientists at the University of Chicago have found a signature at the molecular level of a kind of "arms race" of proteins in people and parasites. These signatures in the human genome indicate that our molecular evolution has involved protein forms struggling for emergence (binding proteins in malaria parasites continually striving to overtake red blood cells). This is demonstrated by the remains of fossil-like forms left from retroviruses struggling to evolve in our DNA.

HIV is a retrovirus, dangerous because of its rapid molecular evolution of large-scale variant forms known as "quasispecies." One possible treatment is to accelerate the molecular evolution of these variant forms of HIV such that they evolve so quickly they self-destruct. By involving substances known as nucleoside analogs, errors in chemical structure of DNA progressively increase with each copy reproduced. With each viral infection in cells, the genetic signal becomes diluted. The progressive dilution of the variant's formative integrity eventually incapacitates the HIV variant's form. The nucleoside analog subtly mismatches the variant form's genetic code introducing a reversal of formativeness towards decoherence and disharmony. The loss of formativeness in the disease preserves the formativeness of self. There is a struggle in life forms emerging, and formativeness of motifs is essential for survival. Maintaining the integrity of one's formative motif is fundamental to one's health.

Ornstein and Sobel (1987) also discuss cancer as emerging at times of genetic and environmental interactions which result in immune system suppression. Tentative theories are reported regarding cancer as a possible result of information underload or overload. That is, individuals vary in their need for novelty and stimulation. In some cases, cancer may be the result of the organism's need for novel excitement in situations of understimulation (boredom). In other cases, mutation of massive levels of cancer cells represents overstimulation of information to the organism. The degree of differentiation in each individual is unique in its complexity. Cancer may represent misalignment of mind/body functioning at unique levels of an individual's differentiation. Ornstein and Sobel (1987) indicate that there is some evidence for such theorizing as individuals with higher intelligence levels seem more susceptible to cancer. Apparently, it may be more difficult to attenuate the right balance of information flow as unique motifs require more differentiated at higher levels. The need for refinement of artistic motifs evolving into increased uniqueness and asymmetry may be required at such levels. The pace and flow of emerging differentiation needs to be aligned with the needs of the individual's motif. Begley (1980) reports on how administering anticancer drugs for leukemia at appropriate times in one's circadian rhythm can multiply its effectiveness. When the pace and flow of one's innate rhythms are out of synchronization, impaired healing can result.

RESILIENT MOTIFS IN HEALING

There are particular traits and variables in resilient individuals that ward off adverse effects of stress and vulnerability to illness. Werner and Smith (1982) studied such traits and variables. They discovered that resilient women had strong concepts of themselves, were nurtured by primary caregivers and held responsible and achievement oriented attitudes.

Such women sought supportive relationships and counsel as needed. They had qualities of being self-righting and accepted change as a part of life. In addition, they could tolerate ambiguity and were cognitively flexible. Their attitude that life was a challenge to be met reduced their perception of stress, increased their sense of self-efficacy and strengthened their immune system.

Kobasa (1984) describes such qualities of resilience in terms of hardiness. In addition to the above qualities, he indicates that hard individuals take a challenge and committed perspective that the task at hand is meaningful and purposeful to achieve.

The caveat to such a courageous profile is that challenge orientations such as the preceding could result in illness if there is a mismatch of resources and task demands (Ornstein & Sobel, 1987). While one can maintain health by viewing a potentially stressful job task as challenging, if the task has many demands that exceed the hardiest of individuals, overwhelming and burnout could result. It is in such cases of mismatched resource and task assignment where health risks are greatest.

Knowledge is power. Yet even the most knowledgeable have blind spots of themselves. The survival value of self-attentiveness as to whether one's unique, evolving motif is ready or not for the task challenge at hand is critical. The hardiest and most resilient of individuals are wise enough to self-attend and elicit feedback from respected others as to the appropriateness of their cause of action. Being open to feedback and self-evaluation in light of one's unique individuality is critical to stress and health management.

The brain's capacity to organize and structure the individual's internal and external world environment is one of its major responsibilities (Ornstein & Sobel, 1987). As noted previously, neurosignatures of schematic designs are organized to filter and streamline incoming stimuli to create meaning and purpose. Antonovsky (1984) utilizes such capacities of meaningful organization into what he refers to as a sense of coherence. A sense of coherence refers to the comprehensibility, manageability and meaningfulness in the individual's life experience. Comprehensibility means that there is an order and design to the task at hand which is consistent, predictable and clearly defined. Manageability implies the range of resources available to handle the task (skills, people, spirituality, etc.), and meaningfulness refers to the worth or value assigned to the task in investing one's resources so as not to present an unnecessary drain of energy.

The sense of coherence imbued through an individual's life implies a high degree of harmony and alignment within one's self and with the self and environmental interactions at large. This may seem to require a massive computer to coherently organize one's life to such a degree. However, inherent, organizing motifs are already operative to order and anchor one's life in meaningful and purposeful ways. Learning and self-attending to one's uniquely ordering, personal experiences (emotional characteristics, cognitive structuring of reality, belief systems, etc.) access operative motifs.

When one's world becomes disrupted, thrown into chaos, overwhelmed by biological and/or psychosocial trauma, tenaciously accessing and anchoring to one's unique core self is essential. The hardiness of aligning (or realigning as needed) with organizing and evolving motifs of one's self is what survivors have learned through trial and tribulation. The courage of belief, faith and emotional assertion in one's unique self maintains the righting and balancing effects of hardiness and coherence.

MOTIFS AND MIRACLES

Motifs are organizing principles constituting the essential or core self. As such, they are self-integrating and evolving, breaking old, rigid rules of perception and cognition. Unique design structures emerge in improvisational configurations effecting and reflecting paradigm shifts in consciousness and behavioral manifestations.

The harmony and synchronization of mind/body design structures facilitate the healing energies from within. Design structures of motif affect synchronicity of alignment in mind/body integration. It is this very synchronicity of mind/body integration which has been identified in what is known as spontaneous remission or miracles (Benson, 1996). These are healing events where patients suffering from serious, debilitating illnesses recover health which appears to defy conventional, medical expectations. Individuals who present for these types of recovery illustrate synergy and shifts in consciousness as underlying processes (Benson, 1996).

Synergy is the individual's capacity to integrate (put together) everyday ideas, experiences, emotions, behaviors, consciousness and so on in his or her own idiosyncratic way such that a new whole emerges (Brigham, 1998). Such a definition is highly congruent with the formative principles of an individual's unique motif. Siegel (1986), Brigham (1998) and others espouse the fundamental role of synergy as a primary foundation for spontaneous miracles of recovery. They describe synergistic operations as occurring at the right brain's level of unconsciousness.

The synergistic integration is a uniquely improvisational solution of brilliance emerging from the uniqueness of one's motif. The individuality of the person is not separating him or her from others or the universe as a larger whole. Rather, we are referring to individuality as a person's essential uniqueness, which distinguishes his or her place in the unfolding whole of relatedness to others and the universe at large. This is not an ego-centered individuality but rather one stemming from unique wholeness. It is rooted in oneness yet differentiated as characteristically distinct in the larger whole. The paradox of individuality is one of being uniquely whole (as Ansbacher and Ansbacher, 1956, expresses, that individual means indivisible or whole) yet discovering uniqueness in the larger than self whole of psychosocial culture and spirituality. It is the Jungian construct of universal self uniquely manifested in the individual self.

The unique, synergistic improvisation of the individual facilitates a sudden shift of consciousness or epiphany (life transforming experience) in spontaneous remissions (Brigham, 1998). Roud (in Brigham, 1998) describes how synergy has helped cancer patients in spontaneous remissions through remarkable shifts in outlook, moving towards their genuine, core self-releasing material fixations. Weinstock and Kennedy (in Brigham, 1998) found curative factors in cancer patients respectively incorporating a deep feeling of hope and increased self-esteem and valuation of their lives. These features reflect qualities that are ingrained in unique formative features of motif in core self evolution. Weil (1995) speaks to these core issues when he describes spontaneous natural healing to be inherent in DNA. It has the design structure to generate enzymes to heal itself.

Dossey (in Brigham, 1998) further clarifies the recovery process through his depiction of what he defines as paradoxical healing. He differentiates paradoxical healing from rational healing as the former focusing on being while the latter is on doing. Spirituality, synergy and spontaneous remissions are indicative of paradoxical healing as they involve a release of trying to make the actual recovery process happen. Release, surrender and openness to new meaning and life purpose evolve at this point. Rational healing involves conventional medicine's surgery, medication and the like. Brigham (1998) indicates the interaction of both being considered in the recovery process. He suggests an enlightened perspective integrating both ends of such a continuum with the caveat that trying too hard can prevent recovery. He emphasizes that the unique needs of the patient be the determinants of what degree of which perspective is utilized. Intriguingly, being as well as doing healing interventions incorporate the being and becoming evolutionary nature of the individual's unique motif. Realignment of mind/body synchronicity involves unique treatment interventions for each patient. Each patient is out of alignment in his or her own way in reference to his or her own mind/body motif. Therefore, unique treatment regimens are required to facilitate reestablishment of inherent, internal synchronicity.

Many spontaneous remissions are followed by an emotional change (Brigham, 1998) known as an epiphany. Falling in love, new insights, near death experiences and personal transformations of self-concept are examples of epiphanies preceding miraculous healings. Hirshberg (in Brigham, 1998) describes being qualities in individuals experiencing spontaneous remissions. These include movements towards autonomy with healing coming internally, expressiveness of emotions, increase in caliber of relations with others, accepting and confronting the disease and increased spirituality among other changes.

Pearsall (in Brigham, 1998) described additional characteristics of patients who were prone to miraculous recovery. These include psychic toughness dealing with crisis in recognizing duality in the nature of events (from hopeful to hopeless), awareness and confidence exceeding logical thinking (the larger than self reality beyond ego), simplicity of life beyond materialism, creativity not just adjustment, willing to think creatively and take risks to achieve dreams and becoming more patient, understanding and truth oriented in a benevolent capacity.

Pearsall and O'Regan indicate that the psychophysiology of patients with these characteristics suggests they are in a unique psychological and emotional form of consciousness. Such uncommon consciousness reflects unique configurations of reality in patients facing crisis.

Consciousness is formative awareness and as such influences psychophysiological reality. Talbot (in Brigham, 1998) describes how the capacity to shift consciousness from one paradigm of reality to another can have physical consequences in the material world in which we live. He presents the universe as in a state of flux where patterns of reality (flesh can be burned by fire) are simply repetitive habits as are physical laws, which our consciousness has also been habituated to accept. He elaborates that while physical laws appear stable, out of the ordinary characteristics (immunity to fire) imply that some laws can be suspended.

Morowitz (in Brigham, 1998) suggests that the new physics (quantum mechanics) of the universe offers a novel paradigm that may account for miraculous recoveries. Pearsall (in Brigham, 1998) presents such discoveries of the new physics as theory of nonlocality, uncertainty principle, complementary principle, levels of reality and so on. Brigham (1994) discusses how Maui spiritual healers depict personal crisis and illness as a process of entrapment in a fixed level of reality. Healing enables the individual to develop access to multiple levels of reality.

Motifs in their improvisational brilliance stretch the everyday consciousness (and as a result formativeness) of ego orientation (fixatedness) of the individual utilizing uniquely inherent organizing (and reorganizing) principles from within. Motifs are inherently capable of facilitating shifts in consciousness (and therefore reality) because of their formative nature. These shifts in consciousness involve altered states which, when potentiated through epiphanies can emerge into spontaneous remissions of serious illness. Grof (in Brigham, 1998) suggests that these altered states could be essential in exacting alterations in physical laws. The depth of emotionally charged belief may enhance critical shifts in consciousness through formative improvisation changes. These changes can be manifested in the reality of the individual's physiology. Bohm (1980) reflects such a mind/body influence interactiveness as he considers the universe as consisting of consciousness (formativeness potentials). To Bohm, reality is manifest in thought. Watson (in Brigham, 1998), a biologist studying paranormal events globally, believes in a similar vein that the construction of imagination is a very large part of reality.

Jahn and Dunne (in Brigham, 1998) of the Princeton Engineering Anomalies Research Lab take the position that consciousness is essential to the distinctive (unique) reality of subatomic particles. As was presented in an earlier chapter, unique formativeness of motif is a distinctive quality at subatomic levels as was described in the theory of strings. The very formativeness of an individual's everyday reality has been theorized (Brigham, 1998) to be a blueprint of intelligent consciousness remaining stable while the physical atoms and molecules are constantly being replaced in the body (e.g., "new" stomach will be just as ulcerated as the "old" one).

The phenomena of multiple personality disorders (MPd) are a classic example of altered consciousness states affecting physical reality. In one state of consciousness one may be allergic to smoke yet in another have no reaction. The variety of subpersonalities illustrates compartmentalization of consciousness in discrete but reified form. The formativeness of motif is interrupted by design structures of consciousness segregated from one another. The family of characteristic features of the unique motif is disrupted in the artificially segmented subpersonalities of the MPd. MPd presents an altered configuration that serves coping needs but undermines core self needs of formative motifs.

EXPRESSIVE MOTIFS

Expressive experiences that access healing formativeness of mind/body synchronicity are advocated by Jean Houston (1982). She utilizes numerous mind/body exercises and guided imagery to facilitate reintegration. Khan (in Brigham, 1998) utilizes numerous meditations to enhance the magnitude of consciousness expansion and integration.

Brigham (1998) in her Getting Well program draws upon expressive therapies. She believes that such treatment elicits externally what is internally experienced. This draws upon the core resource of essential self. Removal of the consensus trance (what is believed by tyranny of the majority to be reality), social conditioning and cultural abuse (resulting from the way social structures are stereotypically organized) through expressive therapies reveals the person's essential self. Expressive therapies facilitate outward manifestations of internal, unconscious imagery representative of core self-motifs. The self can express the source of its own inner truth through the artistic modes of expressive therapy. The unique motif of the core self manifests inherent organizing motifs of the artist within. The formative source of each person's artistry is the unique, organizing principles inherent in his or her artistic motif. As the sculptor creates the figure of marble so the motif creates its self-formativeness. The motif of the artist is the motif of the formative self — the artist within, the healer within.

The modes of expressive therapy include movement, journaling, music, drawing and so on. Brigham (1998) describes how such modalities access right hemisphere activity of creative imagery. It is this imagery and creative visualization that integrates consciousness with physical expression. The individual can then manifest his or her own creative designs as a blueprint or motif in the emergence of core self. The essence of self is in its formative design of unique motifs. Connecting with our present self-artistry is a way of being connected to our core self. This facilitates the unique synchronicity of mind/body healing in the most brilliant of improvisational ways.

One form of expression has been tailored for cancer patients. Achterberg and Lawlis (1984) have developed a technique called the Image–CA. The instrument utilizes imagery experiences where cancerous tumors are visualized as being destroyed by attacking immune cells. Imagery may also include visualizing radiation and other forms of therapy destroying cancer cells. The patient then draws his or her image on paper displaying the cancer, the immune system attacking the illness as well as any other therapy occurring. These imaged drawings are then evaluated along dimensions of vividness, strength and effectiveness of treatment. Image–CA findings illustrate up to 97 percent predictive value of health over a six-month period. The organizational features of the imagery (shape, size, color, symbolic, anatomical) and its way of mobilizing powerful healing designs of the body's defense system can effect positive health outcomes.

Utilizing self-expressiveness stemming from inherent organizing motif assists in generating positive healing imagery. Mind/body alignment of unique organizing motifs enhances healing imagery through empowering critical formative properties affecting the imagery's design structure. Synchronicity of mind/body alignment with the individual's inherent motif can enhance the capacity for inner healing. Aligning these organizing imagery features according to one's inherent, unique motifs enhances one's healing capacity. Congruent articulation of imagery with unique motifs potentiates their healing value. For example, a fifty-two-year-old married male suffering from depression, alcoholism and a history of numerous physical losses was admitted into outpatient treatment. He described how he was missing one of his lungs (from pneumonia) by the age of seven. He was also missing three ribs and lost three inches in height due to the surgery. He missed school until the fifth grade. He also was missing his normal weight at the age of sixteen years (from 160 down to 104 pounds) and lost 19.5 pints of blood (though replenished) due to bleeding hemorrhoids. He was missing his first wife who died, he was missing a functional liver due to alcoholism, and he felt that he would soon be missing his second wife as he was still missing his first wife. He described himself as a concentration camp prisoner drained and depleted. Curiously, his second wife was a nurse in a local prison. The image he projects is that of a prisoner, progressively "missing" (both literally and figuratively) more and more parts of his life. Cuing from his imagery of being a prisoner in a concentration camp and that many of his parts were "missing in action," inquiry was made as to whether the visualization of being the "incredibly shrinking man" withdrawing and caving into smaller and smaller imprisonment was fitting for him. He responded in the affirmative.

His body posture, mood and attitude was one of being slumped down, head resting in a resigned tilt on his left hand and sullen tones of despondent beliefs in his progressive imprisonment of personal "shrinkage" from life. It was suggested further that he had been "shrunken" enough through therapy and that a change in direction was now possible. Instead of visualizing himself as shrinking from missing parts, he was encouraged to visualize in his own way what he gets to have both physically and in his lifestyle. To facilitate this, his motif was utilized.

Since his motif involved design structures of shrinking imprisonment, corollary design structures of expansive freedom were encouraged. Somewhat like unscrewing or unwinding a tightly coiled spring, he was encouraged to sit upright, extend his upper and lower body torso, open his arms in a spreading, outward motion, look upwards and with full minded consciousness, affirm the statement, "I can hit the mark, I can have it, I can get and have more of what I want." Both verbalizations of "getting and having" integrated with corrective body configuration "open, expansive and upward" align with the healing motif of the patient.

This combinational integration of body posture, verbalization of belief and faith and inspiring, upward head positioning with full consciousness absorption was repeated numerous times. Realigning the patient's mind/body organization according to the unique articulation of his motif's design structure resulted in rapid improvement of his psychophysiological experience. He manifested a positive shift in attitude, optimism and reported expectation of feeling better about his physical condition. These are all qualitative variables that have been found highly correlated with improved health.

MEDITATION, MOTIFS AND BRILLIANT WHOLES

Emphasis on healing through meditations of mindfulness is advocated by Jon Kabat-Zinn (1990) who directs a stress clinic on full catastrophe living in Massachusetts. He differentiates healing from curing in that the former involves a profound transformative view of one's self and one's relationship to his or her illness or disease. Such a shift in perspective occurs where the person views the illness from the perspective of his or her wholeness by being fully present in the moment. Wholeness is defined as the patient's connection with how they are already complete or whole in the larger self context (universe, God, etc.).

Such focused, mindful meditations create empowering shifts in the patient's sense of self-esteem, imagery, creativity and sense of inner peace. Increases in these qualities, as mentioned previously, have been related to positive alterations in enhancing immune functioning and lessening severity of illnesses. Such alterations do not promise a cure in the conventional sense of permanently eliminating the illness or disease.

An essential feature of mindful meditations is to focus alteration on the moment, experiencing a way of being whole, not as a way of doing something to the illness. As such mindful meditations are not techniques to achieve something (no deliberate intention to eliminate the illness), but rather a way of assisting the patient in discovering and connecting with ways in which he or she is already complete, intact and together in his or her own way.

Kabat-Zinn (1990) describes how wholeness is a deeply personal and unique experience for each person. Yoga and body scan (attending to sensory experiences throughout body) practices provide the patient a glimpse into his or her completeness in a moment of stillness. Being mindful in meditative attentiveness allows the formativeness of sensory and perceptual design structures to emerge. The patient can discover wholeness in unique, formative designs of seeing how events in his or her life can be viewed in new ways, attending to being part of a whole, here-and-now design flow of sights, sounds and feelings — for example, sensing the smell of flowers, seeing the light of the sun dance upon a glass of pure water and feeling fully alive in appreciating the design of color and shape in that moment of sensory reverie.

BRILLIANCE AND HEALING

Notice that these healing moments are quite similar to what happens in moments of brilliance. The streams of consciousness experienced by Michael Faraday described previously also embody full mindfulness of thought, form, sense and flow. The brilliant motif of his consciousness is mindfulness at its best.

The focusing of mindful meditations actually destabilizes the patient's identification with his or her illness. Kabat-Zinn (1990) presents how patients overidentify with their illness becoming a cancer patient or an AIDS patient and in so doing lose their essential identity. One might suggest that part of what gives illness and disease its power in the first place is when the core self of the person is composed in his or her psychosocial way of being in life (consensus trances, cultural trances, role fixation, etc.) where one's fragmentation becomes distortedly reorganized into unhealthy ways of living leaving one susceptible to disease (the stress-prone type A). In such a scenario, the person is vulnerable to the very disease or illness that symbolizes through its symptoms the person's unhealthy organized way of living. Witness the organ language jargon of the person with heart disease having lost a spouse (dying of a broken heart) or a rheumatoid condition in a person with rigid, fixated ways of thinking and feeling (frozen or stiffness in feeling and expression).

Shifting perspective to one's formative wholeness or brilliant way of construing the moment unique to one's self, accesses the aforementioned healing qualities. There is a shift away from feeling isolated and alone towards feeling whole and complete. Symptom reduction and physical improvement can result. Healing is always a unique, deeply personalized experience (Kabat-Zinn, 1990). Learning to face one's life challenges, coping and adapting involve a form of brilliance that becomes healing in evolving a healthier, formative way of being organized in one's life.

Kabat-Zinn (1990) describes how meditation involves a spiritual form of self-inquiry which has a transforming capacity in encountering and working through full catastrophe life experiences. He makes a key point of the person taking responsibility to adapt the meditative practice to become his or her own way of being whole. It needs to fit the individual's unique life needs. The particular choice of what works in being whole depends on the person's unique life experiences and temperament.

Meditation involves the process of self-attending invoking feedback loops of self-reflexives. The more an individual attends to how and what he or she perceives, the more elaborate and intricate self-awareness emerges. Such was the very process involved with what was previously discussed as the Einstein factor practiced as a means of connecting with one's inner brilliance (formativeness of motif). Self-reflexivity (the self's awareness of its ways of being aware, known as altered states of consciousness) is the result of intricate, formative brain structures in the layers of columns in the cerebral cortex.

As individuals with disease (formerly called patients) access ownership for their unique healing experiences, they can reorganize into their idiosyncratic self. Ownership of one's personal experiences in responsible ways reorganizes formative alignment in mind/body synchronization. The degree to which the diseased (disorganized) individual realigns with inherent, formative motif experiences (ways of being) is the degree to which transformative healing can occur.

Unique improvisations dealing with moment-to-moment novel problems of illness and disease are formative manifestations of motif's design structures. These design structures occur in idiosyncratic formativeness as the core self manifests and expresses itself in unique, mind/body synchronicity. The source of inner healing is accessed when synchronicity of unique mind/body motifs is achieved. The capacity for the immune autonomic and endocrine system to generate homeodynamic balance in healing is enhanced with synchronicity. Realignment in balanced, body/mind metabolic and neurochemical interactions indicates the brilliant moment-to-moment improvisations of adaptive, healing responses.

Rossi and Cheek (1986) describe approaches of idiodynamic responses of mind/body healing. The first step involves assisting the patient to access focused, relaxed altered states with a readiness for exploring healing responses. Suggestions are then given that an inner (unconscious) search for healing responses can occur with the reframing of the illness/disease as a challenge to which inner resources for healing can be discovered. An idiodynamic response (finger may move involuntarily) will signal when this has been completed. Finally, ratification of the learning is suggested to have occurred when the patient awakens from the altered state with post-hypnotic suggestions for continued healing.

The idiodynamic nature of signaling is indicative that something uniquely healing and innovative has occurred within the individual. The idiodynamic signaling of inner healing occurring is also unique to the individual. Instead of a finger lifting, the hand may move or an eyebrow can lift. The uniqueness of inner healing as well as its particular symbols of change occurring involve highly personalized, designed expressions. The internal healing responses and the signals of their occurrence represent uniquely brilliant improvisations of healing. The design structures of inner motifs manifest themselves through the brilliant improvisations of moment-to-moment healing. The idiosyncratic nature of healing is the unique manifestation of the individual's motif.

At the heart of unique healing improvisations is the resilience of coherence, manageability and meaningfulness. Idiosyncratic healing of brilliant improvisations utilizes unique organizing principles, resourcefulness and purposefulness inherent in motifs.

The motif is an unfolding brilliance of creative organizing principles. It is already whole in its moment-to-moment contemplation. Yet, it is always evolving as the wholeness of the unique being is always becoming more of what it already is. Healing, brilliance, evolution and wholeness in the moment are imbued in the unique motif of each individual. It is the uniqueness of each individual that paradoxically allows each person to be both whole in themselves yet a unique part of the large whole of the universe. Connection to one's self and to the larger wholeness through unique motifs is the essence of healing.

MOTIF IN HEALING

The mind/body interaction is characterized by Weil (1995) as what happens above (mind) is what happens below (body). The mirroring of mind and body parallels the symbolic meaning of illness symptoms (dying of a broken heart paralleling heart disease). Parallelism can be schematically illustrated in the following design which incorporates Weil's depiction.

Healing interventions at one level evoke parallel healing at another. For example, someone experiencing loss of a significant other images symbols of darkness, fragmentation and isolation. Symptoms generated may be physical pain, lowered immune resistance, signs of flu (fatigue, aching pain, etc.).

Transformation of these loss images through accessing encouraging resources (one's inherent uniqueness, hope for future relationships, flow of one's unique interests and/or artistic activities, sense of connectedness to others, etc.) generates new mind set images of healing. Perceiving and interpreting one's experience of loss as having been enriched as a unique person with greater wholeness with which to connect in the future creates hope, facilitates grieving and increases self-esteem.

The transformation of physical symptoms may mean reduced signs of fatigue, quicker recovery from illness and reduction in aches and pains. In addition, medications providing some relief coupled with healthier diet and sleep patterns can influence positive mental symbols of how to construe a more optimistic mood.

Bridging the mind/body levels involves comprehending that altering cortical activity of imaging and perceiving (frontal lobes, limbic system, etc.) activates transduction of transformative information flow via the hypothalamic-pituitary-endocrine and immune systems. The transduction (translation and conduction of unique, formative information flow) from mind (cortical activity) formativeness of design structures to body formative changes occurs through neuroendocrine linkages. Neuropeptides, neurotransmitters and neurohormonal chemical messengers convey unique formative alterations from one level to the next (Rossi, 1986).

Bridging mind/body levels requires a sequence of neurochemical alterations that occur over time. There is not one bridge but multiple bridges transducing formative alterations in unique (for the individual) sequential arrangements or designs. The particular bridging pattern design involves that person's idiosyncratic motif. One illustration is provided below:

(Old)	Mind	M1	M2	M3	M4	M5	(New)
(Old)	Body	B1	B2	B3	B4	B5	(New)

In the illustration M and B indicate the first new mind alterations and B the first new body symptom changes paralleling these alterations. Transformative alteration of sequential mind/body interactions progressively occurs over some time interval (either within the moment and/or weeks and months). The point is that the mind and body transformation into health becomes progressively aligned and designed according to one's unique healing motif.

The schematic of the above design can symbolize a unique track upon which the health of the individual traverses. The winding twists and curves in the individual's healing design track are idiosyncratic to one's motif. The arrangement of the images (mind/body transducers) involving interaction of neurotransmitters, hormones and so on emerges as unique design structures of motif. Intriguingly, DNA spiraling strands (the double helix) are linked in unique sequences by complementary pair bonds of amino acids (A, C, T, G). The unique design sequences of DNA linkages reflect unique organizing motifs of the individual. The mind/body linkages also have their own unique sequence of connection involving neurohormonal chemical messengers.

The unique motif incorporated within the DNA sequence is holographic (congruent) to that in the individual's healing design track of recovery. Indeed, the individual's unique motif imbued in DNA sequences and tier layers is the one and the same unique motif imbued in the individual's healing track of mind/body transductions. These are complex tier layers of proteins enfolding in the DNA molecule. There are also complex layers of neurohormonal networks bridging mind/body alterations.

One of the consequences of unique motifs imbued in both DNA and healing tracks is that their very shape and design structures resonate and are in harmony with one another. Parallelism can occur between healing tracks and DNA molecule sequences. This could be one of the contributing factors to what happens when mindful meditations of wholeness and connectedness result in corresponding symptom changes in one's health. For example, one of the contributing factors to cells becoming cancerous is free-radical damage (electron-hungry atoms) to DNA during repair. Here, mutation in the gene occurs because the DNA molecule is not able to repair itself to the required level of integrity.

When the individual accesses and aligns with his or her unique motif of design structuring (during mindfulness meditation), formative changes are initiated at all resonant levels (healing tracks as well as DNA transformations). Motif may enhance health track link designs of mind/body and amino acid connections in DNA molecules. The empowering, organizing properties of inherent, unique motifs may serve to minimize such DNA damage and/or compensate for it through reordering effects. While such propositions need to be researched, studies cited previously regarding imagery and cancer prediction exemplify how unique, organizing motifs are holistically imbued throughout parallel levels of the individual. Unique motifs are resilient in their hardiness and self-righting properties as they are holographic, organizing principles of self. Healing involves creative, moment-to-moment, brilliant improvisations of mind/body motifs readjusting, reintegrating and renewing the unique balance of self.

Chapter Eight

Motifs in Marriage and Family Systems

The self-motif of the individual emerges from the differentiating zygote through a continual selective, environmental interaction (internal biology, womb, immediate and extended family, peers, etc.). The zygote acquires inherent formative properties from parental, biological germ cells (sperm and egg). Therefore, the self-motif's manifest uniqueness emerges from a contextualized, biopsychosocial nature. The growth and development of the child evolve through stages which require age appropriate nurturance and task achievement to progress in the lifelong differentiation process (Piaget, 1979).

Differentiation (Bowen, 1978) of the child's self motif involves his or her being an "offspring" of parental integration. The unique self-motif of the child reflects selective physical and temperamental characteristics drawn from the parents and integrated in the child. The unique self-motif incorporates similarities of both parents but reflects a derivational formativeness (not unlike fractal design structures discussed previously) that "springs off" from each individual parent.

The child then is a unique characteristic motif, derivative from the larger family motif. His or her formative design is derived from parental integration. Remember that motifs can be defined as a family of interactive pattern sets of characteristics and themes (Wittgenstein, 1974) which are similar but uniquely different from one another. Notice that such a description of motif as a family of interactive patterns is both symbolic and literal when dealing with actual family systems. There can be a family of families (extended family), each of which represents unique derivations of interactive characteristics. One might consider such a level of organization as a larger whole above that of the single family.

Additionally, the family with its children is a literal (as well as metaphorical) example of motif (each child is a pattern set of interactive themes and characteristics). Each of its children exemplifies a derivation of the family motif as well as a unique motif at the individual level. This is an example of a "smaller" whole at a lower level of organization (as compared with extended families). Indeed, one could extrapolate that social and cultural levels of organization represent even higher hierarchical levels of larger and larger wholes. Each of these organizational levels of wholes represents motifs within motifs. For example, being American is a motif in itself. Yet, within such an all-encompassing motif are myriad derivations with characteristic design structures (e.g., northerner, southerner, etc.). Design structures can also be motifs (unique wholes) at lower levels of organization. One could go global with such a schema, notably as an earthling motif. Imagine the countless design structures that are the "offspring" of a universal motif. Earthlings will be reclassified as a set of design structures of more universal or galactic motifs.

The point to all this is that the child in the family operates both as a derivation of parental/family motifs and also as a unique, whole motif. This creates a dialectical tension between the individual as a unique entity of motif and as a derivational design structure "sprung off" from the larger family motif. It is at this point of interplay regarding the child (as simultaneously a self-motif and a derivational design structure of family motif) where growth and differentiation occur. The family's motif (communication and organizational structure) needs to evolve and grow in its maturing differentiation to allow parallel growth in the child's self-motif. Transitions and crisis in both marital and family development trigger growth differentiations at multiple levels. Indeed formative motifs in families and individuals within the families will exhibit dialectical tensions. That is, a reciprocal relationship exists between the family as a whole and its individual members. As family motifs at one level press for evolution, individual motifs (design structures of these larger motif wholes) are affected and in turn reciprocally affect family organization. When parents divorce, challenges and disruptions filter down to and back up from their children. As the formative motif of marriage is altered, the effects on the larger whole of family motif and smaller whole of child self-motif are reciprocally set in motion.

Marital and family motifs are dynamic, organizing systems seeking to maintain balance and equilibrium (Minuchin, 1996). To achieve this in times of transition and/or crisis, they need to evolve to a higher level of formative complexity and differentiation. As systems evolve through periods of chaos and creative reorganization, brilliant, healing improvisations are brought to the forefront. While examples of such innovative formativeness will be illustrated later, it is important to elucidate that homeodynamic equilibrium is achieved through the elaboration and differentiation of motif's uniqueness. It is the uniqueness enhanced at multiple levels that facilitates the dynamic maintenance and enhancement of brilliant improvisations of healing and growth.

MARITAL MOTIFS

Enhancing uniqueness of self-motifs in marital relationships requires the understanding that the relationship forms a motif of its own. The degree to which partners can assert their uniqueness in formulating a healthy, unique marital bond is the challenge expressed in the dialectical tension between individual and relationship levels. When there is confusion between these levels, conflict, paradox (Bateson, 1972) and fused entrancement can occur (Feeney, 1999). Paradox involves conflict between class and member levels (Watzlawick, Weakland and Fisch, 1974). For example, the phrase "All Cretans are liars!" expressed by a Cretan creates a conflict between class (the Cretan who expressed it) and one of its members (the statement itself). If all Cretans are liars, the statement is invalidated in that the one who stated it is a member of the very class to which he is referring. Infinite, oscillating feedback loops will ensue (the statement is true when it's false, and false when it's true). Such reflexive dilemmas can occur in marital (or any intimate) relationships.

Partners can learn to share their unique motifs with one another through manifesting individual design structures (their talents, special abilities, proclivities, etc.). When one mistakes one's design structures (talents, roles, abilities, etc.) as being one's whole identity, there is a confusion of class (motif) with one of its members (design structure). Idealization and/or obsessive fixation insisting on design structures to be rigidly predominant leads to an entrancement further fusing and enmeshing the couple.

For example, a wife may be highly attuned to detailed analysis and detective work. She may be able to uncover distinctive language patterns (unique, repeated word phrases) in her husband and detect subtle alterations in when and how he speaks. She is also capable of mixing and matching colors and shapes in designing her home and landscape. The husband may sit back, take a global perspective and see the "big picture." His way of organizing his experience is to let all the details come together, patiently waiting and reflecting, then get to a bottom line summation of what it all means.

The wife may suspect him of having an affair. In her fervor to substantiate this, she can become extremely focused (obsessed) in analyzing and detecting any subtle changes in his way of speaking, acting, smelling (perfume scents), etc. She could even notice different hairs in their marital bed that she claims don't belong to either of them, exclaiming "someone's been sleeping in my bed." She would be so invested in her detective quest she could lose herself and the wholeness of the marriage in the absorbing nature of her talent (design structure) and ability to detect. She and her husband, for example, may have been married for twenty-nine years, raised two healthy, high achieving sons and generally feel respect for what their marriage has accomplished over almost three decades.

Focusing on the wife's motif can be quite helpful. When she is asked her middle name, her favorite color and most enjoyable set of experiences, her entire tone changes. She becomes centered, comfortable and smiles with a warm glow. She becomes reflective of herself as a person rather than as a detective lost in analysis. When asked her middle name, she abruptly comes to a halt with a confused look. She realizes she had totally forgotten herself (lost in design structure) in the fusion of the relationship and her insecurities. As she had insecurely pursued the potential of threat to her marriage with a vengeance, she had fused herself to her ability to analyze and detect. In the process, she lost sight of her needs for warmth, attention and meaningful dialogue. Indeed, she dominated the conversation ignoring meaningful input from outside awareness and became absorbed in her own talent for detecting incongruities with her spouse. For someone who was so talented in generating perceptive distinctions of what mixed and matched congruently or not congruently, she herself went undetected and unrecognized. She lost sight of her own motif. Her paradox was one of acting like a detective who could not detect her own sense of self.

She is asked to consider that so much talent had gone into generating multiple design analysis of her husband's possible behavior that her sense of reality was becoming distorted. She acknowledges that what she needs is personal warmth and attention. Yet, she needs someone to help her set limits and guidelines.

As she had lost her father when she was four years old, there was a childlike quality in her needs of attention and direction. Her motif of being a bright-eyed, outgoing, curious little girl was left somewhat unnourished and "undetected" as a consequence of early father loss. Her husband was somewhat passive aggressive (reserved in attentiveness with a tendency to blurt out his feelings all at once). As she became more focused on being herself (acknowledging her intrinsic attraction to mixing and matching colorful and unique language patterns, behaviors, etc.) she learned to enjoy her generativeness of motif rather than being fixated and obsessed in set patterns of analysis and detections. In extricating her identity of self-formativeness, she frees up her capacities and talents from obsessive fixations. These fixations interfere with her personal needs of love, attention and caring direction (open to her husband's firm but fond levels of attention and affection).

Neil Jacobson (in Wylie, 1999) utilizes an approach known as Integrative Couple Therapy (ICT) in dealing with the "primitive, dark underbelly" in marriages. Couples are assisted in understanding and accepting unique aspects inherent in each partner and how they relate to each other. These aspects remain unchanged but can generate and enrich partner empathy. When partners accept each other's self-motif, they acknowledge and affirm each other's uniqueness. With greater extrication of self-motifs from repetitive, nonadaptive fixations, partners can increase their response range of healing and nurturance. Partners can experience a marked increase in brilliant, adaptive responses to one another in dealing with the complexities of endearing, long-term relationships. For example, when abusive males access core motifs empowering their artistic nature, increased confidence and creative adaptations to stress ensue (Cunningham, 1998). Robert Bly (1992) discusses how males need a sense of rootedness and anchor in connecting with their masculine side. Each man needs to experience his own inner "drumming" or beat (Bly utilizes drum beating as a ritual experience in empowering males). Henry David Thoreau addresses these issues where each man (and woman) moves to the "beat of a different drum." The rhythm and harmony is unique (but not incompatible) for each person. The key is to access the generativeness of core motifs. The individual's uniqueness (and empowered identity) is imbued in self-motifs.

EXTRICATING ENTRANCED MOTIFS

Liberating partners' motifs from paradoxical and entrancing enmeshment involves differentiation of the self (Bowen, 1978) motif. Individuals in enmeshed and fused relationships (with themselves and the significant other) need to "take back" their projected fantasy ideals (Feeney, 1999) to facilitate the differentiation process.

Loving relationships exert and elicit tremendously powerful and often unknown forces deep within and between partners. These forces are felt and sensed but rarely accessed in a conscious and enlightened frame. The energizing field forces of loving (erotic pull of entrancement) invoke a matching and resonance of rapport between partners' minds, emotions, senses and chemistry. These field forces of rapport have a name: entrancement.

Entrancement is an alignment of matching energies and expectations at one of the deepest levels of human experience, which involves attraction, resonance and union between thematically (thinking and believing) similar and congruent partners at many levels of their life experiences (images, feelings, characters, fantasies, chemistry, etc.). Entrancement involves suspension of critical faculties (meaning we lose our mind and surrender ourselves to some strange new girl or guy, then lose sleep because we cannot stop thinking about them). It also involves selective attention (she or he is the only one for me in the entire world of billions of people). These and many other facets suggest that the power of entrancement is hypnotic in origin. Romantic addictive relationships can be comprehended in such a hypnotic framework.

The essential premise is that romantic, addictive enmeshment is the result of what is experienced as irresistible pulls from hypnotic entrancement. Entrancement involves a coming together or fusion of idealized images superimposed upon physical attributes of one partner by another. Each partner brings to the relationship ideals or images of his or her perfect mate. Partners merge their ideal images of love and beauty with the size, shape and contour of their mates. Such fusion unleashes incredible forces far beyond each partner's conscious comprehension.

Romantic relationships intimately parallel hypnotic relationships. Because couples do not realize the presence and power of hypnotic dynamics, they are vulnerable to addictive fixations in their relationships. The main premise suggests that romantic relationships involve, if not require, hypnotic dynamics and forces to sustain them.

A key feature to entrancement is that the more partners act on their fantasy ideal, the more intense and powerful it becomes. Entranced couples may find themselves with partners they really don't like or value. Partners can date each other for years, disliking numerous aspects of one another (talkative, superficial, and rude). Yet they are too frightened to say anything or to leave for fear of being alone. Such tolerance for what is unacceptable intensifies entrancement and submergence.

Partners really don't know the inner dynamics that actually keep them together. Enduring unacceptable, abusive experiences is indicative of entranced "love." The harder partners struggle for control and resolution in the relationship, the less they actually have. Such intense struggles propel them deeper into entrancement with their fantasy ideal. Entranced couples can be entrenched in conflicting positions involving negativity, fear, loss, terrorizing abandonment or smothering engulfment. Partners in such positions believe they are fighting for their fantasy ideal. The reality is that acting on these negative motives only intensifies them and serves to deepen entrancement. The paradoxical consequence is that such intensification of negative feelings makes their fantasy ideal even more elusive than before.

The effects of hypnotic dynamics in romantic relationships are called entrancement. These hypnotic dynamics are what contribute to such paradoxical consequences that result from the perceptual distortion effects of entrancement. Entrancement is defined as a way romantic partners engage and relate, where suggestive imagery and sensory stimuli merge to form a fusion or bond. For example, when a man holds an ideal image in his head of a charismatic, tall, slender, blue-eyed blonde and a woman of that description walks past his visual field, it could be said that a mild state of entrancement has been induced (if the man is in conversation, there may be a silent moment, eye-fixation and a brief head turn attending to the person in question). There is a matching of inner fantasy and outer reality such that the boundaries blur between the two. This type of experience fits the description of perceptual changes in reality occurring under hypnosis presented in the previous chapter. The inner imaginary fantasies and external world of reality (what is real about the other person) collapse and merge together in romantic relationships. This merger or fusion of fantasy and factual reality is called entrancement.

It may be helpful to understand that there are essentially two kinds of entrancement. The first is what was just described and is referred to as a sensory-based trance. The focus is on appearance, personality, language style and other sensory stimuli. This type of entrancement occurs in the beginning stages of romantic relationships. Healthy couples evolve out of this level of sensory entrancement to what is termed character entrancement, which is distinguished by a depth focus. Depth focus means being able to perceive the inner nature or character of a person's real self. For example, a husband beholds the evolved image of his wife's uniqueness as a human being and long-term partner. As she walks past him, he reflects and meditates on her inner beauty and special qualities that make her the unique character she really is and the one he really loves.

It is important to note that evolving from one level of entrancement to another requires time, maturity and progressive, successful stage development. Partners progressively learn to love and respect the inner character of each other by moving from external to internal perceptions of each other's true nature. However, romantic relationships of necessity need to progress through various stages of growth.

At the initial stage of romantic contact, an absorbing, fixating allure may be essential to getting the relationship off the ground. Such an absorbing, fixating allure involves entrancement. Entrancement in a romantic encounter is similar to the initial ignition of a rocket about to launch. There is a need for a fiery, energetic thrust to get the vehicle off the ground.

Entranced relationships become addictive when they are unable to progress successfully from one stage to the next. They experience difficulty in releasing one section or stage of their relationship growth for the next one that would assist them in continuing their journey. It is important to note that most couples are not aware, or are only vaguely aware, of the extent to which hypnotic entrancements operate in their relationships. When couples do not evolve in their entrancement, they experience chronic problems (conflicts, verbal and/or physical abuse and other struggles). It is at this level of restrictive relating that they experience the perverse twist of addictive bonds. Without learning to master, understand and gain a perspective on hypnotic entrancement, couples risk the nightmarish perversion into addictive bonding.

In an addicted relationship, two or more individuals begin to engage in a type of relating and communicating that has a perverse give-and-take quality. For example, partners constantly criticize and harass one another for needing time alone or feel pressured to behave in artificially perfect ways. One partner may demand constant attention from the other through handholding and eye contact and humiliate the other for acting silly in public.

There is usually an obsessive quality of dwelling on and living through the other partner. Partners feel compelled to spend all their time together and feel abandoned and lonely when apart. There may also be a kind of rigid role playing where one partner always tries to be happy-go-lucky, while the other assumes a depressive, almost morbid sadness.

The focus on the relationship, while it may have admirable and well-intentioned beginnings, leads to qualities of obsessiveness, loss of control, frustrations, anger and rage. There are usually various forms of abuse and fixation hallucination. Addictive relationships foster a fantasy ideal or illusion around which the addiction is organized. This is in contrast to the evolved character entrancement, which emphasizes how each partner can enjoy and enhance a sense of self, character and integrity with the relationship. Mature relationships organize themselves on the contributions of each partner's unique character. As such, partners in healthy bonds are in the relationship but do not experience the source of their lives as coming primarily from their relationship. While their relationship is primarily important to both, it is not essential for their lives to continue.

Just the opposite is true for entranced relationships restrictive in their evolution. Partners feel they will die (perhaps literally) if the other one leaves them. In severely addictive relationships, this may be more of a reality than a metaphor, as in the case of one partner preferring to kill the other to prevent the loss. Notice the paradoxical perversity in the entranced logic of loss (to kill the lover to keep him or her). This is where sensory entrancement perversely twists itself into addictive bonding. Figures 8.1, 8.2 and 8.3 depict the positive and negative correlations concerning absorption, entrancement and boundary confusion. Notice that as absorption and sensory entrancement increase, so does the degree of boundary confusion (Figure 8.1). This indicates a progressive loss of reality-testing and problem-solving ability. When observing the relationship between boundary confusion and character entrancement, there is an opposite negative correlation (Figure 8.2). As character trance increases, boundary confusion and its concomitant reality distortions decrease (Figure 8.3).

Addictive partners adhere to fantasized, rigid, close-ended ideals of what their romantic vision of the encounter should and must be. In order to "truly" fulfill and satiate their highly sensitized, emotional need requirements, they lose sight of enhancing their individuality as part of the relationship. This prevents a sense of partnership and oneness where they could learn to be themselves in a relationship. They learn to abuse each other's self in attempting to have this wonderful (so-called) idealistic fixation.

Healthy relationships have a balancing system where each partner's identity and genuine sense of self remain intact. Where they have discovered mutuality and grown together in a common ground of shared experience, partners release only a select sense of self in becoming one together. For example, one couple married thirty years had very unique individual characters yet worked quite well together. The husband was in his early fifties, a former marine and successful in sales with a dry sense of humor, somewhat self-contained and disciplined in character. The wife, in her later forties, had successfully raised with her husband their three daughters and was quite energetic, bubbly and sociable and worked as a secretary. Both valued high standards of living and invested much time and energy in the home and family. Recently, they cleaned their four-bedroom home's carpets, working like a SWAT team together, and they got the job done in almost no time at all. They have their own individual character and style, yet share common values and commitments, mutually releasing distinct realms of their identities to be one with each other.

An entrancing couple, by contrast, tends to thrive on emotional and over-whelming problems. The entrancing couple magnifies and overly complicates daily problem-solving tasks of communication, trust and shared task responsi-bilities. Such couples become polarized with tasks and achievements. They may become either highly ineffective in task completion or obsessed with all-encompassing successes that dominate their relationship lives. Remember that in hypnotic trances, individuals can regress to a childlike level of sensory preoccu-pation and overmagnification of how severe events really are. In this regressed state, they lack mature adult cognitive resources.

Such magnification and cognitive distortion from hypnotic entrancement can be seen in the way couples overgeneralize their problems. This is where one failure in attempting to solve a problem or resolve conflicts in the ideal relation-ship is overgeneralized into all-or-nothing thinking. Couples may think regres-sively that one failure means all is lost. Catastrophizing (prediction that conflicts and problems could mean the end of a relationship) and awfulizing (how terrible such problems are to go through) distortions further confuse and complicate the way entrancing couples solve problems.

Such distortions in thinking, created by entrancement, can lead to taboos in how couples will relate in order to defend against such fantasized disasters. Partners communicate double messages to each other. One partner may assert how beautiful the relationship is while, at the same time, critiquing and ridicul-ing the other's way of dressing and acting in public. Protests from the other

Figure 8.1
Absorption and Entrancement

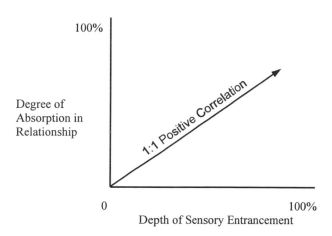

Degree of absorption as related to progressive depth of entrancement.

Figure 8.2
Boundaries and Sensory Entrancement

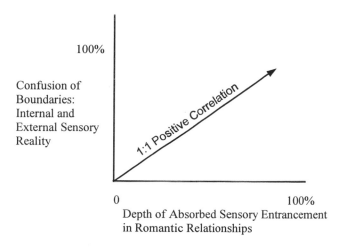

Degree of inner and outer boundary confusion in reality frames as related to depth of absorbed sensory entrancement in romantic relationships.

Figure 8.3
Boundaries and Character Entrancement

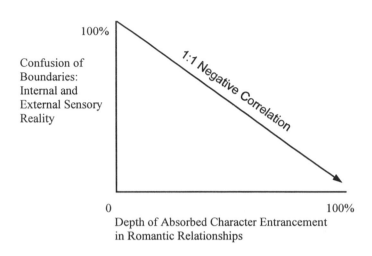

100%

Confusion of
Boundaries:
Internal and
External Sensory
Reality

1:1 Negative Correlation

0   100%
Depth of Absorbed Character Entrancement
in Romantic Relationships

Degree of inner and outer boundary confusion in reality frames as related to depth of absorbed character entrancement in romantic relationships.

partner are met with a quick subject change, establishing the taboo against expressions that might cast a shadow of a doubt on their ideal and beautiful bond.
Such taboos restrict partners' ability to resolve negative communication and
maturely evolve the intimacy in their relationship.

Entrancing relationships are regressed states of hypnosis where partners
symbolically represent childlike images and demanding ways of being treated in
highly individualistic and self-serving ways. If partners are not treated in such
specialized, perfect ways, they experience rejection and loss of idealized love.
Such is the power of regressed, entranced bonds on here-and-now realities. Partners will not feel this rejection from friends and colleagues as they have reestab-
lished mature, adult perspectives being out of entrancement. The instant partners
encounter their entranced relationship, severe and painful feelings are released
as regression from entrancement has set in. Partners can always be hurt more by
the one with which they are in love (or entranced).

In addictive relationships, partners are fixated in their merged positions.
This fixation creates a feeling of being out of control, unrewarded, unfulfilled,
unrequited (which creates miserable experiences for each person). Partners don't
feel free in such a relationship and therefore feel a pressure to try and "break
free" but fail to do so. Partners may insist that their relationship has an essential
fantasy, ideal or hallucination, which is a hypnotic absorption they believe must
materialize to fulfill their needy emotional lives. They believe that being with

one another in some mysterious, special, magical way holds the key to their personal fulfillment.

Partners experience such magical moments when anticipating that being with one another will soothe all their worries and frustrations of the day. Partners believe that the magic (entrancement) of the other's presence lifts them out of the mundane, ordinary routine of daily living. This is a classic example of losing hold of one's creative capacity to create one's own reality. It is not unlike the magic of a mother's kiss upon a bruised knee of her child who has fallen. The belief in her healing power to make it better with a kiss is very real. Such magical powers ascribed to the fantasy ideal are actually hypnotic suggestions empowered by each partner's self-induced belief.

Recall in the previous chapter that a hypnotized individual appears to behave involuntarily (arm rigidity). Yet, if the hypnotic induction suggests a kind of imagining and associating that has a goal-directed purpose (of creating arm rigidity) this will be the outcome. Since critical faculties of judgment are suspended, this allows the hypnotized individual to function at a regressed level of immaturity, preoccupied with sensory gratification without conscious censorship or interference.

Such imaginary, associative, goal-directed strategy and regressed immaturity with a suspension of critical faculties operates in entrancing relationships. Entranced couples appear to act in involuntary, rigid ways, yet the imagery and strategy of their idealism creates a goal-directed outcome. In this case, they have a fixated, rigid way of treating each other so as to maintain the fantasized idealism of the relationship. It's a kind of "arm rigidity" of a fixated mind-set. This can lead to apparently involuntary actions and reactions from each partner. Conflicts can ensue with both being surprised at how they are acting. They are not aware of an unconscious strategy and goal-fixated behavior.

One partner may feel more in control and confident than the other (known as being one-up [Delis & Philips, 1990]). The other partner may feel more vulnerable to losing the relationship. One partner may perceive the other as having more control, feel vulnerable and attempt to secure the other's commitment in more reassuring ways. Various strategies involve moving closer, trying to please or acting distant and detached seeking to enlist attention and interest. Such maneuvering may trigger escalations of equal and opposite reactivity. Quite frequently, entranced couples misperceive and miscalculate the posture of their partners. Each tends to over- or underestimate the other's degree of commitment.

The resulting instability serves only to intensify their preoccupation and their entrancement with one another. The struggle for who is more in control of the relationship, of who will be more independent and less needy to the other's involvement, threatens to erode intimacy and trust. Such a struggle is based on the false illusion that one partner could actually control and make the other partner love him or her. Yet they may both be out of their "control comfort zones," as such struggles and conflicts are actually the involuntary dynamics of entrancement.

The control issues of the maneuvering "one-up" partner (flirtatious and exhibitionist acts seeking to draw the attention of the "one-down" victimized partner) actually mirror their hypnotic dance. These pursuit-withdrawal tactics are designed to maintain the fixated, hypnotic set point.

If one feels bored and needs stimulation to reenergize and reorganize the fantasy ideal, the flirtatiousness of one partner in front of the other can provoke renewed interest and energy. If the man comes across as the passive, one-down needy partner, the woman's flirtatious provocation can incite him to riotous, active interest, bringing him out of his passive, dormant state. The two may have conflicting words about it, which creates painful involvement. This is a way of deepening the entrancement (drawing them closer into the trap of the hypnotic pull). There may then be brief moments of euphoric pleasure (they end up having sex all night to soothe the pain, reigniting the fantasy, and again strengthening the hypnotic pull of enmeshed fantasy). This pain-pleasure alternation maintains a balanced point of set levels of intimacy. Yet such alternating pain-pleasure cycles actually serve to deepen entrancement.

MOTIF: THE CORE ANCHOR FOR MASTERY

Accessing core motifs provides structured anchors and safe places. Without it, partners are vulnerable to illusions. The problem with illusions is they have no flaws. Partners feel trapped in the hypnotic entrancement, enmeshed in the grandeur of ultimate love. They can feel controlled, compelled to bend to each other's will as the only way to maintain this long-sought-after type of "unconditionality."

This type of entrapment happens again and again in entrancing relationships. The first step in this process is the major premise that this relationship fulfills some long-sought-after type of universal need (human beings need unconditional love and acceptance). A partner sometimes tries to fulfill such a need by turning to the other partner as the only one who could ever know or want him or her in this very unique way. Ironically, it is this very uniqueness that partners ignore in themselves that they persist in misattributing to each other. A partner may perceive the other as what they have been waiting for their whole life. A partners may feel the other is able to give him or her what no one else can. He or she may think that the other can make him or her feel like the truly special, unique person that no one else really knows. The second step is that in order to maintain this so-called perfect love scenario, partners pressure one another to adapt and fit themselves into what they believe are the requirements for perfect love. The third step is when the entranced relationship progressively deteriorates through the stages of disillusion, obsession and ultimate rapprochement of each other and the relationship itself. For couples to break free of this entranced entrapment, partners need to awaken from entrancement sufficiently to begin to question the whole situation. This is done by having them stay in the here and now. They are asked to describe their level of present pain in the relationship without trying to make sense out of it initially.

Partners may be tempted to deal with entrancing illusions of conflict, which threatens to resubmerge them into a lost identity of absorption. Partners can become lost in endless ruminations and images of what each could be doing. Entrancement feeds off of anxiety and ambiguity. When partners feel threatened and are unclear about what is a real threat or what is no big deal, they are drawn even deeper into an absorbing, entranced bond.

Motif serves as the master anchor as it accesses unique, structural designs within each partner that, by their very nature of uniqueness, are immune to enmeshment. As parts of each individual may merge and entrance with another, when that part or aspect of the self is experienced as part of the larger whole of motif, reassociation as an integrated whole person is possible. Partners entrance various aspects of their identities with one another, remaining grounded in their unique, sensory motif. Partners can associate to the entranced part dissociated in the relationship by the realization that that part is actually an extension of each partner's unique, greater wholeness and therefore can never be fully absorbed into the other.

LOSING ONE'S MIND, COMING TO ONE'S SENSES

Partners are more effective in their effort to emerge from entrancement if they temporarily suspend cognitive efforts of making sense out of it. This is achieved by simply focusing their attention on what feels and appears to be right and effective in the here and now to relieve their painful responses in the relationship. At first, the ideas that emerge regarding what would help make no sense at all. This may involve a time out (taking a break from being together) or suspension of dialogue. It may involve enjoying a simple laugh when they are supposed to feel miserable. Partners get entranced into their programmed dialogues and verbal conflict patterns, saying the same negative statements to each other without thinking. They need ways to disrupt and break these cycles.

After partners have established a safe place to begin to question why they are in so much pain in what's supposed to be their "ultimately perfect love," they discover just how absurd the design of the relationship is. They learn to realize the futility of trying to change and prove themselves to attain this unconditionally. Of course, every relationship requires mutual adjustment, but not to the extent that it is at the expense of the core self.

The next step is for partners to begin to access what universality (all-encompassing need or quality) they are in search of and learn to give that to themselves first. When they take initiative for this is when they begin to fully awaken from the entrancement. The accessing of sensory motifs is a powerful way in which partners can begin to give themselves this type of universal acceptance. Ways of accessing motifs will be presented later in this chapter.

Resurfacing couples need to get to know each other all over again in their alert, awakened consciousness of self. Such couples need to be quite gentle and patient with one another in the resurfacing process. Many vulnerabilities, sensitivities and untested facets of each other's personalities are revealed. Time, acceptance and a sense of respect for the emerging motifs within each partner are essential in supporting such new awakenings. A sense of openness and receptivity supported by unconditional acceptance and avoidance of rigid expectations are additional factors in the process.

Emerging out of entrancement frees both partners and their relationship to be what they were meant to be in the first place. Couples can have all the love, charm and beauty they desire. Awakening to the call of their inner truth frees them to arise out of the ashes and manifest the true inner and outer beauty of the character they were meant to be.

MOTIF: UTILIZATION AND REALIZATION

Illuminating partners' artistic motifs serves to illustrate how such self-knowledge and understanding can be a powerful resource in developing a healthy, intimate, long-term relationship. By learning how to access and identify with their own motifs, partners are in a healthy and empowered position to participate and contribute to a loving, passionate and mature relationship. Establishing the unique ground of each partner's character enables both to be honest and loving in a growing and enriched bond. Motifs in partners are unique designs that can never fit (because of their essential uniqueness) into entrancement's fantasy ideal of role/image perfection. As motifs are inherent, organizing principles of character, they can be accessed and utilized by partners in times of stress, change and transformation. Motifs provide resilience and empowerment when couples require the courage and stamina to weather the emotional storms of intimate relating. Such empowering designs in partners serve their need to work through another variable in entrancing relationships called hypnotic set points. As motifs are inherent, organizing principles of character, they can be accessed and utilized by partners in times of stress, change and transformation. Motifs provide resilience and empowerment when couples require the courage and stamina to weather the emotional storms of intimate relating.

ENTRANCING SET POINTS

The hypnotically induced relationship, like all relationships, is governed by a set point which determines the degree to which partners can uniquely be themselves in close, intimate relationships. The body's metabolism is governed by a set point of how efficiently it will burn fat calories. Relationships have a similar set point of how high and efficient partners' interactions can burn and heat up their intimacy such that they can come together as their true selves.

Individuals function differently as single people than as partners in a relationship. In relationships, the whole is greater than the sum of the parts. If one partner wants to move closer or farther away, seeking to exert more or less influence and change into the relationship, the set point, if challenged, will require the other partner to exert an equal but opposite reaction to maintain stability and homeostasis. We see this in action when one partner seeks to become more affectionate and intimate than usual and the other partner pulls away, questioning the change.

Increasing this powerful regulator in relationships necessitates three structural changes: (1) mutually encouraging each partner to internalize a higher degree of personal authority and internal focus of self-control; (2) enhancing each partner's unique character and sensory motif; and (3) nurturing the fantasy vision into a real-life "dream come true." There needs to be a mutual and expanding, growing version of the fantasy vision of the basis of the relationship held by both partners. This then needs to be evolved and developed.

This expanding version allows for higher integration and self-differentiation of unique motifs. At the same time, there is increased intimacy at higher levels of love, value and spirituality without precluding lower levels of passion and romance. There is transcendence. This preserves the original romantic qualities in healthy, real-life situations. There becomes an expansion of themes and emotions that are not fixed to any rigid space, time or form. There is a gradual enhancement of each partner's internal sense of authority, operating more from a felt sense of choice.

Partners become increasingly unique and diverse in who they are, taking on characteristics of each other. They have more to share and invest because of their diversity. They feel grounded in their values and more expanded in their abilities to be and express themselves. The motif of the relationship can open up and incorporate the vast, unique universe of both partners. It is the sense of being mutually incorporated in their growing bond with boundaries ever expanding yet inclusive of how they are as unique individuals. Their synergy of coming together provides more facets to share. As long as the relationship is framed as encouraging and enhancing as much uniqueness as each partner chooses, the relationship can and will expand to accommodate it.

The set point increases to accommodate and stimulate two partners developing and expanding their motifs. The synergy of two individuals pursuing genuine, character-structuring motifs creates high-energy rapport, elevating set points to new levels of connection. What prevents partners from growing apart and moves them together is that in accessing motifs they are openly accessing loving qualities. Not only do they love each other for who they are, they can now synergically be guided together by their loving motifs of one another.

Set points can be raised by expanding the space and boundaries of each partner's internal frame of reference. This means that instead of partners having to constantly create new diversions to keep one another interested or go outside the marriage for new challenges, each partner continues to grow and differentiate according to their own unique motif. This allows both partners to evolve in themselves and each other. They learn how to be themselves with their partner in a shared and yet individually creative way.

Set point determines the available degree of genuine intimacy defined as the ability to maintain identity while feeling a sense of oneness with a partner. Accessing sensory motif enhances identity in relationship. It allows partners to release and give themselves to one another, having an inner guidance system to focus them while in the energy field of the relationship. Accessing their motif allows partners to discover balance, knowing who they are while relating with their lover. Neither partner needs to fear either being engulfed or abandoned as they have teamed together to develop the confidence to truly be themselves with each other.

Accessing one's own motif also allows partners to deal more effectively with the issue of attainability. The paradox of relationships is that the more confident one partner is that the other partner belongs to him or her, the less desired the other partner will be. For a relationship to grow, it is important to recognize that full possession is impossible. The myth of possession is entrancing. Partners maintaining their motifs refuse to allow others to possess or fixate them. Motifs eliminate the paradox of possession.

A corollary to possession is attempting to keep the relationship stimulating. Trying to change various features in themselves and in their partners regarding dress, travel, enjoying a different hobby and such may help. However, this type of change is of a basic, first-order level, simply altering the content of their activities and images. It may work for a while, but eventually couples need to change the fundamental way they go about doing things within the relationship to create a real change.

FAMILY MOTIFS

The marital relationship is itself a motif constructed from the integrated birth of two unique individuals emerging into a third, the relationship. The differentiation of the marital motif in families facilitates the differentiation of the other members in the family as well (Bowen, 1978).

The family motif is a higher order level of organization than the marriage. These family motifs are built upon healthy marital motifs which form the differential core of the family constellation (motif). The old adage "as the head goes the body will follow" applies in the case of family construction. Napier and Whitaker (1978) and others refer to the family as a kind of mobile where when one part is pulled the rest vibrates as a whole organized system. The organization of the family manifests its motif in multiple, unique design structures (known as children who are themselves whole motifs of their own).

Differentiation of the family organizational motif requires the marital core to be clearly delineated itself. In this way, distinct boundaries between levels of marital and parental relationships can be established. Healthy families require healthy marital motifs. We are referring to intact families at this point. Single-parent families similarly require establishment of clear boundaries between parent and child but may be more difficult as the marital core is absent. Of course, healthy significant other relationships can supplant as resources in such cases.

Family motifs are as unique as self motifs though more complex at a higher order of abstraction and organization. The characteristic talents and temperaments of parents and children (when in healthy differentiation) exhibit dynamic, creative atmospheres. Whether quiet, subtle and reflective or adventurous, exuberant and risk-taking, there is a motif of family characteristics permeating each of its members. The intensity, degree and proportionality of talent, temperament and nuance is individualized in each member. A classic example is the Kennedy family. Both parents maintained core marital motifs which clearly delineated talent, temperament and nuance for public service, achievement, influence and leaving one's grand mark on the national landscape. Each of the Kennedy children manifested his or her own unique version (offspring of design structure) of such powerful family characteristics.

Problems and difficulties emerge when boundaries and enmeshments (or detachments) ensue. Motifs become distorted in paradoxes and entranced design structures, and the part begins to dominate the whole (the tail wags the dog). The tragedies in the Kennedy family may in part have resulted from parent-child boundary compromises. That is, the father had a highly specific design structure of what he expected from his offspring — that of becoming president of the United States. While this is a magnificent achievement in itself, it is far from clear that this is what the offspring originally wanted for themselves. One needs to be careful what one wishes for because one may just get it. Each member in a differentiated family is able to choose freely the most brilliant, moment to moment improvisation to evolve their unique motifs.

While the child is a member of the family, he or she has also introjected (taken in) a unique interpretation of the family within. Each member of the family will carry in his or her own psyche a constructed version (design structure) of what the "family" means to that particular person (Ansbacher and Ansbacher, 1956). There is not one absolute family but multiple versions of the family. There are as many versions as there are individual members who have their own unique perspective. The point here is that individual self-motifs are still at work even in the complex constellation of family organization. Extrication from fused distortions facilitates the evolution of the self-motif. The self-motif of the child needs to be able to emerge in his or her unique family version.

ENMESHED MOTIFS AS PROBLEM SOLUTIONS

Napier and Whitaker (1978) describes how each family has its own structure, tone, rules and so on. The organizational patterns are established and maintained over many years. Symbols, metaphors, rituals, ceremonies, traditions and such all become established in the ways family members behave with each other. The predictability that emerges from these ingrained patterns, even if painful, is in formative family bonds. To discover one's unique motif when it means challenging and disrupting established predictability requires external support and nurturing design structures of formativeness.

Napier and Whitaker (1978) suggests that the agent (therapy) of change provides a metastructure (temporary scaffolding) to bridge transitions and crises of change (divorce, empty nest, stress, family evolution, etc.). The family crucible, as Whitaker refers to this metastructure, must have a shape and form to provide a guiding discipline of change and evolution.

For example, a schizophrenic son and his mother may operate on multiple levels of communication. The mother may request affection from the son. When he attempts to hug her she smiles but her body stiffens. The son gets a nonverbal message to withdraw and he confusingly falls into a blank trance. Such conflicted communication has been referred to as double binding. Couples may deal with their own intimacy problems by distracting their focus onto an acting out adolescent.

The family behaves with the same type of integrated functioning as a biological organism (Napier & Whitaker, 1978). As such, the individual member participates in the family motif in a homeodynamic way that maintains stability through growth. However, double binding messages, confused boundaries and so on impair the evolution of family motifs which is where the design structure of a "crucible" for change (treatment design) is helpful. Impaired formativeness requires new ordering resources and therapeutic design structures to realign with healthy family motifs.

Minuchin (1996) describes how the family needs to exercise parenting by approximation — that is, learning to move from mistake to mistake, honing in on successful ways to meet each child's unique needs. There are "future pasts" cultivated in parenting where what is experienced in early childhood lays a foundation for future experience. Being sensitive to how the immediate past affects the future formatively shapes the moment-to-moment experience upon which new futures can be constructed.

The family is a web of connections as is the unique complexity of its individual members (Minuchin, 1996). The idiosyncratic movements of individual members are simultaneously choreographed as a whole family dance and design. Enmeshment is reduced when individual self-motifs can emerge in their own, unique version within (and, at times, beyond) the family dance.

The uniqueness of each individual member transforms and is transformed by the family organizing motif. The dialectical tension between the family and individual organization levels reciprocally co-evolves the constellation of motifs. When a mother feels helpless to solve her relationship problems and needs her son to be dependent for her to feel competent, his problems are her solutions. Reconstructing the son's function as "helpless to solve mom's needs" is a powerful resource in encouraging the mother to redesign her life. Such reconstructing juxtaposes competing design structures and is mutually transforming.

ORDERING AND RESTRUCTURING IN FAMILY MOTIFS

There is a need to restructure and reorganize the family design so as to potentiate and access healthy family motifs. The Milan group (Selvini, Boscolo, Cecchin and Prata, 1980) designed innovative ordering and structuring interventions to achieve healthy realignment of family organization. These include interventions known as positive or logical connotations, circular questioning and rituals. Positive or logical connotations are messages to the family from the therapists depicting disturbing behavior as somehow positive and/or logical in the given context. Circular questioning accesses sequences of transactions and emotions that move from one family member to another. These sequences reveal patterns of family organization and structure. Rituals involve ordering problematic family patterns so as to interrupt their simultaneous occurrence and extend them out over time. In this fashion, new formative sequences can be constructed.

Bateson's (1979) theory of pathology involves double bind communications between parent and child (or parent to parent). Self-contradictory messages (stay away but come closer) are problems in epistemology (ways of knowing) where one person can unilaterally control another. Causality in families is circular and multidetermined. Yet such circularity is not meaningfully dealt with by family members due to the organization's inadequate boundary structures. Members become enmeshed and/or detached through endless loops of trying to control one another (Haley, 1976).

The Milan group utilized Bateson's formulations of cybernetic loops acknowledging the unintended consequences of how member's behaviors influenced the greater organization structure of family. They operated from three premises:

1. Families in unhealthy transactions do not acknowledge ongoing games.
2. Games between family members involve unilateral efforts of control.
3. These games need to be discovered and interrupted.

The family organization needed to be restructured in a new, formative way. This involved the interventions described to induce differentiation of clear boundaries resulting from pattern interruption and reorganization. For example, rituals were employed like therapeutic paradoxes (Haley, 1963) such that families couldn't resist being told to continue behavior currently in progress. Telling a family bed wetter to continue to wet the bed on specific nights of the week provoked a paradoxical shift (Feeney, 1984) moving the family organization to new levels of formativeness. In this case, larger perspectives emerged as well as extrication from repetitive, enmeshed behavior. The motif of families sometimes requires an illogical (chaos with hidden order) "jolt" to evolve into new, brilliant, improvisational solutions of differentiation.

Positive (or logical) connotation was used with a young boy whose grandfather died. The family complained he was not doing well in school and was hallucinating. The positive connotation involved verbal and nonverbal messages to the boy of how he was the pillar of strength and balance point in the family. Over the course of family treatment, he began to do better in school and the hallucinations ceased. Addressing homeostatic behaviors in troubled families "jogs" the family organization to healthier levels of formative differentiation. The shape and design of the family patterns evolve into formative growth. Family design is a function of ordering and formativeness. Evolving new ordering paradigms requires interventions themselves to be highly ordered. If the basic unit of family life forms is one of configuration, then order can only grow and evolve through that which is more ordered at synergistic levels. Basic units of order (individuals, couples, families) require ordering interventions upon which to feed and grow. Illogical, chaotic interventions may actually symbolize higher levels of order to which the family unit can be elevated.

The use of circular questioning assist therapists in gaining access to the varying positions of family members' relationships to one another. Circular questioning is a back-and-forth process comparing and contrasting various family members and the systemic organization as a whole. The family pattern (design structure) that maintains the problem emerges and can then be reformulated (new formativeness of motifs) in healthier ways. For example, questions about differences in perception of relationships (who's closest to mother — daughter or son), and degree of difference all access proportionality of organization and type of structural bonds. There may be questions about the future or hypothetical situations (what would have happened to your child if you were to divorce, or not divorce, etc.?). Such questions illuminate sequences of reciprocal feedback loops emerging in circular, nonlinear complex formativeness. Altering the way events are construed (constructed or designed) provides a higher formative ordering which is needed to heal the family. Such innovations in family design involve a change in the way members seek to change one another (second-order change).

The form (design structure) of circular questions induces and jolts transformation of the systemic organization into new generative levels of formativeness. In this way, the individual and family patterns of motif are extricated and evolve in the transformative process.

MYTHS AND MOTIFS

Cybernetic dynamics (feedback design loops in families) espoused by Haley (1977), Fisch, Weakland and Segal (1982), and Bateson (1979) shift attention toward observer-dependent reality constructs and away from "objective" reality. Cognitive biologist Mantura (in Boscolo et al, 1987) proposed the view that reality is a social construct manifest in the "biased" observer's position. The paradox of objectivity is that we are part of what we "objectively" (illusion of separateness) observe. Meaning is therefore a personal/social construct (ordered form).

In families, meaning is expressed in premises (myths or constructs) upon which problem behavior is anchored. Problems may occur in service of the constructed premise of meaning (or myth). For example, a premise or myth that a teenage son is the cause of the entire family's misery is constructed ignoring that the persons making such an observation are themselves part of the misery-making problem. Shifts in the formative meaning of these myths or premises can provoke formative family motifs to evolve and realign the system.

METAPHORS AND MOTIFS

Individuals, couples and families are multidimensional in their complexity of character structure and in their multiple channels of communication (Combs and Freedman, 1990). They are open-ended, allowing for randomness and spontaneous response. This is precisely what is required to permit the emergence of creative, unique solutions which evolve the organism (individual or family) to the next level of formative complexity.

Motifs operate in just this capacity of spontaneous evolution. Motifs are multidimensional in characteristic complexity. They uniquely manifest themselves through multiple levels of the organism (behavioral, verbal, nonverbal, biological, cellular, etc.). Communicating through several channels simultaneously exerts formative nudges that evolve the organism to higher ordered levels.

The vehicles utilized to facilitate these processes are metaphors as expressed in symbols, ceremonies and stories (Combs and Freedman, 1990). Metaphors are "about" other things and refer to them in an indirect, somewhat vague (or random), experiential and strategically utilitarian way. For example, to say that someone is a diamond in the rough communicates metaphorically about their valuable qualities that are not being utilized resourcefully. Metaphor is a way of communicating multidimensional aspects of an individual's experience through indirect multiple channels (verbal, imagery, experiential, sensory).

Erickson (1980a) attended intensely to the patient's subtle, unique, multidimensional nature (word phrases, facial expressions, movements, breathing, etc.). He would intervene utilizing multichannel communications (verbal, nonverbal, pacing, embedded messages, puns, stories, etc.) which resonated to the patient's uniqueness (self-motif). He would choose precisely the right language pattern that congruently matched the patient's formativeness level in such a way that nudged it in the direction of responding with its own brilliant, healing, moment-to-moment solution.

For example, he would see an indirect (nonlinear multichannel) experiential approach with a child who was thumb sucking. He would jolt the closed organized system into an open-ended one with surprising and confusing commentaries. He might suggest that the child give equal time to each finger and tell him to keep doing present, ongoing behavior in ways that loosen his fixations and allow new formativeness of motifs to emerge. As the child's perception was altered to new ways of dealing with thumb sucking, he eventually released it for more unique, personal, satisfying behaviors. Altering the way or formative pattern of dealing with a difficulty evokes motifs. Accessing one's motif initiates healing, self-organizing properties within and beyond the individual.

Metaphor can assist in jolting fixated formativeness. Congruently matching similar themes in behavior but suggesting new orderings can shape new meanings. Erickson would assist couples with sexual dysfunctions using metaphors of hunger and food. He would analogously (multichannel) refer to the dysfunction through interspersing suggestions that the couple "develop a hunger and taste for healthy foods" to nourish them.

It is important to note that metaphors imply form and order. They both capture congruently the essential experience of the patient but at a more complex level of formative development. It is this complex level of formativeness that releases fixation and accesses uniqueness in patient's motifs for growth.

While motifs are self-organizing, they (like plants and flowers) need their own unique nourishment (soil, water, light, fertilizer). Each unique plant has its own special requirements to become more of what it already is. Metaphors, as well as other ordering forms of intervention, need to be uniquely designed to nourish the individual's inherent motifs pressing to bear the fruit of their abundant uniqueness.

Patients experiencing formative enhancing metaphors and the like search their store of memories, images and experiences to shape meaning in their own, idiosyncratic way. Stories, symbols and rituals are multichannel communications that serve to challenge individuals and families to higher ordered formativeness (and healing) in their internal search to construct unique meaning. Such challenges involve formative learning where the self-motif transforms itself through internal search and higher ordering refinements. Formative learning is what is left over after one has forgotten one's education. Complex formativeness of unique motifs continues long after the specific content is no longer present. The muscular shape of motif remains after the conditioning process has passed.

Combs and Freedman (1990) describe how Erickson accessed each person's unique sense of identity in one of his teaching seminars. While looking through participants' identifying information, Erickson verbalized to the group how his daughter once spilled a glass of red wine on a white carpet. He followed up with the comment, "there is always one in every crowd." Such an ambiguous comment encouraged participants to initiate an inner search to shape and design their own personal meaning of what Erickson might have meant. In the process, they relived their own unique experience of how each person could "stand out in a crowd." The course of such an internal search was directed by their self-motif. There is always "one" (accessing each person's unique oneness of motif) "in every crowd" (each person is one of a kind no matter what crowd they are in) nourishes unique formativeness.

MIND AND MOTIF

Bateson (1979) proposed that in mind everything is metaphor. Every thought is about something else. For example, he described how one may see and have an idea of a pig. Yet, no one really has a pig in their head, only a representation of one (even though some people may be known as pig-headed, this is of a different order). Perception is informed through light refraction (skewed representation). This light is transformed into electrochemical activity continuing in metaphorical form through one's neuropathways (design structures). The electrical patterns are, in turn, transformed to chemical patterns (neurotransmitters) flowing through the brain and are eventually transformed into consciousness (formative mind).

The mind-set of individuals, marriages and families (the marital and family organizations have a "mind" of their own) constructs meaningful representations from formative metaphors. These form-inducing metaphors are transformed through the "biological organism" of the patient/family. If these metaphors are aligned with unique self-motifs, brilliant, healing improvisations of evolved formativeness will ensue. If not, disturbances in the formative organization will occur. It is similar to an alien virus infecting the "mind" of the computer.

The family may experience transition, trauma or situational dilemmas in sociocultural conditions. Parents, children or both may be exposed to dysfunctional metaphors, symbols, rituals and so on. Excesses in achievement needs, the hurried child pressed to grow beyond his or her age-appropriate readiness (Elkind, 1981) and families spending less than one-half hour per week of quality time together are breeding grounds for dysfunctional metaphors, symbolic misinterpretations and so on.

For example, one sixteen-year-old boy began to suffer suicidal ideation and major depression when his family became overstressed with multiple tasks. Both parents were employed in highly demanding professions and his siblings, one brother and one sister, went off to school. He was given the message by both his mother and his sister to take care of the home while they were away. His metaphor was to hold down the fort alone until reinforcements arrived. The problem was that the family had reorganized to make him the lone ranger of reinforcements. He was given a new metaphor in family treatment. His job was to awaken parents to the need to return home to "reinforce the fort." He could do this through alerting them by his absence, as he was to join peer level clubs to activate his own fortification and feelings of belonging. The family reorganized with a healthier alignment of achievement and "hurriedness" in hastening to spend more quality time together, with the parents taking the lead.

MAPS AND MOTIFS

Family relationships are organized and configured like the boundaries of a map. How the lines are drawn and how the emerging design structures are juxtaposed creates the structure of the family's reality. However, the map is not the territory   (Boscolo et al., 1987). The mental map (mind formativeness) of the family appears to be the actual reality. Yet entranced paradoxes will emerge when the map is mistaken for absolute truth and reality.

The map of the United States of America in the year 2000 is quite different than that of the year 1800. The discrepancy between the family's map of reality and reality itself needs to be constantly updated and refined as new formative information flows into the system. If this is presented through fixation, denial, fear of imperfection and such, impairment of self and family motif evolution can ensue.

To facilitate healthy reality testing, Bateson (1979) discussed how couples could use binocular vision to provide abductive learning. Abductive learning is where multiple models and forms occur in conjunction with one another and one looks for patterns that connect. Partners who conjunct their individual perspectives together provide depth and reality testing. However, if couples are wearing blinders, they will have great difficulty sorting out their map from the reality of their impaired family design structure.

DISTINCTIVE MOTIFS

Accessing motifs through formative interventions can remove blinders and lead to healing formative improvisations. Motifs involve abductive learning as they are complex conjunctions of a family of interactive sets of patterns. Bateson (1979) described such conjunctions as distinguished patterns of relationships in one complex system (set of patterns) contrasted (family of interactive sets) with other such systems. Bateson's contrasted distinctions between complex systems and motifs are structurally congruent in their hierarchy of organization levels. Bateson was seeking the "pattern" that connects the entire biological universe. His contrasted distinction smacks of the overlapping interactive set of characteristic patterns in motifs.

Bateson's quest for the pattern that connects can be construed in terms of unique motifs. That is, the pattern that connects life forms is not so much a pattern but rather the quality of uniqueness itself manifest in patterned form. In other words, the common bond in the biological universe and all of nature is one of essential uniqueness differentiating one life form from another. Ironically, it is the uniqueness of motif derivatively manifest throughout biological (and psychosocial) levels of hierarchical organization which connects all living organisms. Uniqueness of motifs is imbued throughout the hierarchical organizational levels of life forms.

Comprehending such a fundamental perspective in dealing with the biological organisms of individuals, marriages and families facilitates accessing these inherent, empowering resources. Such a comprehension assists in utilizing formative interventions to activate inherent, self-organizing principles for healing and differentiation of higher ordering in individuals, marriages and families.

PARENTAL MOTIF-ATION

Comprehending inherent organizing principles of uniqueness in biological organisms can be instructive in parenting. While there are numerous paradigms for parenting, there are common themas expressed which address appreciation for a child's uniqueness.

Jenner (1999) suggests that there needs to be a balanced parenting style capable of grappling with the child's traumas and triumphs on a moment-to-moment basis. She indicates that the true secret to parenting is learning to demonstrate one's love for the child in a way meaningful to that particular child.

To accomplish this, utilization of social learning theory involving behavioral consequences is advocated. Developmental stages of growth and sequence of task mastery are addressed. In addition, it is a theory of relationships employed espousing the unique attachment needs of each child. Included are dimensions of how the child thinks about himself or herself, others and the large social world; emotional scope; and general relationship style.

Balanced parenting involves using one's good common sense and sensitivity for establishing psychosocial balance. Emphasis is upon encouraging the child in behaviors of being himself or herself and ignoring negative behaviors with the exception of punishing dangerous ones. There is an interplay of being both child centered (follow the child's lead) and child directive (set responsible limits and needed behaviors).

NURTURING OPTIMAL MOTIFS

Optimizing a nurturing environment requires recognition and focus that each individual (each child) is unique. Achieving this enriched paradigm shift of recognition means the child must be visible and known by significant adults. Taffel (1999) discusses how children do not feel known by their parents and significant other adults (teachers, coaches, etc.). He indicates that the parenting pendulum continually swings from overpermissiveness (parent effectiveness training or PET) to overdirectiveness (tough love); from empowering children to family values and eventually neurobiological diagnostics (attention deficit disorders, etc.). Yet, all of his reviews of numerous research studies in child development focusing on critical variables for healthy child rearing lead to one, remarkable finding. His findings reveal that each child as an idiosyncratic individual, both in comparison with other children and with one's brothers and sisters. He further notes how research in the previous five years reveals this idiosyncratic nature in children to be hard-wired-in neurobiologically. The resulting conclusion is that the multitude of child rearing approaches needs to be judiciously and selectively applied in light of the idiosyncratic nature of each individual child. There is no one-size-fits-all parenting approach to be applied to all children at all times.

The goodness-of-fit concept is then invoked. This means uniquely adapting the right parenting approach to fit the unique needs of the child. For example, one child, sensitive and withdrawn, may respond to a supportive, indirect nurturing (PET). Another child, boisterous and challenging, may need a firm, tough love approach. Taffel (1999) further describes how some children are nurtured through continual, overt positive statements while others may find this irritating. He indicates that children have core, self-involving, intellectual and emotional attributes in constellation form. As each constellation is unique in its formativeness, recognition and self-disclosure is an idiosyncratic experience.

Taffel (1999) describes how nurturance of the child's unique constellation necessitates essential skills fundamental to the core self. These essential skills involve respect for significant adults in the child's life (clear expectations), mastery of emotions and moods (managing stress and utilizing resilience), peer smarts (able to establish healthy friendships and avoid destructive ones) and expressiveness (share meaningful ideas and feelings of fantasies, wishes, friends, feelings, etc.).

Derivations from these include helping children discover personal passion, focus, gratitude, caution and so on. While he denotes ten key skills in all, the overall purpose is to assist each child in experiencing the visible presence and recognition of his or her idiosyncratic nature, the self-motif.

Interestingly, developing core skills such as respect for adults (assisting children in structure and guidelines for behavior) is facilitated through adults expressing their own unique needs and personal boundaries. Parents need to have respect for their own unique core self and not be afraid to responsibly express these to their children. All too often the parent's self-denial and/or overbearing demands deprive the child of honest self-disclosure of the parent's genuine, unique needs. For example, Taffel (1999) cites how a self-disclosing father's request for help and expressing his sadness congruently mirrored his son's sensitivity and facilitated an increase in respect and expressiveness.

It is important to realize that for the unique self-motif to emerge in the child, it needs to emerge in the parent. As the parent expresses in his or her own unique and honest way idiosyncratic needs and feelings, the probability increases of a goodness of fit emerging in the parenting process. The anger and violence is replaced with confidence and competence in parent-child relationships. Parental expressiveness breeds that in children.

Nurturing and cultivating unique, passionate and purposeful endeavors in children activate self-motifs and multiple psychosocial benefits. When parents encourage their children to self-attend and discover activities and interests that are focused, goal directed and encourage absorbing flow states, positive changes occur. For example, a child encouraged to take up a sport and/or hobby (drawing, auto mechanics, etc.) accesses core features of their motif. In so doing, other core features are developed including connecting with others, expressiveness, gratitude, respect for mentors and rules, able to be one's self in groups and so on.

Accessing a child's passion and absorption involves accessing his or her predilection of interests and values. Catching your child in activities and interests that he or she enjoys doing (video games, talking on the phone, sitting quietly alone listening to music) provides clues to his or her unique motif. How does he or she prefer to be involved (with people or alone and to what degree)? What tempo or pace seems to best describe and match your child (quick, moderate, slow paced, etc.)? How does he or she enjoy structure and organization of people, places, things, time and the like? These and other observations and discoveries of your child require attention, time and personal interest. The child that experiences a parent's unique interest in his or her unique qualities and attributes is most nurtured and differentiated.

To nurture the individuality of the child's unique motif is to utilize one's unique motif as well. The old phrase "what goes around comes around" (and then some) is a key principle in families. Parents who give time, energy and attention to discover and give visible recognition to their child's unique, idiosyncratic self foster core self-motifs in their child. Increased self-efficacy, self-esteem, management of stressful emotions and enhanced interpersonal relationships are but a few of the long-term benefits to be reaped by emphasis on unique self-motifs. Recognition of unique formativeness in one's child can be effectively nurtured by parents who themselves are accessing such core formativeness.

It is important to look beyond the child's style, mood and immediate reactivity. While these certainly need to be considered and addressed, such temporary states are not necessarily who your child actually is at the core level. While matching and resonating with such states assist in rapport and communication, little movement can proceed in core self-growth until discovery of your child's idiosyncrasy occurs. For this to happen, attention needs to be directed to the aforementioned features of how, when and where the child orders and organizes his or her time, place and experiences of what is real to him or her. Idiosyncratic qualities involve the ordering and organizing principles of inherent, formative motifs. All too often, these get lost in the cultural, psychosocial roles and images that hide (like the mask of persona) the core motif of self.

Chapter Nine

Motifs: Meaning and Purposeful Self

Each human being has an inherent life purpose operating as a basic guide. As we live true to this purpose, we experience harmony, joy and empowerment. To access and experience life purpose, we need to attend to our sensory systems (i.e., visual, auditory and kinesthetic) as manifest in flow states. An individual's purpose is primarily expressed in what may be called a sensory motif, a unique way of combining and organizing his or her senses manifesting that person's unique character. Sensory motifs are highly visible in flow states. Use of sensory motifs as clinical interventions is illustrated in five clinical cases. It is concluded that to live with purpose and meaning in one's life involves discovering and gaining access to one's sensory motif.

MOTIFS AND THE QUESTION OF PURPOSE

Many clients suffering from anxious and depressing life experiences exhibit difficulties in such areas as sleep disorders, motivation, concentration and so on. One client expressed the overall malaise as "I'm seeking a reason to get out of bed in the morning!" Such expressions and disorders reflect difficulties in living where clients have lost a sense of meaning and purpose. Their struggle to grasp the meaning to why they are here, what they are to do and how it may be done reflects a crisis point in their life development.

Crisis in meaning and purpose is not the sole domain of clients in treatment. Each person at some point in his or her life reflects on what it is all about, why he or she is here and where he or she is going both in this world and the next (if one believes there is a "next"). These nodal points of self-evaluation in one's life present powerful learning opportunities of internal search and discovery. While challenging the presumptions of one's everyday life, nodal points of crisis and change (divorce, adolescence, birth of a child, loss of a job, death, etc.) can provoke brilliant, improvisational solutions in the moment-to-moment encounter.

Leider (1985) describes how meaning and purpose can be discovered by first gaining clarity and having a distinct image of what is wanted. Pursuing images that one believes should be attained but in fact negate the self leads to feelings of powerlessness. Many people develop feelings of helplessness and clinical disorders for just this reason. Clarification of what one genuinely wants (without undue influence of guilt, pride, shame or fear) is the initial step towards living a life of purpose. Gail Sheehy (1977) describes how the people she interviewed were real pathfinders. They were committed to a sense of purpose that was larger than their own individual egos. Such a larger-than-self commitment gave them a sense of meaning as they pursued their life purposes (artistic endeavors, entrepreneurships contributing to the greater good, etc.).

Leider (1985) presents five major ingredients that are the underpinning of life purpose: (1) a purpose which conveys meaningfulness in one's life; (2) a set of life-organizing principles; (3) utilization of personally gratifying resources within; (4) providing clarification of hobbies, interests and vocation; and (5) manifestations of purpose and meaning emerging in unique, unexpected formativeness. The sense of meaning one experiences when committed to a sense of purpose provides fulfillment and relevance for what one is doing and why. Whether it's physical conditioning or commuting long distances during rush hour to and from work, having a sense of purpose gives meaning to these endeavors. Mother Teresa and Martin Luther King, Jr. are classic examples of individuals deeply committed to larger-than-self purposes imbued with relevant meaningfulness in their life work.

Living a life of purpose also orchestrates the multitude of our thoughts, feelings and behavioral endeavors in a coherent way. The organizing principles of purpose are a motif for how one may set and pursue one's goals and objectives. Purpose organizes one's hierarchy of values and endeavors according to the principles of purpose itself. Leider (1985) describes how President John F. Kennedy mobilized the nation with the power of the purpose of sending man to the moon. The enormous organizational design required to achieve this illustrates how ordering principles are critical to long-term projects (such as living one's life).

Purpose galvanizes one's personal resources, talents and skills. Instead of going to one's job with the attitude and experience that work is just "work," one needs to learn to utilize innate talents to experience satisfaction and joy. Motifs encourage the individual to utilize idiosyncratic patterns and resources in ways that talents and skills can be most satisfying in life task areas. This will be illustrated in the cases to be presented later.

Living purposefully assists one in transforming general ideas and ideals into specific manifestations. Clarification of inclinations into behavioral expression is one of the benefits of living on purpose. Leider (1985) describes how this process occurred with Polly Edmunds who transformed values for world peace into the activist organization Women Against Military Madness.

Finally, it is important to understand that purpose can be expressed in surprising and unique ways. Whether it is seeing one's child in a surprisingly unique way (bold and courageous rather than stubborn and obstinate) or the impact of one's work as indeed socially meaningful, purpose can emerge through taking off one's stereotyped blinders to see the world in new ways. Each moment-to-moment experience presents fresh opportunities to discover one's self and interactions with others in delightfully fresh, meaningful and purposeful ways. Motifs operate most powerfully when set in a fertile field of open-mindedness and willingness to risk venturing into uncharted but richly rewarding territory.

Victor Frankl (1963) described how meaning in life could be discovered through action, experience or suffering. One can either wait for life to happen or one can go out to meet and challenge fixed, rigid but unproductive ways of living. Such is the choice each person confronts in his or her life. Motifs are resilient, inherent organizing principles already operating and able to be consciously tapped by those willing to engage them in formative interactions of flow and challenge.

MOTIFS: EMBUING PURPOSE TO LIFE

The premise that there are core organizing features in the self from birth is held among self-psychologies that will be cited. The thesis is that what empowers and facilitates core organization of self is access to events that resonate with that self's life purpose. Life purpose events seem to be accessed initially through unique experiences known as flow. They have an idiosyncratic architecture and artistic sensory design called motif. These sensory motifs are both literal and symbolic metaphors of life purpose.

Accessing sensory motifs in clients activates wholeness and organizing qualities in their lives. This occurs when the client is immersed in the moment of a here-and-now flow state that resonates with that client's idiosyncratic sensory motif. Clients experience a sense of empowered life purpose that energizes and organizes them to achieve individualized goals and objectives. The sense of purpose experienced in flow states that resonate with the client's sensory motif encourages suspension of preconceived ideas or expectations. Clients can then fully enjoy and use sensory motifs in creative and therapeutic capacities.

What follows is an exploration of these concepts and their implications for treatment. Efforts will be made to integrate sensory motifs and life purpose with various theoretical positions. Five clinical cases using these concepts will be presented to illustrate that flow states are purposeful in themselves, manifesting unique sensory motifs that are characteristic of self. These cases will demonstrate that when sensory motifs are accessed and used in treatment, significant transformations are made possible.

TRANSFORMATIONAL MOTIFS

The orientation in these cases emphasizes core self-organizing and empowering features of sensory motifs and life purpose. The orientation serves to empower the totality of the core self using sensory motifs that go far beyond such techniques as reframing or solution-oriented approaches. Although these techniques may use metaphors and models for change, they are at the problematic level. Because motifs access flow states, they function at core levels of self-actualization. Sensory motifs operate at metalevels of transformation, accessing core organization of self. This facilitates generative levels of transformative change and growth. The orientation incorporates problem situations and intervention techniques at the highest level of idiosyncratic self-organization.

Sensory motifs resonate with the configuration and idiosyncratic organization of self. They transcend techniques, promoting empowered self-alignment and an actualized sense of well-being and oneness. Clients can organize and incorporate difficulties and tasks in a manner congruent with the idiosyncratic motif of an actualizing self. Therefore, accessing sensory motifs is self-actualizing to the client. Understanding what has been said thus far necessitates an inquiry of how the wholeness of the client is addressed by multiple treatment modalities.

MOTIFS AND MODALITIES OF TREATMENT

Multiple treatment modalities — for example, neurolinguistic programming (Banaler & Grinder, 1975), transactional analysis (Berne, 1961), cognitive behavioral therapies (Beck, Rush, Shaw, & Emery, 1979), and hypnoanalysis and Ericksonian use approaches (Zeig, 1985) — respect and develop each individual's unique orientation. These approaches are powerful and creative in their skilled and enhanced use of the client's idiosyncratic characteristics. They offer techniques to move the client from present problem states to desired states of functioning.

This implies the assumption that the client is in need of change on some level of functioning (e.g., beliefs, emotions, behavior, etc.). Such a focus can unduly emphasize techniques dealing with correcting deficits. As a consequence, they can miss the subtle nuances of how clients have the seeds of their own harmony and balance already operating in their lives.

There is a need to focus on structural, organizing design qualities within the individual rather than primarily on techniques to access harmonizing resources. The organizing complex of the individual involves more than trance states, yet entire technologies for change evolve around this facet alone. The danger is that the unique organizing principle of self is lost or reduced to a matter of programming.

The paradox is that the technique can prevent use of client resources by restrictive labeling of the client as a problem category, thereby limiting available resources. We see this happening when clients are diagnosed as depressives and neurotics and then compliantly respond by shaping their behaviors to fit the diagnosis.

I believe that people are inherently designed with a motif and intent to harmoniously organize their lives to be healthy and whole. Such a perspective provides new perceptual filters through which therapists can perceive their clients. Focusing on clients' intent to organize their lives in unique, formative ways can direct the therapeutic focus towards the client's idiosyncratic capacities. For example, the therapist can explore and elicit highly idiosyncratic experiences of the client illustrating how the client's sensory systems (visual, auditory, kinesthetic, etc.) operate in unique, formative sequences (motifs). While the syntax and structural design can have wide variances, the client exhibits core sequences of organizing motifs when engaged in focused states of flow. These flow states evoke an aesthetic formative (artistic motif) organization of the client's sensory systems. The idiosyncratic quality, quantity and nuanced interactive patterns in these sensory systems exhibit a unique orchestration for each particular client.

Accessing and utilizing the idiosyncratic sensory orchestration of core self motifs provide enormous, integrative resourcefulness in reestablishing executive level, mind/body functioning in troubled clients. The aesthetic formativeness in clients' sensory systems is not to be confused with talents and/or abilities even though these do come into play. Motifs operate at deeper patterning levels than talents or abilities. They are the archetextural framework or structure upon which talents and abilities manifest themselves. As such, they operate at core self levels of the client's self character.

Clients need to be accepted at the unique holistic level of motif to experience congruence with their own personality ideal. Rogers (1951) advocates unconditional positive regard with clients. This may go against experience with observable mental and physical complaints and disorders. When the client is accessing and expressing unique qualities characteristic of a purposeful self, healing and growth occur. Rogers (1980) describes the fully functioning person, concluding that there is an underlying flow of movement in the self toward constructive fulfillment of its inherent possibilities. Ginsburg (1984) indicates that by attention to the internal constitution of self, one can see that the system already has an advanced level of organization that includes autonomy or self-direction. He discusses the inherent nature of a biological self beyond ego self or object self-image that interacts with the environment. Ford (1991) found significant correlation between behavioral congruence with inherent temperament potentials and self-actualization.

The assessment and evaluation of specific problem areas, although valuable in their own right, can paradoxically misconstrue the presenting experience. What may be construed as problems are actually creative manifestations of this inherently purposeful movement. When the therapist begins to tease out and highlight the client's organizing capacity and innate creative process of bringing to life "something out of nothing," the therapist taps powerful states of functioning. Accessing these states may even obviate the so-called problem. Frustrations with one's inherent creative energies that have their own unique integrity and hidden mosaic patterns can be at the heart of the client's complaints (Maslow, 1968). Ford (1991) relates maladjustment to discrepancies of living one's life in conflict with inherent temperaments of self. Mahler (1982) discusses the separation-individuation process that, when frustrated symbiotically, inhibits ego development. Discrepancy between an individual's personality ideal and his or her inherent sensory motif indicates false idealization of self, psychological pathology and barriers to self-actualization.

When establishing client goals, it is important to note that the client is already pursuing in creative form an innate formative design or sensory motif that is always evolving. Many theories and techniques have been developed and learned from clients based on how they naturally and creatively heal themselves (Rogers, 1951). Clients already possess many techniques and resources (e.g., have abilities to reframe, tell stories, go into trances and access empowered states). These are skills that therapists learn from clients so they can in turn treat the client with what the client already knows. Therapists can give clients what they already have in a more accessible form.

When we appreciate creative movements embedded in the client's efforts, emotions and beliefs, we assist them in accessing and developing their unique sense of self and purpose. It is an unfolding process. As the client begins to access this identity, archetypal ideal qualities of significance (being a part of something larger than self) emerge. In this way, clients take back their projections of seeing these qualities previously transferred onto external objects (e.g., parents, spouses, possessions, achievements). They begin to experience wholeness of purpose, creating order and meaning in life tasks. Buhler (1961) believes that meaning and purpose are the province of psychotherapy.

MOTIF AND PURPOSEFUL FLOW

A sense of purpose and flow of experience in one's life expresses an inherent organizing principle. The sensory design or motif of this principle is its unique character or signature. Enhancing its unique character can strengthen integrity and cohesion of self-identity. In an age of character disorder, emphasis on unique character structure or signature in sensory motifs is self-empowering.

Perls (1971) suggests that the self is constantly pressing for wholeness of the organism to complete its Gestalt. Maslow (1968) refers to self-actualization as peak experiences of unity and organization of self. The identity of self emerges in unique formativeness as sensory-motor connections etch into their unique neural pathways. As emotional effect and cognition integrate with and throughout such configurative pathways, creative consciousness of self and the world at large becomes possible. However, idiosyncratic organizing tendencies exist from the onset of biological life. The client's motif develops and differentiates through formative interactions with external templates (models). For example, clients may require the therapist to provide a formative cognitive and emotional experience (unavailable in the client's "formative" years) known as a role model.

Such a "role model" (template) needs to resonate congruently with the client's unique motif to assist the client's differentiation and emergence of necessary design structures heretofore absent. Motifs require such formative interactions and expressions (aesthetic forms of unique flow) to differentiate appropriate design structures. The healthy development of motifs necessitates creative derivations of design structures. Derivations of motifs into multifaceted design structures creates the idiosyncratic, web-like lattice upon which the family of motif characteristics can be manifest. It is to the derivative elaboration of the client's motif that his or her life purpose is ultimately founded.

Such developing motifs unfold their elaborate archetexture through purposes that have a script, plan or vision. McAdams (1985) refers to a generativity script, a plan or vision (calling or God's will) of what an individual is to do in the future. This is a gift because it generates a legacy to future generations. He suggests that a meaningful identity (Erikson, 1968) requires framework for self-understanding that coherently binds together one's past, present and future and imparts unity and purpose to one's life. There may be cases that some people, because of early, severe stress and deprivation, may lack strongly defined, coherent frameworks. However, this is not to say that inherent elements of the capacity to organize along one's sensory motif are not still available for later generation and actualization.

As the individual begins to access unity and purpose, identity begins to emerge (Erikson, 1968). McAdams indicates that despite obstacles, people do strive for self-understandings that embody unity and purpose as part of their identity. McAdams's model of the life story uses four components: (a) ideological constructs, (b) imagoes, (c) nuclear episodes, and (d) generativity scripts. He explores identity configurations emerging from the arrangement of these components. The concept of sensory motifs as a configuration of design and meaning relates to McAdams's depiction.

Loevinger's (1976) stage model suggests that ego development will affect the variety and complexity of an individual's generativity. Nurturing and accessing generative qualities of meaning, purpose and sensory motifs could strengthen and encourage ego development. The effects of such efforts will be illustrated in the case presentations. McAdams expresses the position that verbalizations are the most appropriate windows into the identity configurations. The case studies will illustrate a rich focus on linguistics as an expression and link to sensory motifs.

Existentialism postulates that existence precedes essence. This article asserts that each person has a unique essence that manifests itself in the process of his or her existing and exercising freedom. The difference between these two postulates of prioritizing existence and essence is more apparent than real (e.g., which came first, the chicken or the egg?). Existence by definition presupposes form, structure, or design. The uniquely individualistic character of each person exists in sensory form and design, implying the presence of essential, formative, inherent schemas or motifs. Existence and essence of self are two sides of the same unique character, inseparable because one cannot be present without the other.

Csikszentmihalyi (1990) discusses how flow occurs through focused sensory and mental interaction, creating qualities of various form and design (e.g., a tennis player's flowing back-and-forth movement creating form, skill and art). Each person may find his or her self-existence in flow experiences that evoke qualities of form and art where they say they really feel alive and exist as their true self. The sensory motif's existence in self is essential for each person's unique sense of meaningful existence. It is equivalent to the essence of self.

Frankl (1963) in logotherapy emphasizes the importance of discovering meaning and purpose in life. Each person's organizing properties seem to have a unique differential signature (or designation) such that some experiences will resonate more with some individuals than with others. When there is resonance, the individual feels like there is purpose in his or her self-experience. This, therefore, can be referred to as purposeful self that resonates or relates when symmetry is discovered in experiences that present properties of their organizing principle. This ordering process, although unique to each client, is essential for the joy of flow experiences to occur in such unself-conscious manifestations (Csikszentmihalyi, 1990). At such times, the client has a sense of joy, absorption or fascination.

It appears that creative variety and flow are very much involved in pl , and sense-of-purpose experiences (Barnett, 1976; Csikszentmihalyi, 1976). The flow state is essential in accessing sensory motifs of design and order. Bohart and others (1993) indicate that empathy responses that focus on future possibilities increase clients' sense of power and efficacy to solve problems. Helping clients keep an eye on their vision of the future in terms of what would be right for them facilitates the working-through process. This emphasis on what feels right (the flow state of motif) can empower change processes.

CASE PRESENTATION

The following five cases illustrate empowering effects of accessing client sensory motifs. Therapeutic effects of alignment with this organizing field demonstrate how resonance with this field generates the joy of flow experiences. The clients were seen in an outpatient setting for eight to twelve weekly sessions in short-term outpatient therapy. It is interesting to note that when the concept of organizing experiences of life purpose was introduced, all clients involved seemed to accelerate in their treatment progress. Clients struggling with a variety of presenting problems seemed to report optimism and energy when accessing experiences of life purpose. They seemed to deal with their issues with a sense of self-acceptance and self-esteem and in each case resolved their presenting problems. The follow-up to these cases was limited to the time frame of the therapy itself.

Case 1

The client was a married subcontractor referred for treatment by the probation department for stress and creating a public disturbance. He had become quite irate and incensed by a contractor, so he stole some of the contractor's tools and machines as compensation. In the sessions that ensued, many issues were explored: (1) feeling powerful, (2) how he seemed to attract conflict and chaos into his life, and (3) how co-dependent his relationship was with his mother. The client became livid, almost explosive, in one session, expressing how frustrated he was in being deprived of his financial compensation. He also felt limited and constricted in his relationship with his mother. It seemed as if he were enjoying perverse pleasure in being deprived of his earnings, which allowed him to go off into one of his expressive tirades.

When asked what he enjoyed doing, what seemed to be purposeful and flowing in his life, he expressed how much pleasure he derived in being able to use his expertise in adhering to building codes. Indeed, his real pleasure in life seemed to focus upon construction: building, arranging and rearranging component parts in construction and reconstruction-like processes. As a child, he enjoyed taking his building blocks apart and rebuilding them into new forms. For him this meant freedom, power and expression. He loved this process and said he could "do it all day." He seemed even to carry a visual image or map of an erector-set-like motif that, like Legos, allowed him to symbolize the layout of the internal structure of wires, plumbing, skylights, sprinklers and the like. He was even able to draw this structure with horizontal and vertical lines, triangles, and right angles resembling the skeletal structure of electronic circuitry. He would use this map as his reference design for what he had created as representative of the ideal building safety feature. His schematic design was creative and he was quite capable of revising this image as needed. He felt everything had to fit, and he loved discovering new arrangements. As a child, he played with his building toys for hours in the attic. He very much enjoyed working with the minute building blocks which he called chips, as he could construct or destruct his creations at will.

When he tapped into this dynamic organizing principle for himself with its sensory motif of building and construction, he realized that much of this emotional rage and frustration represented his misalignment with not living more congruently with this mosaic design. It was suggested to him that he obviously emphasized through his rage and uproar a tremendous energy for being able to "build up" to a certain peak experience and then explode and "tear down" whatever was created in his path.

He seemed to like the idea that he was powerfully able to map out his sense of design in critiquing how his contractors deviated from the "correct blueprint" of their agreement. He began to feel less helpless and outraged. He took great pleasure in intensely focusing on how to build up a price design or schematic of how an agreement, building, sprinkler system or wiring should be structured and then stripping away all the "fat" and "excess" material.

As he identified with this organizing patterned motif in its sensory form, he seemed to integrate many issues related to power, personal integrity and differentiated self. Accessing his organizing motif in a sensory format seemed to liberate him from enmeshed contacts and allowed a healthy detachment invoking humorous responses instead of intense rage. As continued suggestions occurred as to how this motif may be operating in his life, he gradually became more centered and focused.

The outcome manifested itself in terms of relief from stress, coping ability and an appreciation of his own freedom and power for self-nurturance and validation. He seemed to be impressed with his own internal structuring process as if he really had "something to offer" and could let go of hidden dependency needs on motherlike oppressors toward whom he formerly acted out his anger over his alienation from his own purpose. The stress in his life and conflicts with others seemed to diminish in light of his new attunement to the interweaving process of purpose and flow throughout his life.

Case 2

The client was a forty-year-old nurse who came to therapy to deal with her divorce, feelings of lethargy and thoughts of suicide. She had a fifteen-year-old daughter who was on the move in terms of her own adolescence and youth. She was unhappy with herself, felt she couldn't keep up with her wealthy friends, didn't seem to enjoy her nursing job and felt frustrated in not having a boyfriend. She exerted only half-hearted efforts in her job and relationships.

She felt her life was going nowhere and there was just no point to it all. She seemed down, listless and to feel she didn't have much going for her, even though she was an attractive woman, was in good health and had a good job. She was raised to be very educated and intellectual. Her father belonged to a country club, yet she felt she didn't belong there. She felt that she didn't fit into this kind of lifestyle.

It was suggested to her that while she really didn't buy into this intellectual, upper-middle-class value system, she was fearful of taking a stand about what she really wanted. She feared her father's disapproval and her mother's rejection.

She said she didn't know what she really enjoyed except for a stage comedy skit where she played one of the *Saturday Night Live* comedians. She loved performing, the spontaneity of the moment and dramatizing life events to enhance them to larger-than-life experiences. (She dramatized her plight in therapy sessions in a very theatrical, dramatic way.) She referred to herself as Scarlett O'Hara of *Gone with the Wind* and seemed to be acting this part out in real life. She also loved mystery and challenge. Her dramatic portrayal of her problems really embodied her solution in that she loved to act out her depression or any kind of role or character. She wanted to be an actress where she could enact many of her vital creative scripts. She exhibited a motif of a multifaceted diamond needing to enhance each unique facet to some dramatic extreme edge. Acting allowed such enhancement to occur.

Rather than being pathological, this orientation could help her find her purpose in life. She could be creative, artistic and bring her art to life through performance. Her mother was a former artist who killed herself at age forty-three. She felt her mother was full of self-doubt and stopped living up to her own artistry.

It seems likely that the client feared that she might act out her mother's plight and needed to learn to affirm her purpose in the arts and creative acting. I suggested to her that she started out in her life with a negative emphasis on an artistic way of life. She could be more artistic if she let herself attend to and purposefully flow with her own unique art-forming process. She perked up and realized that she could decide to access and experience the joy of acting as it resonated with that deeper sense of self. She needed encouragement to follow her truth and purpose.

She also liked psychology because it allowed her to deal with people who were "acting out" their pathology, which is what she was familiar with in her own family. She found that when psychiatric patients acted out their wild dreams, bizarre delusions and distortions, it gave them a kind of vitality and expansiveness. Such expansiveness was expressive of her motif, which required varied enhancement of her multifaceted nature. She deeply harmonized and related to this. She needed to act and perform creatively in her real life, creating exaggerated dramas so that she could give meaning and purpose to her life. Actually, the presenting problem of acting down, forlorn and depressed was the "resenting solution" of revealing her need to act out and bring to life her many emotions and images.

It was suggested that she really wanted to be an actress. She then sat straight up, smiled, and said she needed to study and emphasize acting as an artistic experience. This seemed to change her current experience of how she could bring to life hidden dreams and yearnings for realizing her private self-expressions. This allowed her to appreciate the harmony, symmetry and organizing motif of a multifaceted personality and how rich and colorful it could be.

Case 3

Carl, a thirty-one-year-old married male with one child, was dealing with recovery issues from alcohol abuse. He was attending Alcoholics Anonymous groups and was having cycles of anxiety and depression. He attempted to purchase the trademark of an established name brand for his organization so he could be his own boss. However, he struggled with depression and worry about how to deal with financial issues and how things would go in a recession economy. He was anxious about getting enough bookings to make a profit, about supporting his wife and children and about dealing with competition. He became anxious about all the tasks and operations of managing his own organization. He then found himself getting so overwhelmed from his initial efforts and multiple concerns that he sank into a depression, feeling hopeless that the enormity of the tasks could never be achieved.

When this depression became so intense that he felt all was falling apart, he shifted towards hysterical frenzy of worry and activity to hurry up and seek to prevent his perceived catastrophe. He came up with some temporary solutions but then thought to himself that these really wouldn't work and started "downing" himself, which led to feelings of depression. This cycle continued until he experienced exhaustion.

In accessing his purposeful state or structural map of how he experienced order and integration in his world, it was discovered that he loved harmony and jazz. His teaching of music involved the study and appreciation of chord patterns and harmonics. For example, he demonstrated that a ninth note in one chord is the second note of another chord and that played in harmony and progression creates beautiful sounds generating other chord sequences. He exhibited a wonderful glow and energy in describing these teaching sessions.

I therefore suggested to him that his sense of order and creative harmony occurs through interrelating chord patterns and progressions that resonate with an internal sense of continuity and meaning. In short, access of his sense of musical reality resonated with his internal map of his own organizing principle.

My intervention intended to associate this purposeful state of harmonizing and creating music with his enterprise of initiating his own band. When he realized he could approach this initiative with a renewed sense of harmony, he became more centered, relaxed and appreciably confident in his efforts. There was an interweaving of realities between his purposeful sense of harmony, balance and order and his roller-coaster type experience of anxiety and depression. With the emerging association of how he could be pursuing his own sense of purpose by starting his own band, the entire process of anxiety and depression shifted toward balance and progressiveness. Instead of panicking and catastrophizing over what was going to happen or how much money he would have to make, he attuned himself toward harmonizing efforts. He appreciated the interrelatedness of his management steps that embodied a similar structured design of purpose and flow, as if he were focused on using jazz chord progressions.

Case 4

Betty was a remarried woman in her late thirties with one child and two stepchildren. The presenting complaint regarded her fourteen-year-old son, who had been rebellious and defiant at home and at school and had been arrested for breaking into a neighbor's home. Betty felt very burdened and took on everyone's problems as caretaker of family and friends. She rarely expressed her own struggles.

She described an anthropology course she was taking and how she wanted to save a particular culture in the Congo region of Africa. She revealed that she has this love of communication with different cultures and different languages. She said she is so good at learning different languages that she can skip the grammar instruction and go into the conversational course. She cited how she can pronounce Spanish and Russian words written down that she has never seen before.

Although this facility with language comes easily to her, she has a hard time communicating her needs. She seemed to become more relaxed and comfortable at the association of her innate wonder for language forms and her own personal needs. She began acting lighter and became more expressive and emotional in the therapy sessions. It was as if she transformed her personal dilemma into the joy and fascination of her innate ability for linguistics and various cultural modes of expression.

She was going to see her son on the following weekend and was encouraged to share her own experiences about linguistics and primitive cultures rather than focus on his needs and issues. In this way, her focus changed from obsessing over her son and opened the communication system more toward a person-centered rather than a problem-centered style.

The whole experience of her love for cultures, linguistics and the realities created operates as expressions of Betty's order, meaning and purpose in life. It serves as an empowering metaphor in loving, accepting and feeling a part of the different generational cultures of parent and child.

Case 5

Max, a thirty-one-year-old white, married male with three children, was employed as a manager in a business firm and described himself as extroverted, enjoying one-to-one working relationships. He was referred for poor job performance because of overreactivity.

He liked people-oriented management, saving employees by taking a poorly performing employee and training him or her into a high-functioning employee. He liked seeing the product of his work and enjoyed interacting with labor unions and frontline employees, although he had difficulty with upper management.

He had a hard time going to meetings where staff talked about how to do things but nothing got done. He was very pragmatic and task oriented.

When asked if he wanted to change his job performance, he indicated he really hated his job and didn't want to change as he found his work revolting. He could play the part while hating every minute of it. The problem became even worse in that the higher up the organization he moved, the farther away he was from a product-oriented frontline approach to problem solving.

Max had thought of law as an alternative and had actually signed up for courses. He liked the thought of taking on the big corporate law firms, like David battling Goliath. This appealed to his need to have a direct, hands-on experience and be able to create his own personal product single-handedly. He very much enjoyed working with his hands, molding clay and building things with wood. His love for a direct, hands-on experience of building good solid human relations at work and getting a good feeling from seeing people grow and develop were being sabotaged in his own life by trying to "play the game." He realized the need to move on towards more personal work and learning to build more positive relationships.

SUMMARY

These five cases illustrate that accessing clients' unique motifs of sensory organization assists them in integrating their conflicts and achieving their goals. It may, at times, be difficult to tease out inherent themes of a client's love for creating a way of life. However, the benefits are well worth the effort. In discovering the clients' styles of making sense of their experiences in aesthetic ways, it is important to note that the issue of what is functional or dysfunctional becomes a moot point. When clients are involved in activities that are part of personally meaningful organizing themes, they feel as if they are entering the gates to a larger-than-self reality and experiencing personal significance, meaning and purpose.

For example, in the last case, we see how the client enjoyed taking things into his own hands and having a hands-on experience. This kind of metaphor serves as a kind of design or motif that kept expressing itself throughout the case in a variety of aspects. In this first step of delineating and identifying sensory motifs, the effort is to develop the sensory organizing qualities that give shape and form to the motif. The sensory motif has both integrity and growth-oriented wholeness, thereby exhibiting the motif's own identity. It is not merely a collection of senses and stimuli. It has its own inherent organizing field of growth and structure.

The second step is focusing on how this motif is manifesting itself in either a healthy or unhealthy manner. Max was in need of developing good, solid products of his hands-on labors in human relations and in the growth of his workers. The reality that he was not staying true to his purpose was reflected in poor job performance and rebellious behaviors.

The final phase is to integrate this sensory motif with the presenting problem in such a way that the presenting dysfunction is now a functional manifestation in sensory form of the client's life purpose. Max reevaluated his poor job performance in light of his new learning of the importance of honest, hands-on work experience. He experienced the valued motif of such productivity and what happens when he strays from this inherent design. In translating his dysfunctional job performance into a reevaluation of how he had lost hold of his sense of purpose, he now recovered a positive orientation to the problem. There is an expansion of his organized field of behavior and experience. Reevaluation in light of the motif expands the range of the motif's power. This is similar to discovering many facets of a diamond "buried in the rough" but now emerging in bright, clear ways. These facets are created by the diamond cutter along the dotted lines of innate character. The client's motif is a gem that needs to be cleansed, valued and empowered to its intrinsic level of expression.

Indeed, the client begins to transform his or her behavior from dysfunctional to functional by appreciating the flip side of this multifaceted nature. The client could experience how shoddy handiwork would be nothing but fluff but that good, solid, honest handcrafting would yield high-quality products. Note how using the motif in a multifaceted range of connotations facilitates the client's transformation from problem-oriented to solution-oriented efforts. Empowerment occurs when the client's motif is continuously expanded on in such multifaceted ways.

It is important to note that what is being accessed is not simply some empowered state of consciousness. Accessing the client's organizing life principle of self offers empowering opportunities permeating all areas of life tasks. Sensory motifs serve as an anchor not to some state of the client but to the client's core sense of self. What operates and motivates clients in recovery is nothing less than accessing core attributes of their organizing principle of self. There is an elusive quality to motif because it dynamically emerges over time in thematically similar yet unique variations. The characteristic form and quality of these unique variations in growth and evolution are the signature of motif and empower the client as a purposeful self.

ACCESSING YOUR ARTISTIC MOTIF AND PURPOSE

Living a life of purpose through activating one's freedom to follow and be true to one's unique motif supports being true and faithful to one's self. This is a classic case of "to thine own self be true and thou cannot be false to any man" (or woman) (Andrews, 1987). Individuals can spend their whole life pursuing their purpose through aligning life tasks with motifs. As they are ever-expanding, motifs are not things ever totally attainable. As such they can be a tremendous source of wonder and stimuli. Individuals begin to realize that over long periods of time, just when they think they understand themselves completely, they do something completely unpredictable.

The power of the motif is that it keeps one alive and alert to the reality that one will never totally attain or understand oneself completely. With a healthy respect for that wonderful motif in all of us, these shocks and surprises can be the rejuvenating forces that enrich and inspire our lives to ever-renewed heights.

As is clearly apparent, knowing and accessing one's sensory motif is critical in dealing with living and recovery aspects. The following outline assists in just that endeavor.

1. What is it that you love to do in a way that seems to happen naturally and just flows? While it may involve real effort, it's what you just find yourself doing or being without having to think about it. Describe three personal experiences as you answer these questions.

2. What about these experiences attracts you? Does it have something to do with the way it looks, feels and/or sounds? Look at each experience and describe what appeals to you, what you get a kick out of. What are the qualities and/or attributes common to all three that you love? Please be specific.

For example, if you enjoy flying, roller skating and team-leading a dynamic sales meeting, what common qualities, themes and/or features do these three experiences have in common? What "figure" and/or design might emerge when you review all three experiences?

What is it that you like about these experiences? What about these experiences absorbs you in some special way? What words, images, sights, sounds, smell, dreams, scenarios emerge that seem to capture unique features about these experiences? Notice the themes that seem to echo and/or resonate throughout the experiences. What structural shapes and/or forms seem to lie within, without or throughout the experiences? Allow nonverbal images, shapes and forms to emerge as you reflect and relive these experiences. How does the architecture configuration of the experiences seem to pervade or move throughout the content of what you experience?

What repeated design motif seems to transform the experience into that which is most meaningful to you? One woman's imaged structure was a beaming bright ball of fire (the sun) emitting radiant energy and warmth. Make an effort to depict your imaged structure of motif in some rough or general way as a beginning step.

Remember, you are seeking to discover some nonverbal constructed image, shape or even geometric design that may capture the way these experiences seem to structure themselves and/or move interactively through and with you. It may help to think and draw upon images, symbols and various architectural structures and objects and/or natural phenomena in nature.

What is important here is to grasp, in some way, the uniquely synergistic combination of patterned events that, even in their variations, embody a repetitive design and structural integrity. Just as you could recognize a Picasso, could you recognize your own signature and your own flowing motif's structural pattern or design?

Remember that just as you are alive, in a unique way so are your motifs. Therefore, your representations could be reflective of a dynamically evolving structuring process. For example, trees are growing, not static. Even buildings are renovated. Your images, scenarios and symbols need to be interactive with your participating in your flowing motif. This is not to say that "being" motifs (unfolding meditative patterns, mandalas, etc.) are not valid manifestations of your unique motifs. Self-interaction can be a quiet reflection of motif in itself.

The motif is a formative blueprint generating its varied uniqueness throughout your life tasks and experiences. You can get a clearer picture of your motif if you imagine it like a unique collage or vast array of your life experiences. What events stand out in areas of work, love and friendship? Imagine how many ways you sign your name. Each signature has some variation from the other. Yet what is it about all your varied signatures that lets you identify them as coming from one and the same source? Your motif's structuring process or patterned movement creates an ever-emerging design that continues to manifest itself in ever-renewing variations.

3. What purpose is served by what you love to do in these three experiences? What do you find challenging about these situations? What do you sense you've accomplished in completing or even taking on this task/endeavor? What does it in some way touch or seem to answer in your inner questioning and/or your vision of that perfect picture of your life?

For example, a thirty-six-year-old female patient claimed she had no real friends, interests or hobbies. When asked what she did for a living, the woman replied that she was a bill collector. She said that was all she enjoyed doing. When asked what purpose this served, she stated that there was a real love of how complete it felt in being able to get something out of nothing. When further explored, it was found that it was like making the desert bloom in actually having debtors come up with "flowing" revenue out of a pocket that was "dry and barren." This motif of making a desert bloom was actually a hidden sense of purpose that was like a secret oasis in her life. The woman could have taken this motif or design and applied that structural theme in various other life settings. Review your experience with this frame of reference in mind. Articulate what sense of completion and/or meaning it may have for you in terms of an inner feeling, question and/or picture.

4. Identify times when you've been remarkably successful and times when you've been remarkably disturbed. Notice that the design patterns of your successes are inside out, reversed versions of the very same design patterns of when you are disturbed.

5. Formulation of essential qualities for meaningful prosperity and success can be depicted. One's unique sensory motif characteristics + external sensory flow experiences (action-oriented artistic activity) + ability to access these two dimensions in psychosocial-vocational settings = meaningful prosperity and success. Such formulation is generative in that once it is in operation, it becomes self-perpetuating and self-emerging. For example, partners can utilize a sensory motif of being the pillars of strength. Such an artful design between partners supports a prosperous relationship.

6. How do you manifest and articulate your motif in terms of career, family, friends and personal life endeavors. To what extent can or do you find your satisfaction? How would you structure or restructure your day-to-day experiences in these areas in terms of

using your unique characteristics, sensory experiences and ability to access these dimensions in the areas of career, family and friends?

7. What resistances exist to doing what it is you love to do? What conflicts, disabling beliefs and so on prevent you from doing what you love?

A. Do you feel guilty for pursuing your own endeavors and leaving others behind? Is there a sense of undeservedness (past acts of transgression) that impairs self-esteem? As a consequence, artificial but self-imposed limits can unwittingly be set that prevent growth past a certain point.

B. What do you fear about your success? Will you be hurting others in terms of making them look bad? Overwhelming others with powerful narcissistic demands from your successes? Overwhelming yourself with your achievements, challenging your identity and boundaries of who you are and how you define yourself?

C. Are you lacking interpersonal skills in synergistically combining self-with-other and self-on-your-own in relating to both family and career/cultural/social systems? That is, do you know how to be yourself when in the company of others and, most important, when by yourself?

D. Are you lacking precision in applications of unique, personal characteristics? What are those unique contexts that most access alignment of your inherent sensory motif? Sometimes we overlook how our specialness can be applied.

E. Have you learned how to utilize past setbacks that tend to disconfirm future efforts? It's time to clean up the past.

What messages have you said to yourself and/or heard and seen from others that may have encouraged you to discount what your unique talents and artistic motifs are?

EXERCISE

The following alignment process utilizes the empowering, organizing and integrating properties of your artistic motif. With this exercise, you can begin to clean up these resistances and utilize them for achievement.

Align yourself with your motif in verbal and nonverbal ways (through those unique movements and/or sensory designs that echo your motif). For example, focus upon the various forms of music, painting, craft or work that strengthen and reaffirm your structural design. Recall the three experiences you love to do. Create a working symbol or design that captures unique structural features of your motif. Now, temporarily align yourself with those negative messages that are limiting you. Ask what they are trying to protect you from? Let yourself notice nonverbal as well as verbal signs, memories, associations, events, past and present dialogues with yourself and others that relate to these messages of unhealthy "protection." If you feel a sense of more or less discomfort, let yourself stay with it long enough so you can give it a symbol, shape or name.

Now take the imaged structure of your motif and saturate it with the uncomfortable symbol and/or shape of unhealthy, negative protection. Notice the contrast between your motif of what you love to do and the awkward and/or uncomfortable response you get from the negative symbol. As you notice this contrast or juxtaposition, embrace the paradoxical, conflicting nature in the context of feeling what you love to do as contrasted with the injunctions that seem to prevent you from doing it. Now, simply continue to focus on the symbols of the motif, the discomfort and the juxtaposition of the contrast itself.

Instead of trying to force any change, just allow the unique design of your sensory motif to guide you in aligning the symbols as they move with each other in an increasingly coherent, unified whole. Let your alignment with all symbols come to be guided by the intricate design of your sensory motif itself. Take all the time you need to allow these symbols to rearrange themselves in ways that most resonate with your sensory motif. This is a synergistic process that will result in a sometimes subtle and sometimes not-so-subtle set of personal shifts. The integration process that takes place is reflective of your core self and innermost character. If there is a sense of "stuckness," then just allow your focus to center on the structural design of the motif, letting the unhealthy "protection" dissolve into the motif.

Like all change processes, this type of integration could occur in a stepwise fashion or in a single step where a sudden and dramatic total transformation results. Such changes can lead to a highly integrated, self-actualized state of being.

TENETS OF PURPOSEFUL SELF

The following tenets describe the major properties of purposeful self. They are expressed in summary form.

I. Inherently self-organizing intelligence manifests and moves in unique, lattice or web-like motifs.

II. The inherent nature of this self-organizing field of intelligence is the core structure of what we have come to know as *real, self, higher self, Christ self,* and so on.

III. Self is purposeful pursuing alignment of one's conscious and unconscious mind in such a way as to harmonize and resonate with its inherent properties of uniqueness of being. This is known as flow.

IV. Purposeful self is the core of "I"-ness and is an identity of being that is expressed in doing its life work embodied in its everyday work.

V. When self-focus is aligned with its own unique interaction inherent with its inner order and purpose of being, the flow state emerges.

VI. Purposeful self evolves as a "strange attractor" (chaos theory) in that they are patterns that reproduce themselves in progressively familiar but different ways that approach but never totally complete or achieve the wholeness (Gestalt) of their being.

VII. Purposeful self is an inherently organized field of intelligence. The self-organizing intelligence pursues unifying life themes that are undifferentiated prior to birth, expands and permeates our lives as we grow and encounter both triumph and trauma in our physical experience and remains unfinished and evolutionary even when we make our transition to the next quantum level.

VIII. The degree to which the individual chooses or to be or not to be aligned with this inherent life-sustaining purpose determines the quality, energy, flow, health, longevity and generative achieved expansiveness (feeling interconnected synergistically) in all life areas: family, work, love, selfhood, success levels, wisdom, guidance and so on.

IX. Inherent, purposeful self involves organizing dynamics of unified life themes operative from conception (or before). As in the Big Bang theory of the universe, one emerges holographically through constant life-evolving, expansive processes of differentiation and integration. The degree to which one allows encounter with chaos to occur facilitates flow states which are needed to achieve a higher ordering of one's universe. The holographic emergence is embedded holism throughout the organism. From the lowest to the highest levels of one's differentiated design structures, one's signature of purposeful motif is imbued.

X. Purposeful Self Theory

A. Inherent self-ordering of dynamic organization.

B. Ever-expanding and differentiating into all life areas.

C. Unique mosaic web-like tapestry of one's own internal perspective of time, space and quantum level of experience and emerging position in the universe.

D. One cannot not be purposeful, in that even when one seems to be doing meaningless activities this is a sign of preparation for higher ordering. In disharmony with one's self, there is pressing for expression: for example, self-hate is self-diffusion needing alignment of self as purposeful.

E. Purpose in life is always present. It is detected through formative, inner-directed right-brain experiences of intuitive wholeness, symbols, images, senses, dreams and so on.

F. It informs what and who one is. It is who one is. It filters one's way of interpreting one's self and the universe in that it creates perceptual positioning from which all experience of self and universe emerges and is formed.

G. When centered in purposeful self, one can experience expanded integration and oneness with the larger-than-self whole.

H. Inherent to purposefulness is the self-organizing capacity of unique, intrinsic ordering motifs. These can be perceived and experienced as the self selectively interacts with the universe. The possible, creative orderings and manifestations are infinite (artist, poet, mathematician, mechanic, etc.).

I. The purposeful self is holographic (holistic) to the uniqueness of the universe in that its infinite potential of possibilities parallel the infinite nature of the expanding universe.

Chapter Ten

Motifs: Soul and Spirituality

The uniqueness of an individual is manifest through his or her idiosyncratic, artistic motif. Such unique artistry of motif has been presented as imbued throughout the multiple levels of body/brain/mind and psychosocial dimensions. Moving from one dimension to another (body to brain, brain to mind, mind to family, mind to meaning) represents a transduction (transfer of formative information) from one medium to another.

Motif provides a formative "bridge" translating meaningful information design structures from one medium level to another. They are holographic, retaining the uniqueness of motif's design structures resonating throughout internal and external levels of individual and psychosocial contexts. The previous chapters have illustrated numerous examples of how the individual's unique motif is congruently transduced from one level to another. They illustrate how the interfacing of body with mind, person with family invokes interactive movements of motif within the individual and between psychosocial contexts. Movement from one level of organization to another is facilitated by the unique artistry of the self's motif.

The foundation has now been established throughout the previous chapters to move to the next level or dimension known as soul and spirituality. Interfacing throughout this all-pervasive medium of mediums presumes one has evolved in personal growth and maturation through previous levels. Such evolution involves progressive alignment and resonant articulation with one's ever-expanding, unique motif. Accumulation of alignment and resonant growth is similar to the concentric rings within a tree trunk. For every year of tree growth, there is a larger ring that expansively encircles all the inner circles that represent previous years of growth. The unique design structure of the most expansive outer ring (which is not a perfect circle) builds upon previous circular designed rings each with their own unique variations and derivations. Yet, there is a similar pattern or motif moving through each of the rings, connecting them in some resonant fashion. Such holographic, patterned movements are representative of the tree's inherent, organizing motif. Upon such accumulation and maturation, the individual can now seek to expand to the next expansive "rung" on the developmental ladder, that of soul and spirituality.

MOTIF, SOUL AND TRANSFORMATIONAL OBJECTS

The presence of formative, flowing motifs transcends physical, concrete levels in the human being. Becker and Seldon (1985) in *The Body Electric* describe their findings of measuring the existence of the body's electromagnetic energy field. In reviewing their research on energy meridians treated by Chinese acupuncture, Becker and Sheldon found electrical measures of current where the Chinese system of body energy depicted these meridians to be. These invisible energy fields were amplified at the denoted places where acupuncturists place their needles to adjust and harmonize energy flow for healing. In addition, they found that each energy point has its own unique mapping or design of energy. These energy fields constitute an internal constellation of energy design structures that flow along the nervous system.

Illness is the impairment or interruption of balanced energy formatively flowing through the human organism. Healing is the harmonizing of energy with the unique formativeness and movement of the individual. These researchers found that these formative, flowing energy fields of motif were conducted through the insulation sheaths (Schwann cells) of neurons.

Such invisible energy fields that harmonize the human organism are transcendent to the naked eye yet can be verified through measurements of electrical potentiation. The distinctive design and flow of such invisible fields are but an example of how formative motifs are imbued throughout physical and nonphysical (energy) levels of the individual. There are distinctive, unique motifs in energy and spirit that formatively flow through the soul of self. The articulation of distinguishing formativeness strikes at the heart and soul of core self.

Depiction of soul in human beings extends formative motifs into highly refined states of articulation. As the human being evolves, internal, formative patterns progress from large, gross levels of expression (two- and four-celled divisions of the zygote known as blastula and gastrula) to refined, internal articulations (millions of intricate neural pathways in the brain's cortex).

Such pathways articulate intricate artistic design structures enabling complex altered states of mental functioning to arise. Crick alludes (in Searle, 1997) to these complexities in describing emergent properties of the brain evolving into mind function. Evolution of complex mind/body articulations allows the self's unique, formative motif exquisite expression. Manifestation of motif's complexity to such a degree strikes at the very soul of self. Soul is not so much a complex function of mind as it is one of mindfulness, which articulates formative, holistic states of being. The greater the manifestations of unique motifs, the deeper access to soul. Yet soul (and spirit) are present at all levels of self and can be awakened through resonating with unique motifs imbued throughout these levels.

Such levels occur in the emergent properties of the brain/mind. The emergence of mind from brain gives rise to mental structures. These mental structures take the form of ego formation at the prebirth level known as the unconscious ego (Bollas, 1987). The unconscious ego does not involve repression of conscious material. Rather, it relates to the formativeness and design of the neonate's unconsciousness. Bollas (1987) refers to it as the ego's idiom, which is an evolution of one's inherent disposition. He states that such inherent designing of the ego is there prior to birth and serves to differentiate and distinguish the neonate's personality.

The unconscious ego is depicted as generating organizing principles in the neonate's psyche. These organizing principles develop in the unconscious ego design structure into an established, complex system. Establishment of a highly complex system of mental structuring precedes cognition (conscious awareness) or presence of one's sense of self. It is what Bollas (1987) defines as the unthought known, which is an existential not cognitive experience.

The underpinnings of the unconscious ego with its own inherent design structure of organization are precisely those of unique motifs. The preemptive, existential experience of inherent organizing principles in such mental structures clearly refers to imbued characteristics of formative motifs.

Development of the unconscious ego's inherent design and organizing principles initially occurs in the womb. It is in the unique interaction of the evolving unconscious ego with the mother's internal environment (indirectly affected by the mother's temperamental disposition) where transformation of the neonate occurs. The first object (significant other) that transforms the neonate's evolving experience is called the transformational object (Bollas, 1987).

The unconscious, organizing ego interacts in selective ways with the mother in manifesting its own motif. Yet the unique experience (filtered through distinctive motifs) of mother as an impetus of development serves to make her a transformational object. The neonate selectively experiences characteristics in its interaction with mother, which becomes its way of manifesting uniqueness. These characteristics become part of a psychosoma memory that is felt or known but not thought or conceived. As such, they are ingrained into the core beginnings of the neonate. It is essential to note that the neonate's unconscious ego interweaves its unique formativeness into the complexities of interaction with the first transformational object (mother).

Some characteristic experiences may be healthy and grow while others may be destructive and abusive (borderline personalities may have such experiences). The point is that some of the neonate's unique, organizing principles are fused and incorporated in such transformational experiences with mother.

These transformational experiences now become psychosoma anchors of preverbal memory. When similar experiences are encountered in the person's adult life, aesthetic, sacred qualities are ascribed to them. For example, if the person encounters a powerful, unexpected sense of connection through walking on a beach, writing a sonnet, climbing a mountain or so on, the impact of such a significant effect creates a sense of the mystical. Yet this is not simply some preverbal memory falsely experienced as a spiritual event. Rather, it is the encapsulation of one's core, unique motif precipitously encoded into the preverbal characteristic memory of the first transformational object. The accessing of one's uniqueness of motif in characteristic transformational objects (mothering-like design encounters) is what spiritualizes the encounter.

There was an old Zenith TV commercial that stated "the quality goes in before the name goes on." Indeed, the uniqueness of motif (unconscious ego) is imbued in encounters with the first transformational object. While the form of the encounter may serve to reawaken ingrained, preverbal, psychosoma memories, it is the embedded uniqueness in these encounters which accesses the sacred and spiritual. The transformational object encounter is the eggshell that contains the uniqueness of motif's egg. The formativeness of the individual's uniqueness can be contained in many forms yet they are merely its container or vessel of the unfolding sacred and spiritual encounters of the soul.

One may describe the soul as being touched by the spiritual experience of an oceanic view. The encounter could be relegated to its similarity with characteristics of the first transformational object. Yet, the oceanic view is only the vessel displaying and imbuing the genuine uniqueness of one's formative motif, which is the core of transformation in all encounters. The structural design of the neonate's unconscious ego is imbued into the first transformational object. That is what makes the first such encounter transforming. While it would be quite difficult to extract the unique organizing motif from its fusion with transformational objects (significant others), it is essential to comprehend that such an object embodies the motif's uniqueness which is recurrently manifest in all future encounters. The oceanic view may reactivate preverbal memory of transformational objects, but it is the embedded uniqueness of motif, then and now, with which the soul resonates with sacredness and spirituality.

Soul is the embodiment of heart, mind and will, exquisitely releasing the essential uniqueness of the self's motif. Soul extracts and forges the embodiment of uniqueness in a human being. The soul of the self seeps into every aspect of our inner and outer life (dreams, myths, archetypes, art, etc.). It involves creative life expressions of one's unique essence. Soul manifests through artistry in ordinary (Moore, 1992) as well as extraordinary life experience. It is the soul that unlocks the David figure that Michelangelo sculpted out of marble. Soul is the connection of one's unique mystery unfolding in the events of an individual's moment-to-moment experience. Moore (1992) describes the soul as the domain existing somewhere below understanding and above unconsciousness. He proposes that the soul's instrument is neither body nor mind. Rather, it is imagination which infuses life events with soulfulness. Imagination, as described previously, involves formative, symbolic entities, which proliferate and expand motif's design structures. Giving imagination to ordinary and extraordinary life events (from doing housework to giving birth to a child) nourishes the formative process of bringing the inanimate to animation or life itself.

The soul's ability to symbolize and inject the uniqueness of individual motif into seemingly inane events is the living miracle of the soul's animation of meaningfulness on life. Through attending to the soul, one can learn to discern meaning and purpose in an otherwise empty and inanimate, thing-oriented, materialistic way of life. Soul attending involves seeing the material world with "soft eyes" opening to multidimensional enrichment. One Reiki healer depicts seeing with the eyes of the soul in the following passage: "When you can see other dimensions — observe them through physical eyes with the aide of your third or perceptive eye [the third eye is the energy center or *chakra* located in the center of your forehead] — you know that which is heavy in light force and that which is light — you see slow moving low vibrations and fast moving high vibrations — to look at the flowering bloom of spring trees and it makes your heart flutter and you can literally feel it dance in your chest" (K. L. Feeney, 2000)

As noted in the previous chapter, meaning and purpose resonate to one's innate, sensory motif. The selective, formative interaction of perceiving sensory experience through the imaginative filter of motifs provides relevance and meaning. Such selective observation and participation in life events invoke creative formative motifs. As one attends and participates, engaging in relationships, career and family events and the like, the soul emerges in creative nuances and subtleties of formativeness.

Motif is the essence of such unique formativeness. Motif is the artistic movement that details the magnificent recognition of nuanced color schemes in a sunset, the miracle of child raising and the exquisite agony of loss and the self-resurrection that happens once you move on, emerge and grow from that loss. It is the individual's unique way of creating formative order and meaning out of chaos. If life is a set of Rorschach cards (inkblots), then motif is the creative mode of construction. Each person selects and constructs in their outer world the embodiment of which is their inner motif. One sees the motif of the soul in the uniqueness of one's artistic creations.

Only by reaching down into the depths of one's felt sense (how one genuinely and deeply feels, constructs and uniquely pulls it all together) can the soul's motif manifest itself. Moore (1992) describes this process as a mysterious journey not unlike that of Ulysses in Homer's *The Odyssey*. The hero, Ulysses, endures a complex and arduous journey before he is able to return home to reign as father of his household.

The whole premise of spiritual evolution is based upon this. No situation is presented nor challenge created by one's higher self and co-created with and by interactions with others unless one is sufficiently spiritually mastered to handle it. One will always have the tools to handle opportunities to evolve. One will not have loss without spiritual resources of strength and endurance to deal with it. One will not have suffering unless it is best at the time. It takes great confidence in the universe to believe this. Such confidence in this paradigm or motif of readiness is otherwise known as faith. Such an epoch endeavor is the soul's journey gathering the rich variety of qualities needed for its own emergence. Indeed, in going within, challenging and encountering one's demons and dragons, there is discovery of a hidden maze or labyrinth (one's subconsciousness) from which emerges access to the soul's motif.

If life is difficult at any given time, then learning to do the good work of inner search and discovery of the soul's motif can ease the load. Everything that goes on outside reflects some unhealed part of an individual. Until one takes the responsibility to understand and resolve what is behind the things and events not working in life, their reoccurrence is inevitable. After resolving unhealed parts of ourselves through inner motif alignment, external events almost effortlessly will align themselves in healthy ways through entrainment of motifs. If your kitchen is falling apart, spending more time domesticizing motifs enhances attentiveness towards creating a sense of home. When one does the good work of soul searching, alignment with meaning and purpose simultaneously occurs. In such instances, healing and brilliance of improvisational solutions to life's problems literally flow into one's consciousness. Alignment with one's soul requires intense hard work and courage. Yet it is the lack of inner search and discovery of our inner labyrinth that makes the challenge of life appear so overwhelming.

Attending to one's inner motif provides a context of framing, shaping and designing one's life experience. To exist is to manifest essence of one's formativeness and uniqueness. When this is understood at a sensory level of embodied uniqueness (experience of ourselves in an idiosyncratic mode), alignment of our soul's motif reveals creative formations, resourceful in our movement through life. For example, one twenty-five-year-old woman had a traumatic encounter when her boyfriend of four years abandoned her after he had promised to stay with her after delivery of their child. She was an honor roll student with numerous high quality colleges pursuing her with scholarships. She turned them all away deciding to have what she believed would be a marriage and family. When her boyfriend abandoned her, she felt devastated and victimized, becoming bitter and resentful towards everyone including her child.

With a great deal of soul searching and inner work, she aligned with her inner need for intimacy and individual recognition. Her inner work involved reviewing her early childhood with a caring but distant, unavailable father and a critical, unhappy mother. Her high level of performance in high school had left her feeling empty in her success. Success did not mitigate her loneliness. She accessed her inner mode of operating through careful attendance to the sacred complexity of her motif of connection. She reformulated her life complex as one which now nourished her lifelong abandoned inner child. The way she had been treating her own offspring echoed the way her inner child had been raised. Accessing her unique sense of self and mode of operating liberated her to self-attend and self-care. She learned to love and care for her both inner and outer child.

The soul's motif encourages deep exploration of the unknown and mysterious both within and outside the individual. Brilliant and healing improvisational perspectives become possible in such explorations. As Moore (1992) suggests, it is important to allow one's life drama to unfold itself in its more unique and idiosyncratic ways. As in the case of the twenty-five-year-old single parent, she allowed herself to encounter and engage her drama and her darkness, and let it play itself out working it through to its most unique, profound meaning and learning. In letting our dramatic (and traumatic) experiences grow and mature, the implied themes, symbolic implications and creative unique formulations and reformulations are made possible.

The potentiation of unique reformulations can be enhanced through the creation and utilization of sacred space (Pearsall, 2000). Such sacred places can be any uniquely meaningful area (garden, church, special area of one's room, etc.) where being and/or meditating with one's self is possible. Pearsall (2000) describes these places where wish consciousness conditioning can occur. Individuals can focus upon a unique desire or wish in their lives. In so doing, the sacred place where the unique wish is requested (through reflection, affirmation, meditation, etc.) takes on coherence or formative ordering. For example, Pearsall describes how tiny, electromagnetic devices are energized by concentrated thought (purposeful thinking and/or prayer). The ordering or formative increase of coherence effected through focused thought at the sacred space (wish imbued area) potentiates the wish coming true. The wishing space is formatively more coherent after such focused thought. As such, the sacred (wishing) place functions like an antenna drawing in needed resources.

The intriguing findings (Pearsall, 2000) indicate that focused, formative thought affects major physiological alterations. Changes in blood samples, Ph levels, liver enzymes and even DNA configurations have all been detected. DNA functions as a toroidal coil (Pearsall, 2000) folding back on itself (formative motif). Such enfolding is similar to an atomic mushroom cloud. Subtle alterations in DNA's formative enfolding may be affected by formative thought of intention. The intense, deep focusing of formative thought (purposeful wishing) can resonate throughout mind/body levels of formativeness. Dropping a pebble in the middle of a pond sends out formative wave alterations through the body of water. When the sacred place of "the body of water" is attuned (coherent) to formative thoughts, new orderings of formativeness can ripple throughout the system. The depth of formative focus can reach the soul of the self. The deeper one delves into his or her unique formative motif, the more the soul is invoked to do its work.

This kind of work invoking the soul's motif unfolds unique characteristics with its own roots and wings of internal design structures. The inner motif work engages and entrains with external people, places and things in ways that lead to synchronicity of events (Jung, 1971). Such synchronicity has been previously described as uniqueness of motif in action. The fortuitous unfolding of manifest, unforeseen yet beneficial events is the soul's complexity motif at its most profound depths. Such depth of synchronicity results from cultivation of one's artistic complexity.

Interestingly, Moore (1992) describes the soul as a font (design) of what one is. The formative aspects of soul's motif in extricating one's uniqueness are strongly implied in such descriptions. Motif is not an operation of one's ego or willpower. Rather, motif is the formative will of soul creating through artistic design structures transformative meaning and renewal in one's life experience.

MOTIF AND SOUL NURTURANCE

Moore (1992) depicts artistic facets in nurturing one's soul. He describes the careful selection of places to walk, scents, oils, where to live and so on as affecting the quality of soulful engagement. These and other specific facts of one's life experience are unique derivations of the soul's motif. Cultivating and nurturing the unique arrangements and design structuring of soul's motif enhance one's quality of life and spirituality. He advocates depth and attentiveness in ordinary, daily experiences as nurturance of soulfulness. Such depth involves imbuing ordinary events with symbolic meaningfulness and sacred rites which enhances the soul's care. Such an approach actually infuses common experiences (washing a car or paying bills) with symbolic meaning representative of one's formative flow of unique patterning. Creative symbolism and imagination construct a domain of possibility. Such a domain liberates unique formative patterns of one's motif to project themselves onto the confusion and ambiguity of life events. Discovering the healing meaning of one's life is to unleash the inherent formative motif manifest in the grains of sand of our time in this world. Life means what our soul's motif projects it to mean. The seeds of our design flower in the fertile cultivation of the artistry of our motif.

HUMANE MOTIFS

The soul's motif accesses what is humane and redeeming within our mammalian nature. While human beings have instinctive survival (flight or fight) mechanisms, primitive biological mechanisms can be overcome. Paradoxically, this involves incorporating primitive biology (rather than its denial) through accessing higher ordering design structures in the cerebral cortex. The intricacy of design and artistic organization (columnar arrangements and multiple layers of complexity) provide pathways to higher formative consciousness. The soul's motif is imbued not only in one's day-to-day events but in the very core of one's psychophysiological design. When the nature of one's being is accessed, it is the inherent formativeness of unique motifs soulfully manifesting themselves through every level and fiber of the individual's biopsychosocial level.

Formativeness is, as previously noted, in the vibrational subatomic components of matter itself. Problems and crisis manifest themselves when fixations and rigidities prevent the soul's formative flow of unique derivations to mature and proliferation. One might suggest that evil is the result of truncated growth and development of formative motifs.

Eating disorders such as anorexia nervosa have their own soul's expressions. When allowed to grow and mature (allowing the deviated motif to evolve into fruitful derivations), the story and drama emerge in a symbolism all its own. The narcissism of self to gain control of one's needs evolves into the soul's hunger to align with a self-direction that cultivates its own artistic satiation without guilt or shame. Reformulation of complex life entanglements is potentiated through soulful engagement and alignment with the font of unique individual motifs.

SOUL'S MOTIF AND CIRCULARITY

Moore (1992) depicts working with the soul as a circular process. For example, dreams reveal a structure that is continually repeated and reviewed. Cycling through such a design process grows, materializes and extricates symbolic and formative meanings that are resourceful in one's life. The person recovering from alcoholism is encouraged to repeat and retell his or her story endlessly to literally and figuratively realign his or her his-story. The reformulation of his-story alters the meaning, structure and symbolic form enhancing recovery. Alcoholics acknowledge alcoholism as "who they are" and, ironically, are liberated from trying to control. In the surrender experience (giving up ego control), the person is freed of self-conflicting constraints releasing uniqueness of self. The controlling ego has been lifted out of one's way facilitating genuine self-expression.

Circular processes are also involved in the type of questioning utilized in the treatment of dysfunctional family organizations. As previously described, families exhibit formative patterns of interactions. The use of circular questioning strikes at the family soul (honing, shaping and maturing healthy innate formative motifs).

GRACE AND SALVATION THROUGH THE SOUL'S MOTIF

The conversion and healing experience through soul-searching journeys reveals hidden creative orderings of unique motifs. The experience of conversion and recovery is what is referred to as grace and salvation. Through soul work of formative motif realignment, the sense of being blessed by the grace of God and salvation from evil emerges. The soul's motif is resonant with a larger-than-self higher power. Alignment with the soul's motif involves a parallel transcendence in alignment with a higher power. The larger-than-self experience augments the union of soul and spirituality. It is from such spiritual and holy union that grace and salvation arise. One does not earn grace or salvation. One surrenders soul's motif with spiritual union, and there by the grace of a power greater than one's self-ego may conversion in spirituality arise. The Bible refers to dramatic experiences of the Christian slayer Saul being struck down off his high horse by a bolt of lightning. When he arose, he was a changed (altered formativeness) man, so to speak. The symbolism is both literal and figurative. Going down from one's ego control and arising renewed, realigned with his soul's motif effected Saul's conversion. Obviously not all transformations need be quite so dramatic. Yet, each of us experiences symbolic forms releasing, trusting and evolving faith in intrinsic, transformative evolutions.

THE MOTIF'S SHADOW

Moore (1992) describes two kinds of shadows (the dark side of existence) that Jung (1971) also depicted. The first was how an individual might reject or turn away from the soul and the other involved evil as an absolute existence within both the person and the world at large. Willingness to deal with these shadows is part of the soul's work and evolution of its spirituality. The courage and persevering quality of aligning with soul work both acknowledge that evil exists and extricate genuine motifs from false deviations.

Acknowledging idiosyncratic and even eccentric aspects of an individual's uniqueness is the soul's motif acknowledging itself. Movement to the light (spirituality) evolves when unique articulations of an individual resonate with a sense of sacredness (accessing artistic motifs). Unfolding the uniqueness of soul's motif evolves over the course of one's life. When all is said and done, such unfolding may be the Purpose of one's life purpose. Each individual evolves his or her own soul's motif version of this Purpose of life purpose.

The soul's sacredness can be expressed as a working or crafting of one's artistry. Moore (1992) refers to Plato's expression *techne tou biou*, "the craft of life," in depicting the sacred craft or artwork of the soul. If art is the soul's sacredness, then motif is the "soul" of its artistry. The soul's motif is the artistry of one's uniqueness crafting itself in the large and small events of one's life. The skill and attention involved in such crafting require sensitivity to one's sensory experience of self as well as observation of the world at large.

Attentiveness to nuances and subtleties in observing such events as a child playing, sunsets, swimming, love making and cleaning house activates unique sensory experiences of the moment-to-moment unfolding. Meaning and flow unfold in keen attention and sensitization in the art and craft of being one's unique self in the mindfulness of the moment.

The soul's motif crafts moment-to-moment encounters as brilliant unfolding improvisations of unique, formative manifestations. As such, walking through the woods becomes an I-thou encounter of renewal (Buber, 1958). The light through the trees, the wind, the smell of fresh pine cones all unveil a beautiful cacophony unfolding as if for the first time. Intensity and vividness infuse the experiential encounter as the senses come alive in unique, formative observations. Learning to see and experience daily and life events as if for the first time (the child's innocence of fresh observance) unveils the uniqueness of ourselves as manifest in the uniqueness of what is before us. For some, the beauty and mosaic designs of a peacock's tail or colorful rainbow may convey the soul of their motif. For others, it may be the brilliant flash of lightning or white water rapids of the Colorado River. Each person manifests his or her soul's motif in deeply personal, unique ways of observing, engaging and infusing symbolic and creative improvisations. The ubiquitous, formative expressions available to each individual parallel his or her soul's motif of artistic expression. The possibilities are omnipresent at the soul's level of unique, artistic motifs.

Motif is an artistic concept in itself referring to a style and/or set of themes in how one's creative art is manifest. The soul's artistry has its motif reaching the depths of universal and spiritual sacredness. At such far-reaching depths and breadths of formativeness, accessing one's soul motif resonates with the omnipresence of spirituality. It is with such resonance that the soul's motif embraces and embodies the sacredness of spirituality.

The soul's motif reveals complexity and at times confusion. The difficulties of human existence require soulful engagement. Encountering conflicts, dramas and dilemmas in one's life requires inner search and deep soul searching. Repetitive experiences of unresolved dramas begin to artfully weave their web of unfolding, learning evolution and involution (self-integration). The soul's love embraces complexity in one's life, engaging fear, insecurity and guilt. As redundant encounters replay themselves in one's life (divorce, rejection, hurt, failure, loss, etc.), new discoveries and learnings unfold. It is the soul's artful work of honing and shaping a multitude of derivational, multifaceted encounters and perspectives.

It is the soul's motif artfully crafting itself through trials by fire that is the cutting edge of the sculptor's blade releasing the omnipresent artistry from within. Honing, shaping, designing multifaceted design structures of one's unique motif is the soul work of one's life. The beauty in the beast of each individual necessitates the soul's working its motif grasping and encountering numerous facets of such juxtapositioning. The inner search and journey of the soul's designing and carving its own motif reveals through maturation the beauty in the beast of human complexity.

The numerous contradictions of life (rational/irrational, order/chaos, love/brutality, etc.) are configurations with which to struggle, challenge and mature. In seeking resolution to life's dilemmas, the soul's motif is honed, designed and manifest in a multitude of derivational intricacies. The weathered features of elderly wise men and women soulfully glowing with the artistic patina of age reflect not answers to life, but answer the soul's calling to artistic living with life. The soul's motif is the way of the artist in its most symbolic formativeness. Whether an Einstein, Picasso or person in any walk of life, artistic grace under fire is the soul's motif in courage and brilliance of formative living.

The sacredness of working the soul's motif involves ordeals, rituals and journeys of vast complexities. Raising a child as a teenager, divorcing after twenty-five years of marriage, recovering from addiction, the death of a lifelong spouse and other life experiences represent nodal points of change embracing the formative work of soul's motif. These and other occurrences in the outer world — in one's past — and things stored inside of oneself cannot be fathomed unless one were to seriously delve into the depths of one's consciousness. The way that you perceive and deal with the world around you today, in the here and now, is a direct reflection of your past and of your healed and unhealed parts — of your complete being from the first time your soul came into manifestation to the time and place where it now exists. The now that you perceive is the result of what you have created in throughout your lifetime. If what you see now is something you do not like, all you have to do is discover what unhealed part of yourself is creating it.

Each occurrence in your life, good, bad, beautiful or ugly, is the most wonderful opportunity your soul can have to challenge itself, to confront itself, to push itself, to bring everything into the light. See it all without judgment from a place of safety, of complete alignment with our unique motif, of complete protection from all that is higher. Then and only then can you see God in everything. Then can you know that God is everything. Your emotions become your tool rather than your ruler when your body becomes your sacred vessel aligned with unique motif. While bad things can happen to good people, answering faith in our spiritual motif allows us to remain untouched — safe from pain, fear or anything that might distract us from our spiritual course — that is, unless we choose to put faith and belief into these things. How we choose to interpret some event gives it its meaning and reality to us. As Eleanor Roosevelt once said, no one can hurt you unless you let them. Absolute belief and faith can work wondrous miracles and move mountains. Such intensity and fever can access and generate brilliant and momentous improvisational solutions. Remember the hidden empowerment tapped when a mother lifts a car to save her child and the inner healing powers within individuals accessing moments of remembered wellness. Committed to faith in our God-given, spiritual motif we experience protection and safe places. Nothing "bad" can ever happen to us — only growth can happen to us — only spiritual evolution can happen to us. This is true on an individual level and on a mass level. This is not to say that crime, holocausts, famine, and such do not occur. It is to say that, while one may walk through the "valley of death," walking in the light of spiritual alignment allows one to "fear no evil." This truth has been evident throughout the ages. Rossi (1986) reports that when the United States dropped the atomic bomb on Japan, only one house was left standing at ground zero, and it was known to be one of exceptional spirituality. It is the journey into one's heart of darkness that reveals the intrinsic ordering and spiritual meaning of one's soul work. Stripped of social roles and cultural supports, individuals who have lost everything through a series of disasters discover inherent principles of formative designs. Note the resilience of holocaust survivors and those suffering in totalitarian societies.

The journey or odyssey down one's life path unfolds unique, formative opportunities for the soul's motif to reveal its intrinsic presence. Its artistry is a route of discovery through the maze of illusions and distractions of what Rheinhold Nieburh (1980) calls little "g" gods (domination, materialism, hedonism, fear, anger, etc.). Learning to discern the soul's motif in both the everyday and the major crises of life reveals intrinsic formative and ordering properties grounded in spiritual sacredness. Only when the sun goes down (crisis, loss, encountering the unknown, etc.) does heavenly artistry of stellar constellations reveal itself in the night sky. In darkness, there is light.

Whatever one's religion, artistry is manifest in its writings, cathedrals, synagogues, temples, paintings, sculptures, rituals, prayers, psalms, robes and so on. When the Pope authorized Michelangelo to paint the Sistine Chapel in Rome during the Renaissance, the motif of creation was Michelangelo's soul crafting its artistic sacredness. The background in Michelangelo's famous scene of the finger of God reaching out towards Adam's finger reflects the precise design of the human brain (Meshberger, 1990). It is motif synchronistically manifesting itself in art and science. Michelangelo's hand moved through uniqueness of motif. It was a sacred movement of creation and oneness. As he painted God's finger reaching to Adam's, there was a slight gap (or synapse) between the fingers. It was almost like the synaptic gap between neurons in the brain (neurons never actually touch but are mediated by the "spark" of electrical neurotransmitters). The spiritual "spark" occurs in the artist through the uniqueness of creation motifs.

Michelangelo, in connecting with his unique motif of creation (for the Sistine Chapel), was actually reflecting his own synaptic connection with spiritual union. Mediation between spirituality and soul is "sparked" through core uniqueness of motif. Michaelangelo painted through his core unique motifs of creation and therefore painted with (in resonance to) the hand of God. The uniqueness of our handwritten signature reveals the signature of Divinity. The unique motif of our signature reveals the Holy Scripture of our lives. Uniqueness of motif is the spiritual spark that transduces formativeness of information from level to level. As such, soul and spirit unification is scientifically and artistically imbued throughout the multilevel organization of the individual self.

Connection and access to unique motifs may necessitate assistance and revelation in the form of a mentor or guide. There is a guide or daimon involved in the soul's work (Moore, 1992). The soul's work is crafting its artful expression of unique sacredness. Symbolic representations, whether from internal or external sources (inner voice and/or significant person) serve to assist the individual in resonating with their unique motif. Uniqueness of the soul is its motif of formative grace and courage journeying through trials and tribulation. The inner search and challenge of motif matures and reveals itself. In the minuscule, moment-to-moment event or major nodal point of change, the soul's motif is in the unique, improvisational sacredness of artful living.

MOTIFS: TRANSFORMATIVE BRIDGES OF SOUL AND SPIRITUALITY

Soul is the mysterious existence of one's multitude of complex sensory experiences and perspectives. Spirituality involves a transcendence of formative values in a reality larger than self (one's higher power). The holy union of soul and spirituality is the liberation of one's entranced self (or ego illusion) into the harmony of sacredness. It is the soul's awakening in the larger self. The alignment of soul and spirituality is a union of multiple complexity aspiring into higher ordering of harmonious oneness. Such a union is never complete but moves in a dynamic of dialectical tension approaching but never achieving perfect harmony in this world.

The soul's complexity reflects a multidimensional God (values) in one's life. Such multifacetedness is reflective of the soul's complexity that transcends into a spiritual harmony of oneness (higher power). The soul's capacity for multiple perspectives represents a nuanced range of differentiated, sensory facets in one's experience. Witness the reverie and sensory reverberations of one's walk in the woods or watching children play. Spirituality is the confluence of harmonic union as the cacophony of the subtle and nuance orchestration into symphonic wholeness. Moore (1992) utilizes the cathedral as a metaphor of such union. The rich sacred carvings, sculptures, chapels and interior body of the cathedral gracefully come together in intricate transcendence as the steeple rises into thin air.

The interactive union of spiritual soulfulness is not one of all or nothing but rather one of degree. The extent to which the complexity of soul's motif is imbued in the sacred art of spiritual transcendence is the extent to which this union exists in one's life. The harmonic orchestration of the soul's complex differentiation into spirituality's transcendent wholeness represents the organizational principles of unique motifs.

Motifs differentiate themselves through derivational design structures (shades of meaning, variety of perspectives, variations in one's signature, etc.). At the same time, motifs intricately orchestrate through expansive formativeness of intricate web-like configurations, harmonizing these design structures as unfolding (or enfolding) organisms. The interplay of complex, derivational design structures with intricate holistic configurations is the "motif" of motifs. It is also the motif of soulful/spirituality. Motif is imbued throughout the mind/body system of the individual. Therefore, one could state that soulfulness/spirituality is incarnatively imbued throughout the mind/body interface. Imbued incarnation of motif resurrects the body and spirit of holy union.

The spirit or soul represents a higher ordering level beyond mind and body. However, movement from one level (or medium) to another occurs through bridging motifs. The design structures (cell assemblies, columnar cortex layers, neurotransmitters, hormones, etc.) transduce formative information from one level of organization (mind, brain, body) to another. The intricate harmonizing of differential design structures through expansive, formative motifs is precisely the way soulful spirituality transcends into sacred holy union. The mind/brain/body system is the incarnation (temple or cathedral) of sacred soulfulness and spirituality. Each distinctive human being is the blessed, unique vessel, which embodies universal sacredness.

Motifs are the transformative bridges throughout the organizational levels of each human being. Increased alignment and harmony with one's unique motif and its derivational design structures send an outward harmonizing and higher ordering transcendence throughout one's hierarchy of organization. It's as if a pebble were dropped into a pond sending expansive, circular waves outward throughout the medium. The movement of motif expands throughout the body, brain, mind, soul and spirituality.

Movement of motif's design structures is embodied in different formative manifestations while preserving the design's integrity. These various formative manifestations are organizationally or medium specific. The body level involves physical body shape and form, internal organization of tissues and organ shape, size and so on. Brain level organization involves the complexity of neural pathways, various brain structures, cell assemblies just to name a few. Mind functioning involves design structures related to intelligence (multiple), brilliance (talents), emotions, temperament and so on. Awakening spirituality in the soul involves attentive observation and participation in one's unique design structures imbued in the self, the world and one's higher power.

The multiple media of one's organizational levels transduce formative design structures from one shape and mode to another while maintaining the holistic integrity of unique self throughout. The homeodynamic consistency of transducing motifs reflects the unique integrity of the individual body, soul and spirit. Motifs are transformative bridges unifying complex differences into ever-expansive, formative uniqueness.

Transduction through one medium to another (water to air) involves altering the mode or manifestation a wave or energy form may take. This is exactly what happens in transformative motifs. When one's prayers, meditations and visualizations embody sacredness, what is called spiritual healing occurs, which is the activation of healing transduction motifs of a higher ordering.

The experience of higher ordering transformative bridges can assist in faith and trust in one self as surrendering to a power greater than oneself. This can occur without a sense of lost integrity and with a discovery of a reality greater than one's experience. One can then feel at first lost (death) and then found (rebirth). The conversion experience of Saul being struck down by lightning off his high horse (metaphor for the ego) and arising with a new form of purpose (aligned intrinsic motif with larger than self reality) reflects the death and rebirth experience.

Awakening the soul's motif in alignment with one's sacredness of art initiates transformation. As alignment increases in complexity and intricacy, bridging expands from one medium or organizational level to another.

The soul's movement toward sacredness involves the mystery of higher ordering. The motif is not knowable in a purely intellectual fashion. Intuitiveness of personal experiences surrendering to complexity and intricacy reveals unique, transformative movements of the soul's motif towards spirituality.

Motifs of intricate complexity and harmony in the soul's spirituality can be clearly perceived in the structure of the brain. At its highest level of organization, the cerebral cortex is a layered and columnar lattice (or web-like) structure with multifaceted complexity of design. In these neural strata, which orchestrate higher ordering mental functions, are design structures of intricate motifs. These intricate motifs resonate with complexity and harmony of formativeness characteristic of the soul's motif. The ordering and crafting of the soul's artistic motif involves an ever more complex yet intricately harmonizing higher ordering. Such evolving formativeness of the complex, unique motif is the essence and characteristic of spiritual sacredness.

UNIQUE MOTIFS AND RELIGION

Uniqueness of motif can be found in the various religions of the world. Major religions of the world are grounded on similar, all encompassing truths (monotheism, ascendance towards higher levels of being, union and oneness, etc.). Yet each of the major religions (Christianity, Judaism, Islamic, Hinduism, etc.) manifests its own unique, special meaning and facet of spirituality.

Kenneth Woodward (2000) quotes the philosopher George Santayana who expresses the marked idiosyncrasy of each healthy, living religion. The unique message embodied in each religion conveys a special and surprising message through "the bias which that revelation gives to life" (Woodward, 2000). New vistas and mysteries revealing other worlds are available through each of the world religions. Therein lies the unique motif of each particular religion capturing mysterious and wondrous visions of dimensions and realms of realities far beyond common sense experience.

Through the description of miracles occurring in various religions' historical accounts, Woodward (2000) describes the unique meaning and message that miracles reveal in each religion. He describes miracles as stories and accounts of events that only make sense within larger-than-self realities.

Christianity's God of the New Testament is different from any other. The New Testament reveals the Holy Trinity of God as the Father, Son and Holy Ghost (spirit). Jesus Christ emerges as grounded within all three facets of the Trinity of God. Other distinctions can be discerned between the Tanakh (Hebrew Bible) and the Christian Old Testament. In the former, the scriptures are sequenced and designed with a perspective of the coming of Christ fulfilling the Hebrew prophecy.

The progressive disappearance of miracles in the movement from old to new testaments is cast in a different light. Jesus used more miracles than prior prophets. The Matthew writings depict the view of Jesus Christ as the new Moses. This can be understood through His teachings, signs and wonders (miracles). Jesus surpasses Moses from the Gospel perspective, presenting Himself as possessing miraculous power reserved only for God. Moses hears the voice of God. As scriptures developed, there was a shift from God speaking directly to prophets towards one of Him speaking indirectly through them. His prophets and eventually His Son spoke for Him. This is an interesting development in religion. It is as if God's voice was becoming more differentiated and uniquely expressed as time evolved. This is not unlike the evolution and differentiation of unique motifs. The unique complexity of each religion's faceted perspective of spiritual infinity offers rich diversity and differentiation in the unfathomable realms of omnipresence.

MOTIF: EVOLUTION AND INVOLUTION

The spiritual motif of complexity and harmonious intricacy is reflected in Paramahansa Yoganando (1974). He expresses that creation in evolution goes away from God and then comes back to Him again. He describes how evolution moves from gross forms of inert materials to some refinement of sensations in plants, to some consciousness in animate beings and eventually to human beings with consciousness. The further evolution differentiates into complex forms, the closer the higher ordering of intricate motifs resonate with a universal or cosmic consciousness of oneness with God.

The derivation of complex, unique design structures (human beings) from gross beginnings (simple forms) moves away from its origins only to return through higher ordering of intricate oneness. The farther one evolves from his or her beginnings, the more intricate the complexity and thus the closer to the core.

This movement suggests a spiraling motif of moving away from one's initial core only to return to one's core being at a higher level of ordering. One can leave home as a child, go off to pursue higher education and return home again yet more complex and intricate. One can become more of what one already is at the core level of self. The spiraling structure of evolution is also that of the DNA molecule which embodies a biological blueprint of formativeness. Cathedrals have spiral staircases symbolizing spiritual pathways and blueprints to higher orders of reality. The spiraling motif resonates its sacred formativeness at multiple levels of existence (biological and architectural structures).

The evolution of one's soul motif is the involution (integration) of intricately orchestrated complexities. Involution is the inherent organizing property of unique motifs. The more one moves outward, differentiates and derives new complex adventures, discoveries and life meanings, the more intricately integrated is one's spiraling, transformative motif. There is an undulating movement in one's maturation of increased complexity and expansive harmonization as a whole, spiritual being. The wisdom of an elder statesman in world policy making can illustrate depth of inner complexity as a consequence of expansive vision in global perspectives. The universe has been described by many scientists as expanding and contracting (big bang and big crunch). The motif of spiraling evolution, involution, complexity and holistic intricacy may be a motif resonant within both the individual and the universe. Motifs are transformative in the evolution and involution of the soul's journey of spirituality. As such, they can serve as transformative bridges over difficult times and troubled water.

MOTIF AND THE LUCIFER PRINCIPLE

The Lucifer principle refers to the concept that nature inherently uses violence and aggression to foster higher levels of ordering and life forms. From the smallest microbe to the Chinese Cultural Revolution, evolution necessitates competition among organized entities for the purpose of developing ever more complex forms of order (Bloom, 1995).

Bloom (1995) refers to MacLean's (1973) triune brain (reptilian, mammalian and neo-cortex) as depicting a biological basis of aggression, war and emotional bonding in groups. Such a basis suggests that groups of individuals acting collectively (superorganisms) engage in competitive violence and war to propagate their children and thus their genes. In addition to genes of individuals in a group, the culture of a group has its own distinctive ideas and principles of beliefs (memes). Memes are the social group's blueprints or "genes" at the interpersonal level of organization. Bloom describes how cultural and religious "memes" such as Catholicism, Islam, Protestantism, rock and roll, hippies, communism, capitalism and so on compete to survive and expand. He presents numerous examples of how principles and ideals (memes) can be perpetuated through rationalizing and justifying mass destruction of those different and thus alien. For example, he describes how Mohammed professed that in the name of Allah (God) there were only two worlds, faithful and infidels. The holy wars waged in the name of religion have resulted in massive deaths, cruelty and devastation.

Bloom bases his Lucifer principle that nature (as discovered by scientists) fosters competition and the evils of violence, murder, cruelty and destruction upon five concepts. The first is the principle of self-organizing entities or groups, which he calls replicators. Examples are genes and assembly systems that generate goods and services that can make others obsolete. The second concept is that of the superorganism which invokes the collection of individual components. The third concept is that of the meme, which Bloom (1995) describes as a self-replicating cluster of concepts. They provide a distinctive design organizing civilizations and cultures. The fourth concept is what he calls the neural net, which is like a group consciousness influencing our emotions and behavior. The last concept refers to pecking order, which is a dominant hierarchy of organization in both animal and human groups.

Throughout his work, Bloom depicts nature as a battleground of forms, whether of chemicals, microbes, animals, fish, humans or cultures. The consistent theme throughout is one of living forms pressing to an ever higher ordering of complexity and organization facilitated by violence, competition and destruction. He describes how human biology (illusion of control, hormones, immune system) is advanced in such a process.

He perceptively keys in on how evolution is concerned with developing increasingly complex, higher orderings of life forms. He is keenly aware of how at both the biological (genes) and psychosocial (memes) levels, self-organization and proliferation are operative. He astutely focuses the concept of orderings of individuals into ever-higher forms such as superorganisms, pecking order, hierarchy, and a neural net, web-like group mind. However, his treatment of the individual as a component of a group (as he compares cells within an organism to individual "cells" within a social organization) is fraught with major errors. For example, he identifies how each living cell has a life and purpose of its own. Yet, how the cells do their work together is the collective way the organism functions.

While cells may serve a limited range of purposes and contribute to the whole organism, individuals are not so specialized. There is within the individual a unique motif capable of multidimensional design structures. When an individual joins a group, selective design structures are accessed (finding resonant forms in rhythm of a rock band) while others remain dormant. Even cells can have multiple functions (original germ cells have the plasticity to take on many forms). They can become so specialized as to lose their formative capacity to become many diverse forms. If this happens to a human being, loss of formativeness can be disastrous.

Individuals are multidimensional and not so easily slotted like cells into a superorganism. The uniqueness of self in individuals requires a multifaceted range of connections. This means being associated with a wide range of groups, systems and/or affiliations. For example, a musician in a band may also be a nonpracticing Catholic, part-time father or a world traveler focused on the spirituality of ecumenical councils. How can such diverse individuals totally fit into any one group at all times? It is similar to the Rubik's Cube puzzle. How to solve the puzzle requires being able to achieve multiple alignments simultaneously of various numbers in three dimensions (and that's just for a cube). The multiple facets of an individual's unique motif are vastly more complicated than those of a three dimensional puzzle.

Indeed, evil does exist. It exists when the unique motif of the individual is rigidly and oppressively truncated in obsessive, mindless, stereotyped (loss of individual consciousness) groupings. Evolution selects for complexity of higher ordering yet moves toward multidimensional integration. Variations and mutations are ways evolution is advanced. A child is the offspring of two parents with different genetic sequences integrated into one unique design. When variation and difference are prevented or missing, stagnation and death result. Notice what happens with in-breeding and distortions in the genetic pool.

The same is true with cultures. Memes that are allowed to develop derivations, offshoots and the like persist much longer and stronger than truncated ones. Witness the strong, multicultural diversity in America as compared to the rigidity in totalitarian, communist countries.

Evolution moves through formativeness not through form. Formativeness is not static but rather dynamically derivational. That is why motifs are inherent in individuals, cultures and evolution itself. As evolution evolves its complexity of motif, a natural higher ordering of multidimensional formativeness emerges. While it is true that there exist warring factions, competition and violence, this is not the result of inherent evil. It is the result of primitive and concrete limits in ordering possibilities. After the initial Big Bang signaling the beginning of the universe, only atoms and particles were available. There were initial limitations in arrangements of ordering. As particles and atoms formed the chemical elements of the universe, there was an exponential increase in the ordering patterns available. As formativeness potentials expand, so does the capacity for sacred evolution and the progressive movement towards higher consciousness ways of co-existence. Witness the biological dimensions in the way nature evolves its sacred formativeness. Evolution could be seen as selecting for spiritual capacities as having biological advantages.

The biological benefits of spirituality were illustrated in a previous chapter. It is interesting to note that a center in the brain (left temporal lobe) called the God-spot has been discovered (Ramachandran and Blakeslee, 1998) which assists the brain in consciously experiencing spiritual phenomena. The flooding of the left temporal lobe connected to limbic (midbrain) and frontal cortex interaction leads to a process called kindling (creation of new neural pathways). Spiritual experiences resonate with formativeness in brain pathway development. The soul's spiritual motif is imbued in the psychoneurological motifs of the brain's neural pathways.

As individuals enhance their uniqueness and cultures advance in diversity and multicultural web-like intricacy, competition and violence will become less necessary for formativeness to evolve. When Michelangelo carved David out of marble, he had to destroy the surrounding excess marble to "release" the David within. In a way, this was an act of evil according to Bloom in that disassembly of the marble block had to occur to release the artist from within. When Native Americans hunted buffalo, there was no waste as they utilized all parts of the animal for their survival. This represented their respect and sacred treatment of God's creatures. This was a highly spiritual endeavor. Could Michelangelo's block of marble have been carved in such a brilliant, healing way as to have utilized every ounce of matter? Instead of carving could it have been remolded to release multiple design structures of the David such that nothing was wasted?

Violence and war may have initiated form selection early in evolution. Through higher ordering, evolution requires less violence and greater cooperation. Increased capacity for complex design strives not to exclude one form of species over another but to derive the highest ordering from both. Rosen (1997) discusses how sperm cells do not compete but rather cooperate in potentiating one another so that one will reach the egg cell. Far from competition, there is a team effort involved in the fertilization of evolutionary development. There may come a time when the lion can lie down with the lamb. There is an evolutionary effort to move away from aggression and violence as modes of resolving differences in living forms.

Today, many are moving away from eating other living animals all together. It seems that every day we are becoming more conscientious of how we treat other life forms. There may come a day when formativeness has evolved to an advanced level where the universe as we know it will manifest its full motif.

MOTIF AND MULTIDIMENSIONALITY

The capacity for multidimensional organizations to accommodate the unique complexity of the individual implies fulfilling utilization of people's talents. A place for every living form is the inherent infinite complexity of the universe's evolved motif. As Yogananda (1974) says, the farther away from God evolution moves, the closer it is to Him. Evolution leads to involution. As the motif proliferates its intercomplexity of higher ordering design structures, multiple dimensions orchestrate themselves in an internal intricacy of harmonic oneness.

Stephen Gould (1977) observes that there are more genes that are nonfunctional on the human chromosomes than are statistically expected based on Darwinian natural selection for the individual. Bloom (1995) proposes that these "useless" genes reflect survival at the social group level of organization where individuals could not function without group affiliation. Intriguingly, genetic structure and design evolution may evolve such that "extra" genes serve as ways of interfacing with a variety of life form adaptions. Such an ability for one's genes to interface or "fit" at a variety of levels (individual, family, group, etc.) may illustrate genetic capacity for multidimensional, simultaneous connections. The capacity for simultaneous connection, operating at multiple levels at the same time has been demonstrated by researchers (Yam, 2000). They illustrate how subatomic particles can be at two different levels simultaneously.

Evolution enhances complex capacities for multilevel, higher ordering, and motifs express precisely the formative design properties with which to increase multidimensional complexity. With motifs, nothing is wasted. There is no competition. There is a holistic unfolding of interrelated, derivational design structures capable of multilevel, simultaneous connection. The human zygote is an example of such differential derivation. As the fertilized cell continuously divides, it becomes ever more complex and synergistically holistic in structure and coordination of function. Originating gamete cells do not compete with one another but work cooperatively to make room for one another in an ever-expanding, differential whole. Complexity and intricacy are the involutional (spiritual) movements within evolving life forms. When nerve cells migrate to various parts of the growing fetus to establish the neural tube, there is a synergistic potentiation. Instead of competing for what gets where first, each nerve enhances the other's growth spurring one another on in a team-like spirit (spirituality).

This is similar to the process of sperm cells seeking to fertilize the egg cell. What appears to be a kind of sperm warfare or competition is actually a sophisticated form of cooperative design structuring moving towards greater complexity of motif.

MOTIFS AND FORMATIVENESS

The point of all this is that far from competition and violence, evolution moves to a higher ordered level of cooperative, complex life formativeness. Such complexity in unique motifs moves away from an evolution through violence towards one of spirited multidimensionality. Formativeness is the derivational capacity of motifs to evolve a family of similar but different patterned thematic design structures (offspring, children, etc.) which are multidimensional in complex ordering. In other words, with evolving complexity of motifs there is room and time for the intricate co-existence of a myriad of derivationally designed structured life forms. Witness the multiculturalism emerging with greater global networking. Evolution operates as a universal motif proliferating uniqueness in all its artistic crafting.

As evolution advances, there is enhanced formativeness such that nothing is lost or wasted. There is a gradual transformation from the natural to the supernatural (spiritual). Such transformations access the inherent ordering potentiations of infinite, derivation design structures innately interfaced with one another in complex, multidimensional facets. America has fifty highly diverse states yet has evolved into a highly complex, ordered union. Our global village (as the world is sometimes called) is a metaunion of diverse countries such as the United States. Seeking to establish a world order, making room and time for all, implies grasping the vast interplay of multidimensionality of metamotifs at the international level. Paradoxically, there needs to be a place even for rigid, fixated forms of thinking and living. Such tendencies seem to be part of human nature. As perfection is an illusion, providing a safe place for rigidity maintains flexibility in a multidimensional world. Alexis de Tocqueville (*Democracy in America*) would be pleased with the elimination of the tyranny of the majority.

MOTIF VS. FIXATION

When genes and/or memes become fixated and rigid, formative evolution at the individual and global level is thwarted. It is at such points where the spirit or spirituality of a religious and/or cultural ideal becomes obsessive and perverted into harsh and cruel violence. How Christian were the so-called holy wars, and what violence is brought upon family members in the name of love and adoration? Psychopathology is the loss of formativeness in evolutionary motifs. This is the real evil. The inherent formativeness of an ordering universe seeks to transcend and transform such reifications and fixations.

Individuals may become pathological in terms of violent behavior due to abnormalities in brain structures and/or abusive environmental conditions. Included in the latter are *in utero* conditions where the fetus is exposed to various material toxins. Variables like these interfere with the formative evolution of unique motifs. The very soul of the individual can be impaired.

Cultural memes can become truncated into violent, obsessive behaviors and perceptual distortions. Nazi Germany arose through Adolf Hitler's dictatorship. He took an oppressed, impoverished country, installed the meme of a vain supremacy (superman concept) and rebuilt the German consciousness (as well as their military power). By projecting blame onto minority groups for Germany's difficulties and charismatically directing attention towards images of superiority and domination, Hitler's twisted memes gave birth to modern-day darkness and evil. Hitler was an abused, adopted child. His megalomaniacal passion to overinflate himself and an impoverished Germany were a match made in the hell.

Ironically, Hitler was an accomplished architect and designer. He had a talent and an art for building and structuring. It may have been this set of talents that built and engineered the Third Reich. Yet, his art was distorted and fixated by his need for narcissistic power and domination. Because of such fixations, his innate talent and art lost the critical quality of formativeness which strangulated unique manifestation of motif. Many of his military errors occurred from faulty strategizing. Instead of listening to his generals, he listened to his madness (fixation of motif). In losing the essential quality of formativeness in motif, he was damned before he started. What brought him to power (entrancement of power) also took it away.

There is inherent beauty and brilliance in human beings. When one's inherent motif is crippled by a will towards power rather than the will towards creative choice, manifesting motifs is thwarted. One can choose to have faith in the uniqueness of unfolding motif or contain the limits of choice to some fixated ideal in the immediate physical world. Hitlerian choices of an idealism based on total dominance go against innate artistic ideals of formative motif.

Motifs emerge over time and are evolutionary at both the individual and collective group level of organization. To evolve, formativeness is essential in the transformation of motifs. The multidimensional ordering of evolution requires motifs that develop through derivational design structures. These design structures co-exist in multiple dimensions within and beyond the physical time and space that one calls the material world. For example, string theory (presented earlier) depicts eleven multiple dimensions of reality. As this is beyond what is considered the common sense nature of existence, multidimensional realities could be considered meta (above) physical or supernatural levels of ordering.

Human beings need to learn to exercise free will in choosing what is intrinsically valuable to them. Exercising a muscle strengthens it. Exercising free will in choosing behaviors that honor what one intrinsically values strengthens the musculature of one's character. Such choices honor intrinsic motifs as well as one's unique soul. Multidimensional realities may represent a "kingdom of heavenly" possibilities through the open doorway of the soul's unique motif.

MOTIFS AND MULTIPLE FRAMES IN SPIRITUALITY

There is an old saying that all roads lead to Rome. No matter which motif one chooses or uniquely manifests, the more one exercises choice, the stronger the character of manifest motif. For example, choosing to work and develop one's artistic talent (one does not have to be a conventional artist to be artistic) enhances ever-expanding design structure derivations. The actor Anthony Quinn was painting and sculpting into his eighties. George Burns continued to expound and expand his range of talents in living his unique motif by writing about how to live to be 100 (he said you first have to get to age ninety-nine).

Developing multiple frames of expressing and deriving one's unique artistic motif enriches the soul's spirituality. As one's range of derivational expressions increase, so one's spirituality is strengthened.

Howard Gardner, as noted previously, identified multiple intelligence frames inherent within individuals. As these have neurobiological design structures, they serve as evolution's support system for one to attain multifaceted frames of enriched, spiritual motifs. When children are very young (two to four years old) they know of only limited ways of getting their parents' attention (misbehaving, crying, etc.). As they get older, they learn to differentiate multiple frameworks in which to elicit parental responses (adolescences are quite creative in eliciting parental responses).

As adulthood is reached, individuals have learned (hopefully) to establish their own goals, objectives and sense of purpose. They understand long-term goals and sense of life purpose. Their range of behavioral repertoire becomes broader and broader regarding how to reach various goals and outcomes, as they learn alternative, healthier ways towards achievement. There comes a point in their maturation where multiple frames of how to reach their goal or purpose become an intrinsic (for its own sake) end in itself. For example, a musician playing in a band for prestige, money, fame, attention and so on discovers the intrinsic value of playing music (state of flow) for its own sake. There is a convolution of means and ends such that there is a higher ordering of meaning (joy in intrinsic playing of music as a domain of reality itself). Actually, children seem to possess this intrinsic quality, but psychosocial conditioning weeds it out to some extent.

Evolution involves both becoming as well as being. They are reciprocal, mutually enhancing facets. The striving to play music with the initial purpose of external rewards and validation shifts towards a more present focus. The purpose now becomes doing the artistic motif of music for its own validation. By the same token, learning to derive larger purposes for music (soothing for others, stimulating appreciation for music, symbolizing realities, etc.) evolves into a becoming process. Both domains reflect an expanding, larger-than-self reality.

MOTIFS AND LARGER-THAN-SELF REALITIES

Motifs open the individual self to other realities and dimensions. These dimensions involve web-like networks of intricate connections. These web- or lattice-like design structures reflect larger-than-self realities of motif (motifs of motifs in a hierarchy of organizational design). Examples may be one's professional field of endeavor (writer, teacher, tool and die maker, any crafted expertise) and/or other formative realm which resonates with one's unique motif (universal consciousness, tao, etc.).

When early Christians unflinchingly believed in life in the hereafter (their larger-than-self reality), they faced the Roman lions with joy and faith. Interestingly, biological processes support such faithful endeavors (faith experiences) by increasing endorphin levels and rerouting pain signals, raising thresholds for pain tolerance. The strength of belief and faith can be seen in a mother protecting her child, perhaps by picking up an automobile that has pinned her child to the ground, thus the cliché "faith can move mountains." Such incredible adrenalin rush and activation of other biological mechanisms are at the service of each individual. When faith is aligned with one's motif (one's larger-than-self reality) vast resources of far beyond one's expectations are available for transcendence and transformation.

The congruence of such an alignment is empowering in one's life. Juxtaposing this vast oceanic reservoir of energy in concentrated form upon obstacles blocking one's path (limiting beliefs, depression, traumatic memories, etc.) elicits transformative reformations in one's life. The cerebral cortex (with its lattice-like, columnar layers) is capable of remarkable, symbolic transformations (alterations in meaning, abstractions of patterned forms, etc.). When synergistically activated with the hypothalamic midbrain (emotional energy), alterations in perception and reality interpretation can now manifest themselves. What seemed at first impossible now becomes incorporated in innovative, brilliant and healing solutions.

The biblical story of Saul, the Christian slayer, being struck by lightning and falling from his (high) horse (or ego), is a classic example of an improvisational, brilliant solution. Enlightenment, like grace, is received, not taken. Being open, aligned and engaged in one's soulful motif invites such spiritual enlightenment into one's life as well as others' (through sharing one's motif which is prayer).

The organization of the human brain suggests how evolution does not destroy but builds upon what is created. The triune brain (MacLean, 1973) evolved not by eliminating primitive brain structures but by building upon previous structures to ever expanded refinements and complexities. The mammalian brain assists in social groups through emotional bonding. The neo-mammalian brain (neo-cortex) builds upon this providing creative, symbolic capacities for abstract formativeness. In this way, artificial boundaries between groups can be transformed for both differentiation (respecting individual states of unique motifs) and integration (facilitating unions between these states in holistic fashions). The more evolution moves away from God the closer it is to Him.

MOTIF: MICROCOSMS AND MACROCOSMS

Motifs are operative at both subatomic levels (string theory) as well as macrocosmic levels (constellations, galaxies, etc.). Ancient civilizations such as the Egyptians designed architectural structures (pyramids) as pathways to the afterlife. The pharaohs constructed pyramids in a way that would prepare them for transcending into the next life. Findings by archeologists and astronomers (as reported by Discovery Channel programs, March, 2000) indicate that three pyramids (one of which is the great pyramid of Gaza) are built in a certain aligned configuration. Two of the three pyramids form a straight line. The third is angled off to the side forming an elbow-shaped design. It seems that ten thousand years ago the constellation Orion was also uniquely aligned. The belt of Orion has three stars that, in the sky over Egypt of ten thousand years ago, had the precise elbow-shaped design as did the three pyramids.

Intriguingly, the motif of the three pyramids and the three stars on the "belt" of Orion resonate. To the Egyptians, this resonance provided the pathway to the afterlife. Similar resonant configurations have been found around the world (Southeast Asia, England, etc.). While one needs to be careful in speculation over these matters, the symbolism of such findings is quite suggestive. Do motifs designed on earth have resonant patterns in the universe (stars, constellations, "heavens," etc.)? Are motifs guides or daimons of one's soul towards multidimensional, spiritual realities larger than self?

One thing is certain. Motifs are formative, universal design properties permeating the mind, brain, body and environment in our everyday lives. Resonance with motifs at the minuscule and the macro levels of the universe is prolific. It has been said that God, Allah, the higher power, Yahweh, or however such omnipresence is referred to, exists at the infinitely small and infinitely large. These are the two great arcs of the universal circle. Motif may be the bridge that traverses these arcs in holy union of the soul in spiritual sacredness. The Hindu religion (Chopra, 2000) relates to the soul as both Jiva and Atman. Jiva is the personalized, subjective manifestation of soul in unique human form. Atman remains as purity of unformed formativeness in union with the larger-than-self reality. The bridge between these two aspects of soul is the unique formative motif that transcends and guides the subjective soul to the larger oneness. Each human has these two facts of soul. Each person has a guiding resonance, a unique formativeness that can lead the earth-bound soul to that unique constellation of his or her higher paralleled Atman imbued in oneness.

MOTIF IN EVOLUTION

The evolution of one's motif is the holographic resonance with that of the ultimate superorganism, the universe. The soul of one's spirituality is in the holy union manifesting itself through the sacred artistry of one's spiritual motif. Uniqueness is the signature of one's sacred motif. Motif is the inheritance of the soul's spiritual evolution through sacred uniqueness.

John Eccles (1991) proposes that uniqueness is not the prerogative of genetics or of environment. He suggests that the uniqueness of the individual's self is the soul, which enters the human being some time between conception and birth. Such a proposition, while enlightening, begs the question of just how soul is incarnate in human kind. It is not until one addresses the properties of formativeness in motifs that the imbuing of soul into humankind manifests itself. Formative motifs become operative at the time of fertilization and reveal their initial manifestation some time before birth. Formative motifs are the vessels of the soul's spirituality incarnate in human existence and are its evolutionary ground of being and becoming.

The being and becoming of the self imply that individuals are not perfect but rather move towards resonance with what makes them unique. The moral concept of right and wrong needs to incorporate the "rightness" and "wrongness" for what attitude/behavior resonates with individual uniqueness of motif. This is not meant to imply that one should do one's thing regardless of harm to self or others. Rather, it is meant to imply that each individual needs to develop spiritual as well as moral responsibility for extracting the very uniqueness of his or her motif, which resonates with universal omnipresence.

The inherent imperfection (unfinishedness) in each human being has been aptly characterized by a saying on a bumper sticker: "Be patient . . . God is not finished with me yet." The inherent imperfection in human beings is matched with their inherent uniqueness of motif as guiding, organizing principles of personal evolution and spiritual alignment. It would appear that the more one engages in an intrinsic leap of faith in a power greater than one's separate self, the more one needs to believe in the inherent (God-given) uniqueness of one's motif. It is the core motif of uniqueness which guides and aligns the individual with his or her higher power. It is in this resonance where the uniqueness of individual self becomes transformed into the complexity of oneness.

It is interesting that the original, generative cells of the human embryo are called germ cells. While germs are labeled as mostly disease oriented, it is germ cells which lead to germ-ination of plants, animals and people. These germ cells (which reflect our unique "imperfection") are what imbue growth and maturation into life. The original germ or sin in human beings is that each of us is "infected" with the "contaminated" seeds of uniqueness of motif. In this way, we appear to deviate (though actually we are derivatives) from each other. The ideal state of perfection (whatever that is) is challenged by our "deviation" of uniqueness. Our original "sin" is the germination of our originality of unique motif.

If we follow the first commandment "Thou shalt not have false gods (little 'g' gods) before Me," we will strive to evolve with the formative omnipresence of our God-given uniqueness of artistic (and scientific) motif. If there is such a thing as an ideal state of perfection, it would seem to involve our unique motif. By being true to ourselves, our uniqueness, we cannot be false to anyone else (or God).

Throughout the previous chapters, the self's unique motif has been illustrated as imbued at multilevels of organization. Such unique formativeness of motif throughout the organism illustrates that the spiritual soul of the self is imbued holistically. The harmony of soul and spirit is omnipresent through the unique motif of self. It is the unfolding designed spaces between the places where sacred formativeness of unique motifs resonates in transformational self.

Bibliography

Abravanel, E. D., & King, E. (1985). *Dr. Abravanel's body type program for health, fitness and nutrition.* New York: Bantam Books.

Acheterberg, J. (1985). *Imagery and healing: Shamanism and modern medicine.* Boston: New Science Library.

Achterberg, J. & Lawlis, G. F. (1942). *Bridges of the body mind.* Champaign, IL: Institute for Personality and Ability Testing, Inc.

Achterberg, J. & Lawlis, G. F. (1980). *Bridges of the body mind.* Champaign, IL: Institute for Personality and Ability Testing, Inc.

Achterberg, J., & Lawlis, G. F. (1984). *Imagery & disease.* Champaign, IL: Institute for Personality and Ability Testing.

Ader, R., & Cohen, H. (1975). Behaviorally conditioned immunosuppression. *Psychosomatic Medicine, 37,* 333–40.

Allen, A. (1998, March/April). Equal but separate. *Family Networker, 22* (2).

Amen, D. G. (1998). *Change your brain, change your life.* New York: Random House.

Anderson, M. (1988). Inspection time, information processing and the development of intelligence. *British Journal of Devel-Psych, 6,* 43–57.

Andrews, L. (1987). *To thine own self be true.* New York: Doubleday.

Ansbacher, H. L. & Ansbacher, R. R. (1956). *The individual psychology of Alfred Adler.* New York: Harper and Row.

Antonovsky, A. (1979). *Health, stress, and coping.* San Francisco: Jossey-Bass.

Antonovsky, A. (1984). The sense of coherence as a determinant of health. In J. D. Matarazzo, S. M. Weiss, J. A. Herd, N. E. Miller, & S. M. Weiss (eds.), *Behavioral Health* (pp. 35–74). New York: John Wiley.

Antonovsky, A. (1987). *Unravelling the mystery of health: How people manage stress and stay well.* San Francisco: Jossey-Bass.

Atwater, P.M.H. (1996). *Future memory.* New York: Carol Publishing Group.

Aziz, R. (1989). *C. G. Jung Psychology of Religion and Synchronicity.* New York: University of New York.

Bandler, R. & Grinder, J. (1975). *The structure of magic I.* Palo Alto, CA: Science & Behavior Books.

Bandura, A. (1982). Self-efficacy mechanism in human agency. *American Psychologist, 37,* 122–47.

Bandura, A.; Taylor, C. B.; Williams, S. L.; Mefford, I. N.; & Barchas, J. D. (1985). Catecholamine secretion as a function of perceived self-efficacy. *Journal of Consulting and Clinical Psychology, 53,* 406–14.

Barber, T. X. (1984). Changing "unchangeable" bodily processes by (hypnotic) suggestions: A new look at hypnosis, cognitions, imagining, and the mind-body problem. *Advances, 7–36.*

Barker, R. D. J. (1992). *The Principles of cell energetics.* Mass: Butterworth-Heinemann.

Barnett, L. (1976). Play and intrinsic rewards: Reply to Csikszentmihalyi. *Journal of Humanistic Psychology, 16* (3), 35–51.

Bartrop, R. W.; Lazarus, L.; Luckhurst, E.; Kiloh, L. G.; & Penny, R. (1977). *Depressed lymphocyte function after bereavement,* Lancet 1: 834–39.

Bates, E. (1999). Research. *Newsweek,* March 15, 59–63.

Bateson, G. (1972). *Steps to an ecology of mind.* New York: Ballantine.

Bateson, G. (1979). *Mind and nature: A necessary unity.* New York: Dutton.

Beck, A. T.; Rush, A.; Shaw, B.; Emergy, G. (1979). *Cognitive therapy for depression.* New York: Guilford Press.

Becker, R. O., & Selden, G. (1985). *The body electric.* New York: Quill/William Morrow.

Begley, S. (1999, September 27). Shaped by life in the womb. *Newsweek, 134,* 13, 51.

Begley, S., with Carey, J. (1980, December 1). The clocks within us. *Newsweek.*

Benson, H. (1996). *Timeless healing.* New York: Fireside.

Benson, H. & Klipper, M. Z. (1976). *The relaxation response.* New York: Avon Books.

Bernard, J. & Sontag, L. (1947). Fetal reactions to sound. *Journal of Genetic Psychology, 70,* 209–210.

Berne, E. (1961). *Transactional analysis in psychotherapy.* New York: Grove Press.

Berne, E. (1972). *What do you say after you say hello? The psychology of human destiny.* New York: Grove Press.

Berninger, A. & Richards, S. (1999). Research. *Newsweek,* March 15, 61–63.

Besedeovsky, H.; Sorkin, E.; Felix, D.; & Haas, H. (1977). Hypothalamic changes during the immune response. *European Journal of Immunology* 7: 325–28.

Bickerton, D. (1990). *Language and species.* Chicago: University of Chicago Press.

Black, S. (1969). *Mind and Body.* London: William Kimber.

Bloom, H. (1995). *The Lucifer Principle.* New York: The Atlantic Monthly Press.

Blum, S.; Noble, E.; Sheridan, P., et al. (1990). Allelic association of human dopamine D2 receptor gene in alcholism. *Journal of the American Medical Association, 263,* 2055–60.

Bly, R. (1992). *Iron John.* New York: Vintage Books.

Bohart, A.; Magallanes, M.; Guzman, R.; Smiljunich, E.; Aguallo, S.; & Humphrey, A. (1993). Emphasizing the future in empathy responses. *Journal of Humanistic Psychology, 33* (2), 12–29.

Bohm, D. (1980). *Wholeness and the implicate order.* London: Routledge & Kegan Paul.

Bollas, C. (1987). *The shadow of the object.* New York: Columbia University Press.

Boscolo, L.; Cecchin, G.; Hoffman, L.; & Penn, P. (1987). *Milan systemic family therapy.* New York: Basic Books.

Bouchard, T., et al. (1990). Sources of human psychological differences: The Minnesota study of twins reared apart. *Science, 250,* 223–28.

Bowen, M. (1978). *Family therapy in clinical practice.* New York: Jason Aronson.

Bowlby, J. (1969). *Attachment and loss,* Volume 1–3. New York: Basic Books.

Bresnitz, S., ed. (1984). *The denial of stress.* New York: International Universities Press.

Briggs, J. (1988). *Fire in the crucible.* Los Angeles: Tarcher.

Brigham, D. (1998). *Imagery for getting well.* New York: W. W. Norton.

Brody, S., & Axelrod, S. (1970). *Anxiety and ego formation in infancy.* New York: International Universities Press.

Buber, M. (1958). *I and thou.* New York: Charles Scribner's Sons.

Buhler, C. (1961). The goal structure of human life. *Journal of Humanistic Psychology, 1*(1), 8–19.

Buzan, T. (1974). *Use both sides of your brain.* New York: E. P. Dutton.

Calvin, W. H. (1996). *How the brain works.* New York: Basic Books.

Campbell, D. (1997). *The Mozart effect.* New York: Avon Books.

Caprio, F.; Berger, J.; & Miller, C. (1998). *Healing your self with self-hypnosis.* New York: Prentice Hall.

Cheek, D. (1981). Awareness of meaningful sounds under general anesthesia: Considerations and a review of the literature, 1959–79. In *Theoretical and Clinical Aspects of Hypnosis* (pp. 92–104). Miami, FL: Symposium Specialists.

Chomsky, N. (1967). Recent contributions to the theory of innate ideas. *Synthese, 17,* 23–39.

Chopra, D. (2000). *Perfect health: practical system of mind/body system.* New York: Crown Publishing.

Clayton, G. (2000). *Hare brain, tortoise mind.* New York: Harper Perennial.

Combs, G. & Freedman, J. (1990). *Symbol, story and ceremony.* New York: W. W. Norton & Co.

Condon, W., & Sander, L. (1974, January 11). Neonate movement is synchronized with adult speech: International participation and language acquisition. *Science 14; 1,* 99–101.

Cooper, J. (1999). *Body Code.* Old Tappan, NY: Pocket Book.

Cousins, N. (1980). *Anatomy of an illness as perceived by the patient.* New York: W. W. Norton.

Cousins, N. (1983). *Anatomy of an illness.* New York: Bantam.

Cousins, N. (1986). Introduction. In S. Locke & D. Colligan, *The healer within,* 1–28. New York: E. P. Dutton.

Craik, K. (1943). *The nature of explanation.* Cambridge: Cambridge University Press.

Csikszentmihalyi, M. (1975). Play and intrinsic rewards. *Journal of Humanistic Psychology, 15*(3), 39–54.

Csikszentmihalyi, M. (1976). Replay to Barnett. *Journal of Humanistic Psychology, 16* (3), 73–81.

Csikszentmihalyi, M. (1988). Memes vs. genes: Notes from the culture wars. In John Brockman (ed.), *Reality Club,* 102–9. New York: Lynx Books.

Csikszentmihalyi, M. (1990). *Flow.* New York: Harper & Row.

Csikszentmihalyi, M. (1997). *Creativity.* New York: First Harper Perennial.

Cunningham, J. B. (1998). *The stress management source book.* Los Angeles: NTC/Contemporary Publishing Group, Inc.

Dabrowski, K. (1967). *Personality shaping through positive disintegration.* Boston: Little, Brown.

Dabrowski, K. (1970). Positive and accelerated development. In K. Dabrowski, A. Kawczak, and M. M. Piechowski (eds.), *Mental growth through positive disintegration.* 27–61. London: Gryf.

Dabrowski, K., & Piechowski, M. M. (1977a). *Theory of levels of emotional development: Vol. 1. Multilevelness and positive disintegration.* Oceanside, NY: Dabor Science Publications.

Dabrowski, K., & Piechowski, M. M. (1977b). *Theory of levels of emotional develop-ment: Vol. 2. From primary integration to self-actualization.* Oceanside, NY: Dabor Science Publications.

Darwin, C. (1871). *The descent of man and selection in relation to sex.* London: John Murray.

Dawkins, R. (1976). *The selfish gene.* New York: Oxford University Press.

Deacon, T. (1993). The symbolic species, *Science Mind.* MIT, MA.

Delgado, J. (1971). *Physical control of the mind: Towards a psychocivilised society.* New York: Harper & Row.

Delis, D. & Cassandra, P. (1990). *The Passion Paradox.* New York: Bantam Books.

Derogatis, L.; Abeloff, M.; & Melisaratos, N. (1979). Psychological coping mechanisms and survival time in metastatic breast cancer. *Journal of the American Medical Association, 242,* 1504–8.

Dillon, K. M.; Minchoff, B.; & Baker, K. H. (1985–86). Positive emotional states and enhancement of the immune system. *International Journal of Psychiatry in Medicine, 15,* 13–17.

Dilts, R. (1988). *Reimprinting.* Workshop handout, Changing Beliefs, Oak Brook, IL.

Dilts, R.; Hallbom, T.; & Smith, S. (1990). *Beliefs: Pathways to health and well-being.* Portland, OR: Metamorphous Press.

Dobzhansky, T. (1973). Nothing in biology makes sense except in the light of evolution. *American Biology Teacher, 4,* 35, 125–29.

Dossey, L. (1982). *Space, time and medicine.* Boston: Shambhala.

Dossey, L. (1999). *Re-inventing Medicine.* San Francisco: Harper Books.

Ebersole, P., & Quiring, G. (1991). Meaning in life depth: The MILD. *Journal of Hu-manistic Psychology, 31* (3), 113–24.

Eccles, J. C. (1991). *Evolution of the brain.* London: Routledge.

Edelman, G. M. (1987). *Neural Darwinism: The theory of neuronal group selection.* New York: Basic Books.

Edelman, G. M. (1989). *The remembered present: A biological theory of consciousness.* New York: Basic Books.

Edelman, G. M. (1992). *Bright air, brilliant fire: On the matter of the mind.* New York: Basic Books.

Edelman, G. M. & Tononi, G. (2000). *A universe of consciousness.* New York: Basic Books.

Efran, J.; Greene, M.; & Gordon, D. (1998, March/April). Lessons of the new genetics. *Family Networker, 22* (2), 27–59.

Eliot, L. (1999). *What's going on in there?* New York: Bantam.

Elkind, D. (1981). *The hurried child.* Menlo Park, CA: Addison-Wesley.

Elman, J.; Bates, E.; & Johnson, M. (1996). *Rethinking innateness: A connectionist per-spective on development.* Cambridge, MA: MIT Press.

Erickson, M. H. (1980a). Hypnotic investigation of psychosomatic phenomena: A con-trolled experimental use of hypnotic regression in the therapy of an acquired food intolerance. In E. L. Rossi (ed.), *The collected papers of Milton H. Erick-son on hypnosis: II. Hypnotic alteration of sensory, perceptual and psycho-physical processes* (pp. 169–74). New York: Irvington. (Original publication 1943.)

Erickson, M. H. (1980b). Hypnotic psychotherapy. In E. L. Rossi (ed.), *The collected papers of Milton H. Erickson on hypnosis: IV. Innovative hypnotherapy* (pp. 35–48). New York: Irvington. (Original publication 1948.)

Erickson, M. H., & Rossi, E. (1980). Two-level communication and the microdynamics of trance and suggestion. In E. L. Rossi (ed.), *The collected papers of Milton H.*

Erickson on hypnosis: I. The nature of hypnosis and suggestion (pp. 430–51).
    New York: Irvington. (Original publication 1976.)
Erikson, E. H. (1950). *Childhood and society.* New York: Norton.
Erikson, E. H. (1968). The life cycle: Epigenesis of identity. In E. H. Erikson, *Identity,
    Youth and Crisis* (pp. 8–26). New York: Norton.
Etcoff, N. (1999). *Survival of the prettiest.* New York: Doubleday.
Eysenck, A. J. (1981). *The intelligence controversy.* New York: John Wiley.
Feeney, D. J., Jr. (1984). A model framework for alcoholism counseling: cyclic process
    of intensification, paradoxical shifting and differentiation. *American Journal of
    Drug and Alcohol Abuse, 10* (3), 403–15.
Feeney, D. J., Jr. (1996). Purposeful self: accessing sensory motifs as empowerment in
    flow states and clinical interventions. *Journal of Humanistic Psychology, 36*
    (4), 94–115.
Feeney, D. J., Jr., (1999). *Entrancing relationships.* Westport, CT: Praeger.
Feeney, K. L. (2000). Reiki healing session personal consultation. Chicago, IL.
Ficino, M. (1980). *The book of life.* Translated by Charles Boer. Dallas: Spring Publica-
    tions.
Fisch, R.; Weakland, J.; & Segal, L. (1982). *The tactics of change.* San Francisco: Jossey-
    Bass.
Ford, J. (1991). Inherent potentialities of actualization: An initial exploration. *Journal of
    Humanistic Psychology, 31* (3), 65–88.
Fossey, D. (1983). *Gorillas in the mist.* Boston: Houghton Mifflin Co.
Frankl, V. (1963). *Man's search for meaning.* New York: Washington Square.
Friedman, M. (1978). *Type A behavior.* New York: Springer-Verlag.
Gallagher, W. (1994, September). How we become what we are. *The Atlantic Monthly,*
    42.
Gardner, H. (1993a). *Frames of mind.* New York: Basic Books.
Gardner, H. (1993b). *Multiple intelligences.* New York: Basic Books.
Gershon, M. (1998). *The second brain: The scientific basis of gut instinct.* New York:
    Harper Collins.
Geschwind, N., & Galaburda, A., eds. (1984). *Biological foundations of cerebral domi-
    nance.* Cambridge, MA: Harvard University Press.
Ginsburg, C. (1984). Toward a somatic understanding of self: A reply to Leonard Geller.
    Journal of Humanistic Psychology, 24 (2), 66–92.
Golden-Meadow, S. (1999). Research. New York: *Newsweek,* March 15, 58.
Goldman, J. (1996). *Healing sounds.* Boston, MA: Element Books.
Gonick, L. & Wheelis, M. (1991). *The cartoon guide to genetics.* New York: Harper-
    Collins.
Goodwin, B. (1963). *Temporal organization in cells.* New York: Academic Press.
Goodwin, B. (1994). *How the leopard changed its spots.* Weidenfeld & Nicolson.
Gould, S. J. (1977). *Ontogeny and phylogeny.* New York: Belknap Press.
Green, B. (1999). *The elegant universe.* New York: W. W. Norton.
Grof, S. (1993). *The holotropic mind.* New York: HarperCollins.
Grosberg, A. Y. & Khokhlov, A. R. (1997). *Giant molecules.* San Diego: Academic
    Press.
Haldane, J.B.S. (1946). The interaction of nature and nurture. *Annals of Eugenics, 7,* 13,
    197–205.
Haldane, J.B.S. (1968). The origin of life. *Science and Life* (pp. i–ii). Pemberton Publish-
    ing. (Original publication 1929.)
Haley, J. (1963). *Strategies of psychotherapy.* New York: Grune & Stratton.

Haley, J. (1976). Development of a theory: A history of a research project. In C. Sluzki & D. Ransom (eds.), *Double bind: The foundation to the communicational approach to the family* (pp. 59–104). New York: Grune & Stratton.

Haley, J. (1977). *Problem-solving therapy.* San Francisco: Jossey-Bass.

Hall, H. (1983). Hypnosis and the immune system: A review with implications for cancer and the psychology of healing. *American Journal of Clinical Hypnosis, 25,* 92–103.

Hall, H.; Longo, S.; & Dixon, R. (1983). Hypnosis and the immune system: The effect of hypnosis on T and B cell function. Presented to the Society for Clinical and Experimental Hypnosis, 33rd Annual Workshops and Scientific Meeting, Portland, OR.

Halpern, S. (1978). *Tuning the human instrument.* Belmont, CA: Spectrum Research Institute.

Hamer, D. and Copeland, P. (1994). *The science of desire: the search for the gay gene and the biology of behavior.* New York: Simon and Schuster.

Hardie, W. (1968). *Aristotle's ethical theory.* Oxford: Clarendon Press.

Hawking, S. & Penrose, R. (1996). *The nature of space and time.* Princeton, NJ: Princeton University Press.

Hebb, D. O. (1949). *The organization of behavior.* New York: Wiley.

Hess, B. & Mikhailov, A. (1994). Self-organization in living cells. *Science,* 264: 223–24.

Hopkins, F. (1913). The dynamic side of biochemistry. *Nature,* 92, 213–23.

Horgan, J. (1999). *The undiscovered mind.* New York: Free Press.

Houston, J. (1982). *The possible human.* Los Angeles: J. P. Tarcher, Inc.

Hubel & Wiesel (1979). Brain mechanisms of vision. *Scientific American* 241: 150–62.

James, T. & Woodsmall, W. (1988). *Timeline therapy.* Cupertino, CA: Meta Publications.

Jenner, S. (1999). *Parenting game.* New York: Bloomsburg.

Jensen, A. (1980). *Bias in mental testing.* New York: Free Press.

Jung, C. (1960). *The structure and dynamics of the psyche: Vol. III. The collected works of Carl G. Jung.* Translated by R.F.C. Hull. Bolingen Series XX. Princeton, NJ: Princeton University Press.

Jung, C. G. (1963). *Memories, dreams, reflections.* Translated by Richard Winston and Clara Winston. New York: Vintage Books.

Jung, C. G. (1964). *Man and his symbols.* New York: Bantam Doubleday.

Jung, C. G. (1971). *Psychological types.* Princeton, NJ: Princeton University Press.

Jung, C. G. (1973). *Memories, dreams, reflections.* Edited by Aniela Jaffe and translated by Richard Winston and Clara Winston. New York: Pantheon Books.

Kabat-Zinn, J. (1990). *Full catastrophe living.* New York: Doubleday Dell.

Kagan, J. (1994a). *Galen's prophecy.* New York: Basic Books.

Kagan, J. (1994b). *The nature of the child.* Basic Books.

Kasl, S. V.; Evans, A. S.; & Neiderman, J. C. (1979). Psychosocial risk factors in development of infectious mononucleosis. *Psychosomatic Medicine* 41: 445–66.

Kauffman, S. (1995). *At home in the universe: The search for laws of complexity.* New York: Viking.

Keen, S. (1992). *Fire in the belly.* New York: Bantam.

Keller, E. F. (1983). *A feeling for the organism: The life and work of Barbara McClintock.* San Francisco: W. H. Freeman.

Kendel, E. (1982). Steps towards a molecular grammar for learning. Explorations into the nature of memory. Presented at the bicentennial symposium of the Harvard Medical School. October.

Kiecolt-Glaser, J. K.; Garner, W.; Speicher, C.; Penn, G. M.; Holliday, J.; & Glaser, R. (1984). Psychosocial modifiers of immunocompetence in medical students. *Psychosomatic Medicine, 16,* 5, 7–14.

Kirsch, I. (ed.). (1999). *How expectancies shape experience.* Washington, DC: A.P.A. Books.

Klaus, M. (1970). Human maternal behavior at the first contact with her young. *Pediatrics, 46* (2), 187–92.

Klaus, M. (1972). Maternal attachment: Impotence of the first post-partum days. *New England Journal of Medicine, 286* (9), 460–63.

Kobasa, S. (1984, September). How much stress can you survive? *American Health, 3,* 64–77.

Kobasa, S.; Maddi, S.; & Kahn, S. (1982). Hardiness and health: A prospective study. *Journal of Personality and Social Psychology, 42,* 168–77.

Koestler, A. (1964). *The act of creation.* New York: Hutchinson.

Lamarck, J. B. (1914). *Zoological philosophy.* London: Macmillan.

Leider, R. J. (1985). *The power of purpose.* New York: Ballantine Books.

Lienhart, J. (1983). *Multiple personality and state dependent learning.* Doctoral dissertation, U.S. International University, San Diego, CA.

Locke, S. & Colligan, D. (1986). *The healer within.* New York: E. P. Dutton.

Locke, S. E.; Kraus, L.; Leserman, J.; Hurst, M. W.; Heisel, J. S.; & Williams, R. M. (1984). Life change stress, psychiatric symptoms, and natural killer cell activity. *Psychosomatic Medicine* 46: 5: 441–53.

Loeb, J. (1964). *The mechanistic conception of life.* New York: Belknap Press. (Original publication 1912.)

Loevinger, J. (1976). *Ego development: Conceptions and theories.* San Francisco: Jossey-Bass.

Lovelock, J. E. (1979). *Gaia: A new look at life on earth.* London: Oxford University Press.

MacIntyre, F. & Estep, K. W. (1993). Sperm competition and the persistence of genes for male homosexuality. *Biosystems, 18,* 31, 223–33.

Mackintosh, N. J. (ed.). (1995). *Cyril Burt: Fraud or framed?* London: Oxford University Press.

MacLean, P. (1973). *A tribune concept of the brain and behavior.* Toronto: University of Toronto Press.

Maddi, S. R. & Kobasa, S. C. (1984). *The hardy executive: Health under stress.* Homewood, IL: Dow Jones-Irwin.

Mahler, M. (1982). *Selected papers of Margaret S. Mahler,* Vol. 1 (2nd ed.). New York: Aronson.

Manier, J. (2000, March). Darwin reaches final frontier. *Chicago Tribune* 1–29.

Mar, T. T. (1974). *Face reading.* New York: Signet Classics.

Maslow, A. (1968). *Toward a psychology of being.* New York: Harper.

Mason, R. C.; Clark, G.; Reeves, R. B.; & Wagner, B. (1969). Acceptance and healing. *Journal of Religion and Health, 8,* 123–30.

Masters, R. (1994). *Neurospeak.* Wheaton, IL: Theosophical Publishing House.

Masters, R. & Houston, J. (1978). *Listening to the body.* New York: Delacorte Press.

McAdams, D. (1985). *Magical Child Matures* (2nd ed.). New York: Bantam.

McClelland, D. C.; Floor, E.; Davidson, R. J.; & Saron, C. (1980). Stressed power motivation, sympathetic activation, immune function, and illness. *Journal of Human Stress, 6,* 11–19.

Mendel, A. (1947). *Personality in handwriting.* New York: Stephen Daye Press.

Meshberger, F. L. (1990). An interpretation of Michelangelo's creation of Adam based on neuroanatomy. *Journal of American Medical Association, 264*, 1837–41.

Minuchin, S. (1996). *Family kaleidoscope.* Cambridge, MA: Harvard University Press.

Monod, J. (1971). *Chance and necessity.* New York: Knopf.

Moore, T. (1992). *Care of the soul.* New York: HarperCollins.

Myers, I., & Briggs, K. C. (1977). *A guide to the development and use of the Myers-Briggs Type Indicator.* San Diego, CA: Consulting Psychologist Press, Inc.

Napier, A., & Whitaker, C. (1978). *The family crucible.* New York: Harper and Row Publishers, Inc.

Nieburh, R. (1980). *Nature and destiny of man.* New York: Prentice Hall.

Nomi, T., & Besher, A. (1982). *You are your blood type.* New York: Pocket Books.

O'Leary, A. (1985). Self-efficacy and health. *Behavioral Research and Therapy, 23,* 437–51.

Ojemann, G. (1983). Electrical stimulation and the neurobiology of language. *Behavioral and Brain Science.* 6: 221–26.

Oparin, A. (1938). *The origin of life on earth.* New York: Macmillan.

Ornstein, R. E. (1986). *Multimind.* Boston: Houghton Mifflin Co.

Ornstein, R. E. (1986). *The psychology of consciousness.* New York: Viking-Penguin.

Ornstein, R. E. (1997). *The right mind.* San Diego: Harcourt Brace.

Ornstein, R. E., & Sobel, D. (1987). *The healing brain.* New York: Simon & Schuster.

Ornstein, R. E., & Thompson, R. F. (1984). *The amazing brain.* Boston: Houghton Mifflin.

Osgood C., et al. (1971). *The measurement of meaning.* Urbana: University of Illinois Press.

Pearce, J. C. (1986). *Magical child matures.* New York: Bantam Book.

Pears, D. F., & McGuiness, B. F. (1995). *Tractatus logico-philosophicus: Wittgenstein.* London and New York: Routledge.

Pearsall, P. (1988). *Super immunity master your emotions and improve your health.* New York: Fawcett-Division Ballantine.

Pearsall, P. (1999). *The heart's code.* Westminister, MD: Random House, Inc.

Pearsall, P. (2000). *Wishing well.* New York: Hyperion.

Pelletier, K. R. (1977). *Mind as healer, mind as slayer.* New York: Delta.

Pelletier, K. R. (1978). *Toward a science of consciousness.* New York: Dell.

Perls, F. (1971). *Gestalt therapy verbatim* (8th ed.). Lafayette, CA: Real People Press.

Piaget, J. (1979). *Behaviour and evolution.* London: Routledge & Kegan Paul.

Piaget, J., & Inhelder, B. (1964). *The early growth of logic in the child.* Atlantic Highlands, NJ: Humanities Press.

Popper, K. (1959). *The logic of scientific discovery.* New York: Hutchinson.

Pressman, J. (1999). *Last resort.* New York: Cambridge Press.

Progoff, I. (1973). *Jung's psychology and its social meaning.* Garden City, NY: Anchor Press.

Rael, J. (1993). *Being and vibration.* Tulsa OK: Council Oak Books.

Ramachandran, V. S. & Blakeslee, Sandra. (1998). *Phantoms in the brain.* New York: Quill/William Morrow.

Rauscher, R.; Shaw, L. J.; Levine, L.; Wright, E. L.; Dennis, W. R.; & Newcomb, R. L. (1997). Music training causes long-term enhancement of pre-school children's spatial-temporal reasoning. *Neurological Research, 19,* 208.

Reich, W. (1949). *Character analysis.* New York: Orgone Institute Press.

Renoux, G.; Biziere, K.; Renoux, M.; & Guillamin, J. M. (1983). The production of T-cell-inducing factors in mice is controlled by the brain neocortex. *Scandinavian Journal of Immunology, 17,* 45–50.

Restak, R. (1984). *The brain.* New York: Bantam Books.

Restak, R. (1995). *Brainscapes.* New York: Hyperion.

Rogers, C. (1951). *Client-centered therapy.* Boston: Houghton Mifflin.

Rogers, C. (1980). Psychological shocks and creative moments in psychotherapy. In E. Rossi (ed.), *The collected papers of Milton H. Erickson on hypnosis: IV. Innovative hypnotherapy* (pp. 447–63). New York: Irvington. (Original publication 1973.)

Rose, S. (1997). *Lifelines.* New York: Oxford University Press.

Rossi, E. (1980). Psychological shocks and creative moments in psychotherapy. In E. Rossi (ed.), *The collected papers of Milton H. Erickson on hypnosis: IV. Innovative hypnotherapy,* 447–463. New York: Irvington. (Original publication 1973.)

Rossi, E. L. (1986). *The psychobiology of mind-body healing.* New York: W. W. Norton & Co.

Rothman, B. K. (1998). *Genetic maps and human imagination.* New York: Norton.

Rutzky, J. (1999, Fall). *Coyote in a bottle.* Peoria, IL: Paradigm.

Sardello, R. (1991). *Facing the world with soul.* New York: Lindisfarne Press.

Savage-Rumbaugh, S. & Levin, R. (1994). *Kanzi: the ape at the brink of the human mind.* New York: Wiley.

Scheele, P. R. (1997). *Natural brilliance.* Wayzata, MN: Learning Strategies Corp.

Schmale, A. & Iker, H. (1966). The effect of hopelessness and the development of cancer: I. Identification of uterine cervical cancer in women with atypical cytology. *Psychosomatic Medicine, 28,* 714–21.

Schmale, A. & Iker, H. (1971). Hopelessness as a predictor of cervical cancer. *Social Science and Medicine, 5,* 95–100.

Searle, J. R. (1997). *The mystery of consciousness.* New York: New York Review of Books.

Seligman, M. (1975). *Learned helplessness.* San Francisco: W. H. Freeman & Co.

Selvini Palazzoli, M.; Boscolo, L.; Cecchin, G.; & Prata, G. (1978). *Paradox and counterparadox.* New York: Jason Aronson.

Selvini Palazzoli, M.; Boscolo, L.; Cecchin, G.; & Prata, G. (1980). Hypothesizing-circularity-neutrality. *Family Process,* 15, 19, 73–85.

Shakespeare, W. (1987). *Hamlet.* London: Oxford.

Shavit, Y.; Lewis, W.; Terman, G. W.; Gale, R. P.; and Liebeskind, J. C.; Endogenous opioids may meditate the effects of stress on tumor growth and immune function. *Proceedings of the Western Pharmacological Society* 26: 53–56.

Shechy, G. (1977). *Passages.* New York: Bantam-DoubleDay.

Sheldrake, R. (1981). *A new science of life.* New York: Blond & Briggs.

Sheldrake, R. (1988). *Presence of the past.* Rochester, VT: Park Street Press.

Siegel, B. S. (1986). *Love, medicine and miracles.* New York: Harper & Row.

Smith, M., & Jones, E. (1993). Neophobia and existential choice. *Journal of Humanistic Psychology, 33*(2), 90–107.

Spence, D. (1984). The paradox of denial. In S. Bresnitz (ed.), *The Denial of Stress.* New York: International Press.

Sperry, R. (1964). The great cerebral commissure. *Scientific American,* 210, 42–52.

Sperry, R. (1985). Consciousness, personal identity, and the divided brain. In D. F. Benson (ed.) In *The dual brain* (p. 19–73). New York: The Guilford Press.

Steen, R. G. (1996). *DNA & destiny.* New York: Plenum Press.

Steinberg, R. (1985). *Beyond I.Q.* New York: Cambridge University Press.

Sternberg, R. (1985). *Beyond I.Q.* New York: Cambridge University Press.

Taffel, R. (1999, September/October). Discovering our children. *Family Therapy Net-worker*, 35–74.

Thomas, L. (1979). *The medusa and the snail*. New York: Viking.

Thompson, D. W. (1961). *On growth and form.* London: Cambridge University Press. (Original publication 1917.)

Thompson, L. (1998). *Personality Type*. Boston: Shambhala.

Thoreau, H. D. (1985). *Walden.* New York: The Library of America.

Tocqueville, A. de. (2000). *Democracy in America.* New York: Harper Collins.

Toufexis, A. (1996, January 15). What makes them do it. *Time.*

Verny, T., & Kelly, S. (1981). *The secret life of the unborn child.* New York: Dell.

Von Foerster, H. (1981). *Observing systems.* Seaside, CA: Intersystems.

Watson, J. D., & Crick, F.H.C. (1953, April 25). Molecular structure of nucleic acids. *Nature, 737.*

Watzlawick, P.; Jackson, D.; & Beavin, J. (1967). *Pragmatics of human communication.* New York: Norton.

Watzlawick, P.; Weakland, J.; and Fisch, R. (1974). *Change: Principles of problem for-mation and problem resolution.* New York: Norton.

Weil, A. (1983). *Health and healing: Understanding conventional and alternative medi-cine.* Boston: Houghton Mifflin.

Weil. A. (1995). *Spontaneous Healing.* New York: Ballantine.

Weil, A. (1998). *Natural health natural medicine.* New York: Houghton-Miflin.

Wenger, Win, & Pol, R. (1996). *The Einstein factor.* Rocklin, CA: Prima Publishing.

Werner, E. (1992). *Overcoming the odds: high risk children from birth to adulthood.* Ithaca, NY: Cornell University Press.

Werner, E. E., & Smith, R. S. (1982). *Vulnerable, but invincible: A study of resilient children.* New York: McGraw-Hill.

Wickramasekera, I. (1985). A conditioned response model of the placebo effect: Predic-tions from the model. In L. White, B. Tursky, & G. Schwartz (eds.), *Placebo: Theory, research and mechanisms.* New York: Guilford Press, 255–287.

Williams, R.J.P., & Frausto da Silva, J.J.R. (1996). *The natural selection of the chemical elements.* London: Oxford University Press.

Wittgenstein, L. (1974). *Tractatus Logico-Philosophicus.* New York: Routledge.

Wolinsky, S. & Ryan, M. (1991). *Trances people live.* Falls Village, CT: The Bramble Company.

Woodward, K. L. (2000). *The book of miracles.* New York: Simon & Schuster.

Wylie, M. (1999, September/October). Neil S. Jacobson *Family Therapy Networker, 23,* 3, 14.

Yam, P. (2000, April). Two places at once. *Scientific American, 32.*

Yogananda, P. (1974). *Autobiography of a yogi.* Los Angeles: Self Realization Fellow-ship.

Zeig, J. (1985). *Ericksonian psychotherapy: Vol 2. Clinical applications.* New York: Brunner/Mazel.

Index

About the Author

DON J. FEENEY, JR. is a licensed, clinical psychologist and Executive Director of Consulting Psychological Services in Chicago. He is a diplomate in clinical psychology and has practiced in the field for over 25 years. Feeney has authored numerous articles and presented many seminars on transformational change and creative, self-organizing properties on the unique, purposeful self and is also author of *Entrancing Relationships* (Praeger, 1999).